The Results

Obsession

D1457091

The Results Obsession

ROI-Focused Digital Strategies to Transform Your Marketing

By Karen J. Marchetti

ISBN 978-0-578-68686-8

Cover design by Karin Wilson

Printed by Response FX in the United States of America

First printing edition 2020

Response FX, a division of
Strategic Marketing and Advertising, Inc.
1725 S. Rainbow Blvd #16-126
Las Vegas, NV 89146

www.responsefx.com

Introduction

All the Digital Marketing Success Factors in One Place

If you're looking to boost your results from every digital marketing effort, this book gives you a step-by-step roadmap.

- **You'll focus your efforts on the elements that have the biggest impact on results**

And emphasize the digital marketing channels with the highest ROI:

- Your website
- Search Engine Optimization (SEO)
- Email
- Pay-per-click (PPC) advertising

You'll start by correctly **diagnosing** your progress from **Traffic to Leads to Sales** – so you'll know exactly how to improve results.

- You'll understand what to review in *Google Analytics* (with step-by-step instructions)

- And learn the *Marketing Metrics* to evaluate every marketing effort (with easy-to-follow formulas included)

You'll have winning "formulas" to *make every element of your copy really sell!* And you'll learn to *strategically craft Offers* for a big change in results.

You'll also discover easy ways to *"test your way to success,"* so your marketing becomes more effective with every effort!

Finally, if you rely on outside resources, you'll learn how to evaluate every marketing proposal to choose better partners and solutions.

Results are the key in marketing.

> *"Does it matter if the artwork was stunning,*
> *or you thought the copy was amazing,*
> *if the effort didn't bring in leads or sales?"*

When you focus on results from every effort, you'll find ways to make every effort more successful.

Part 1: Analyze, diagnose, and plan

DIAGNOSIS (*Chapter 2*) – To improve results, first diagnose your situation or problem. You'll go step-by-step through simple analyses of your website's **Traffic, Leads, and Sales** (including exactly what to analyze in Google Analytics). You'll also learn the factors that most affect results in SEO, email, and Pay-Per-Click (PPC) advertising. Once you understand the key elements that drive results, you'll know exactly how to improve.

BUILDING BUYER PERSONAS (*Chapter 3*) – Do you know why your customers buy? This objective data-based approach will give you actionable insights to drive Offers and Content. You'll outline the key characteristics, problems, questions, and "why did they buy" of each of your key customer groups. You'll use simple analytics, information-gathering, sales interviews, and customer interviews to create a one-page summary for each Persona.

Part 2: Driving leads and sales

LEAD GENERATION STRATEGIES (*Chapter 5*) — A huge percentage of websites have the objective of Lead Generation – but don't actually FOCUS on Lead Generation. To drive leads more effectively, use more enticing Offers. You'll learn how to match your Offer to your specific objectives, and "merchandise" it so it sounds irresistible. Plus, you'll determine how much you should spend to generate each lead.

OFFERS *(Chapters 4, 6, 7)* — The key to planning effective Offers is to consider your different types of customers and what they might value at each "Buying Stage." You'll get a major education on the strategies behind crafting Lead Generation and sales Offers. If you're not regularly testing different Offers beyond white papers and discounts, these chapters will give you DOZENS of ideas.

SELLING IN COPY *(Chapters 8-10)* — When you're driving traffic, generating leads, or driving sales, you're selling with words. Learn how to translate the steps in the Sales Process to your Content. You'll learn how to craft a unique Brand Message, follow proven Copy Approaches, and incorporate the seven Emotional Drivers. You'll learn the characteristics of great marketing copy, including: secrets to writing fabulous headlines, how to craft a compelling lead-in, and "wordsmithing" to help you create the most effective copy of your life.

Part 3: Your marketing hub

WEBSITE NAVIGATION AND CONTENT *(Chapters 11-13)* – Do you need a new website – or just a tune-up? Learn the characteristics of a great website and how to measure them. You'll evaluate and plan more effective

Navigation and Content by page. Then you'll work on the most important element of your website messaging, craft Content for different types of pages, make your copy sound and look enticing, and plan effective blog Content.

Part 4: Driving traffic

SEO, ONLINE ADVERTISING, EMAIL *(Chapters 14-17)* —
For each digital media channel, you'll learn the key factors that have the most impact on results and how to evaluate them. You'll cover the key components of effective SEO (and how to measure them), how to evaluate your pay-per-click advertising, key metrics for email effectiveness, and how to plan and write effective email campaigns.

Part 5: Test, measure, and staff

TESTING YOUR WAY TO SUCCESS *(Chapter 18)* — Setting up tests in PPC, email, and your website is easier than ever. Learn how to test different Offers, headlines, descriptions, benefits, and more. You'll analyze results step-by-step to identify what's working (and what's not). You'll never again think *"Testing is too hard," "Testing is for bigger companies"* or *"Testing won't work for us."*

THE NUMBERS *(Chapter 19)* – How should you plan your programs to be profitable before you spend a dime? How should you analyze each effort? What metrics should you track regularly? You'll walk through an easy Break-even Analysis, and learn how to calculate Cost Per Order, Lifetime Value, Marketing Contribution, and marketing ROI. And, you'll identify the metrics that justify your marketing budget.

THE NEW MARKETING LEADER *(Chapter 20)* – What are the success characteristics of the new marketing leader? What is Marketing's strategic role in your company (and what should it be)? Why are some Marketing departments so much more successful than others? Learn how to put together the right Marketing team, and become a more educated marketing buyer.

When you **measure the cost-effectiveness of every effort** (through Cost Per Lead or Cost Per Sale), you'll develop forecasts and marketing budgets grounded in actual numbers.

When you can do that, Marketing becomes a strategic resource for your company, rather than an expense.

> When you *develop a Results Obsession*,
> your marketing,
> your team and outside resources,
> your Marketing ROI,
> and Marketing's reputation within your company
> will all be the most effective they can be.

■■

Where did the title "The Results Obsession" come from?

I met with a client I hadn't worked with in a while, and he said with a smile, "I always remember what you told us — *if you can't measure it, don't do it.*"

When you obsess about constantly improving results, it's amazing how your results improve.

■■

Chapter 1

The Results Obsession for the Digital Era

A re you 100% confident that you're getting the most from every marketing dollar? Do you focus on maximizing return on your marketing budget?

Is every marketing effort as effective as it could be? Are you striving to improve results constantly?

The answers to these questions tell you whether you're investing wisely in marketing – or not.

If you're not, why not? What prevents stellar marketing results? Usually, it's due to two strategic gaps:

Lack of focus on results (and ROI)

- You may not be focused on **Traffic, Leads, and Sales** — the three basic pillars of your marketing "funnel."
- Your team may not be **analyzing progress step-by-step** through those pillars
- You're not identifying where key problems and opportunities lie

1

Lack of Testing

- You may not be learning what works in your marketing – and *"testing your way to success."*
- You may not understand *what's actually driving your* Traffic, Leads, and Sales.
- And you may not know **what's most important to your audience(s)**

These two gaps lead to the cardinal sin that drives most marketing disasters: the *misdiagnosis.*

"When you misdiagnose your marketing situation or problem, you waste money on everything you pursue."

When there's no **testing and step-by-step analysis**, your team makes incorrect conclusions about what's actually going on – and what you really need.

When you "misdiagnose," you send your marketing efforts off-course

It's the number one thing that drives wrong turns.

You may continue spending money where you shouldn't, or keep using something that could be so much more effective if you revised it.

You may look for the wrong solution to a problem, make the wrong decisions about tactics, and use the wrong resources. And the unfortunate cycle begins of wasting huge amounts of time and money — on **solutions that never had a chance of fixing your original problem**.

Have you decided a particular tactic (or maybe even your website) "doesn't work for us" – without diagnosing why?

The most common (and costly) misdiagnosis debacles are variations of:

> *"Our website isn't generating enough (leads, sales, organic traffic, etc.), so we need a new website."*

You may embark upon a lengthy and costly website redesign project. But no one analyzes WHY the website isn't generating enough (leads, sales, organic traffic, or whatever) — and the web developers don't ask. Nor do they suggest a review of your website analytics to find out.

Maybe you don't specifically ask the web developers how they would solve a (Lead Generation, sales, organic traffic, etc.) problem.

And that's a shame, **because just a few elements typically cause most results problems.**

Because you don't identify the original problem, the website redesign project has little chance of solving it.

Why does this happen?

We misdiagnose . . . because:

We don't analyze step-by-step, and
We don't understand what drives Traffic, Leads, and Sales, and
We don't understand the elements that have the most impact on results . . . because
We don't test, and
We don't track results.

If you're not testing, you may also be suffering from three other related strategic gaps:

Lack of Lead Generation expertise

If you're not selling directly from your ecommerce website, then you likely have a "Lead Generation website." But you may not have Lead Generation expertise among your Marketing team. *If no one understands the elements that drive leads, you're wasting your budget.*

Lack of understanding of your customer types

Not understanding what **your different types of customers** need, what's important to them, and **why they buy from you** means your marketing is likely shooting in the dark.

Lack of a unique sales message

You need a **unique messaging** strategy to set you apart from your competition and *answer "why should I buy yours?"* And it should be relevant to your different customer types.

In most companies, it's the overall system that's broken – or lacking. It's a lack of the right STRATEGIC approach to your marketing.

Yet, we have more analytics available today (website, email, social media, etc.) than we've ever had in the history of marketing.

We have access to an overwhelming amount of customer information (more than we ever had in the pre-digital era), but we still struggle with understanding our customers.

Isn't it the first day of Marketing 101 class where we learn that marketing should be "customer-focused?"

Plus, there's so much "how to" information online. It's amazing that everyone hasn't become results-obsessed!

If you're going to devote marketing budget to any effort, *shouldn't you know what you got for that budget?*

Don't you want to show your boss how you've improved results – and return on marketing investment?

Shouldn't *knowledge of your particular customers drive your marketing?*

Doesn't it make sense to test, rather than guess, so you can identify the most effective direction?

What's holding you back?

Why doesn't every company, marketer, agency, and freelancer have "The Results Obsession"? Why don't you focus on continuously boosting your marketing ROI?

What *has* been holding you back? Do any of these situations sound like you and your team?

The "Marketing Production" assembly line

Some Marketing teams don't see beyond just "getting the project done." You focus on just completing the steady stream of marketing activities to keep things moving.

Maybe you're *not planning how to track results* – because it's not a priority, no one thinks it's part of the job, or maybe you're not sure how to do it. No one does an analysis to see what's working and what isn't.

There's *no Testing* because that would get in the way of "getting the projects done." So, no learning happens.

The Marketing Production assembly line just keeps going.

"We just create leads that we pass on to Sales"

Are you always focusing on the next campaign? Have you forgotten about nurturing leads and *maximizing the Lifetime Value of customers?*

Marketing doesn't end when you create a lead – or a customer.

5

If you have a Lead Generation website, you're in the Lead Generation AND Nurturing business.

You need a continuous marketing system – to create a steady flow of new leads, qualified leads, and sales.

One marketing director recently lamented to me:

"Oh, but then we'd have to create a follow-up system for those leads.

Yeah! That's a critical role of Marketing when you're in the Lead Generation business.

Lead Nurturing isn't something to be afraid of. It's the education stage of Lead Generation where you help move Early Stage prospects through your Sales Process. *Effective lead nurturing* can give you a MAJOR competitive advantage *(with an incredible ROI!)*

"We don't really see the value of Testing"

Maybe your Marketing team hasn't bothered with Testing because:

- No one is pushing you or your staff to test
- You never learned how to test
- You don't think you have time to test
- You don't believe you have the budget to test
- You don't think your audience or traffic is big enough for Testing
- Maybe you don't think a particular tactic you're using is appropriate for Testing

Your team just continues to "get the work done" without analyzing results and trying to constantly improve them. But, **if you're not constantly Testing, you're wasting marketing dollars with every effort.**

When you test, you learn: which words get higher response, what Offers generate more qualified leads, and which product/service benefits drive more traffic and sales. You learn what's important to your customers and how to communicate more *relevantly*. You **stop guessing** — and start generating **breakthrough results.**

6

To drive continuous improvement, you need to be testing constantly. It's the best way to get the highest return for your marketing budget.

"We don't really track results"

Maybe your boss doesn't ask for reports, because he or she just assumes Marketing doesn't actually generate measurable results.

By not tracking how effective your marketing is or isn't:

You miss incredible learning opportunities.

You miss ways to improve and get more from every dollar you spend.

You also miss opportunities to PROVE to management how effective your marketing is. And you perpetuate the perception of marketing as just an expense, with a team that may not know how to drive positive ROI. (If you struggle to get marketing budgets approved, this is why.)

If your boss or client asks for reports or more specific tracking, it's an OPPORTUNITY — to prove your expertise, and illustrate how smartly you're managing the company's or your client's budget. Never brush off this type of request – it's the fastest way to ensure they'll bring in someone else who does know how to track and analyze results.

"We can't measure that," "I'm not a numbers person," or "We're not looking for volume"

You can measure just about every marketing tactic in some way. The key is to *take a step-by-step approach, so you see **exactly** what happened*. Most email systems, social media sites, and websites have simple-to-use analytics.

What if you're a marketer that cringes at the thought of marketing analytics? Even if you're not a *"numbers person,"* you'll find analyzing most tactics doesn't really require much math at all. The sooner you become familiar with the metrics — and get over your allergy to *"marketing math"* — the faster you'll really jump-start your results.

Analytics track how visitors use your website — what pages they visit (and don't visit), and where visitors come from. You're missing opportunities – and problems – by not reviewing your visitors behavior.

Over-reliance on "philosophy" or "best practices" — versus Testing and real results

Marketers, agencies, freelancers, copywriters, graphic designers, web developers – we all have our particular knowledge or "philosophy" of doing things based on our experience. When we can continue to build that knowledge by seeing actual results, it makes each of us that much more effective.

- But when a marketer doesn't base philosophy on **tested, proven results** – and when your **knowledge doesn't constantly grow** – that philosophy isn't leading to the most effective marketing.

What about "best practices"?

Best practices are where you start, if you're using a new marketing tactic or working with a new client.

But as soon as you see actual results, you'll see exactly what works for YOUR product or service to YOUR audience.

Experience is highly valuable – but it's not a substitute for actual results from your particular audience.

That's because every audience type is different, each will buy a product or service for a different set of reasons, and the effectiveness of different tactics is always changing.

No matter your philosophy, knowledge of best practices, or experience – *you may still spend marketing budget ineffectively if you're not actively testing, tracking, and analyzing results.*

Each of these reasons prevents your boss (and others) from *viewing your Marketing team as contributors to positive company ROI.* Without a focus on results, you paint your Marketing department as an expense. It's why the company reduces your budget at each economic downturn. And, it prevents Marketing from having a strategic role in the company.

Marketing can – and should – **show a direct relationship between marketing activities and sales increases**. The more quantifiable you can make that relationship, the higher your value rises in your company.

What's holding YOU back?

How The Results Obsession will transform your marketing

To generate consistently great results – and maximize the return on your marketing budget — you need a change in focus to:

1. Constantly improving your *Traffic, Leads, and Sales*

2. T*ailoring Offers and Content* for your particular customers at their particular "Buying Stages"

3. *Constantly testing*

4. *Tracking and analyzing results step-by-step*

In the process, you will:

- *Become your company's expert on your customer types*
- Create a *system that generates a continuous flow* of qualified leads and profitable sales
- Pinpoint opportunities to *continuously improve* your results
- Learn exactly *what marketing elements work best* for you, so you can apply them across media channels
- *Prove how cost-effective and valuable your marketing is*

This new focus elevates the Marketing function to a more strategic role. When you can dazzle your CEO and CFO with your ROI focus, you become an incredibly valuable resource for your company.

You learn from every effort, so every future effort becomes that much more effective.

That's the value of a Results Obsession.

6 Results Obsession strategies to drive your marketing

To develop The Results Obsession, you'll build expertise and skills in six main strategies throughout this book:

Results Obsession strategy #1: Diagnose step-by-step

Step-by-step analysis is the key to diagnosing your marketing situation. You'll focus on three main metrics: **Traffic, Leads, and Sales**.

When you analyze step-by-step, you solve:

- The struggle to find out what solution you need to fix a problem
- Wondering how to improve your website or any other tactic
- Wandering from tactic to tactic, looking for one that works
- Constantly changing agencies and other resources in search of better marketing results

Taking a step-by-step approach to diagnose correctly is the first step to a more positive marketing ROI.

Results Obsession strategy #2: Develop a true understanding of your customer types

The idea of developing customer "personas" or Buyer Personas has been around for several decades. But its implementation used to be highly flawed.

The agency or consultant would get senior executives in a room and ask them key questions about customers. The session wouldn't be over until the group arrived at some "group think" beliefs. (No wonder some executives shudder at the thought of developing Buyer Personas.)

When you use a smarter system to learn about your customers, you develop a key competitive advantage. The keys to acquiring this priceless knowledge are: use your own *objective behavioral data, individual salesperson insights, and comments directly from your customers.*

Armed with true customer insight, you'll start looking at everything from your Buyer Personas' perspective. Your Content, Offers, and website will become laser-focused and highly relevant for your audiences.

When you build Buyer Personas, you invest in a clearer roadmap for all of your marketing.

Results Obsession strategy #3: Design systems for continuous Traffic, Leads, and Sales

To create a steady stream of sales, start with marketing that delivers a continuous flow of *qualified traffic*.

Once you've created a continuous traffic system, you may need a continuous flow of *leads*. Then, you'll follow-up those leads with *"nurturing" to help move them through the Sales Process.*

For ecommerce, your website, email nurturing, and customer loyalty messages should create a continuous flow of *sales*.

Results Obsession strategy #4: Continuously learn and improve through Testing

When you focus on continuous improvement, you realize your marketing isn't going to be most effective when you *"set it and forget it."* For most companies, creating a single untested "campaign" to run for a few months (and not as part of a test) is an ineffective way to invest marketing dollars.

To improve continuously, you need to be testing constantly. Some media are great for quick tests. You can take what you learn and apply it to other media channels.

By testing constantly in "quick test" media, you'll drive continuous improvement. And you'll wonder how you ever did your job without it.

Results Obsession strategy #5: Measure every step you can measure (which is more than you think)

You have tremendous tools available to look at your website results. You can see the sources of traffic, number of clicks on particular buttons or links, number of visitors that got to your Offer or individual product page, number of visitors that started the checkout process, and more.

Many media channels have their own built-in tracking, like email and pay-per-click advertising. You can test different headlines, different benefits, different Offers — and learn **which individual words work best**! Measuring marketing has never been easier — you just have to analyze the data to arrive at the right conclusions.

Results Obsession strategy #6: Equate your costs to results whenever possible to get to ROI

The key is **"cost per action."** You can measure just about every marketing effort in terms of actions taken. When you can count the number of actions, you can compute cost-per-action.

Effective marketers never spend money before understanding how likely a program is to at least break even. You'll learn how to calculate everything from *Cost Per Order* to *Marketing Contribution*, true *ROI*, and *Lifetime Value* to dazzle your CFO.

To implement these 6 Results Obsession Strategies, you'll need to build or hone some particular skills.

3 skills that drive leads, sales, and superior effectiveness

Few marketers seem to understand *exactly what elements drive leads and sales overall.*

Similarly, few marketers understand *what drives the success of each individual marketing tactic.*

It may be because marketing has so many different areas to learn. We tend to rely on agencies, web developers, writers, designers, or consultants for particular expertise.

> *But, if those outside resources aren't actively testing, they aren't constantly learning.* They may not be driving the most cost-effective results for you.

To drive superior results, you (and your team and outside resources) need to become experts in:

Lead Generation – a skill too many marketers lack

Lead Generation is a specific body of knowledge. C-suite executives assume their SVP of Marketing knows how to manage it. Marketing managers assume their agency or web development team understands it.

But it's more than just slapping up a white paper Offer or "sign up for our e-newsletter" form to capture email addresses.

When the main purpose of your website is Lead Generation:

> Your Marketing team (and outside resources) *should understand everything there is to know about Lead Generation.*

That includes how to balance Lead Quantity with Lead Quality, how to develop a plan for A-B-C leads, how to drive leads from appropriate Buyer Personas, and how to capture leads in the Early Buying Stage.

Offer construction – what drives the lead

Whenever you have a Lead Generation problem, it's usually due to the Offer you're making (or not making). The Offer drives the lead.

> *If you have a Lead Generation website, crafting Offers is the key skill you (and your team) need to develop.*

You'll want to craft Offers for each Buyer Persona by Buying Stage. Crafting Offers that drive action is a skill set that goes FAR beyond discounts and white papers.

There are DOZENS of types of Lead Generation Offers you could be using. How many have you tested?

With ecommerce, the Offer is the something extra that encourages the sale NOW. To drive ecommerce sales, there are also DOZENS of different types of Offers you could be using, to move far beyond percent-off discounts.

Selling with words – crafting effective Sales Content

When you're driving leads or selling via ecommerce, you're typically selling with words. (You'll sell some products primarily visually – like home furnishings and clothing. But you'll sell many other products and services primarily with words.)

Your copy in your email and website needs to SELL. That copy should sound exactly the way you'd say it if you were face-to-face or on the phone. And your Sales Copy should follow the Sales Process – the same process you'd follow if you were selling in person or by phone.

Is that how your copy reads? Some say you can't be good at both Lead Generation and Brand Messaging. I say, *"why not?"* Effective Brand Messaging should permeate EVERY marketing effort.

When you bring a Results Obsession to every marketing effort, results improve

These are the ROI-related strategies and tactical skills you need to transform your marketing. You can use them across media to continuously improve your results – and help invest your marketing dollars more effectively.

You'll learn a proven framework to **diagnose** your challenges more accurately, "do it yourself" more effectively (if you choose to), and identify the right team members and outside resources most likely to improve your results.

14

You'll re-orient your focus to the key elements that drive leads and sales – to smarter Lead Generation, Offers, and Sales Copy. And, you'll learn how to carefully Test and Analyze results to give you concrete steps to improve results in any media channel!

Plus, you'll finally become the expert on your customers that your company needs.

Start today to incorporate The Results Obsession Strategies and Skills you may have been missing. Never misdiagnose a marketing problem or miss an improvement opportunity again!

> *"Advertising . . . must now become accountable.*
> *Advertising . . . must become an investment in profits."*
> Lester Wunderman.

References

Wunderman, L. (1997) *Being Direct: Making Advertising Pay.* Random House

Chapter 2

Diagnosis: Opportunities to Boost Traffic, Leads & Sales

When you're not achieving the marketing results you want, the first step is to diagnose where the real problem (or opportunity) lies. This seems to be where a huge majority of marketing efforts derail, before they even begin.

Too many times, marketers conclude *"we need a new website," "our online advertising isn't working,"* or *"email is a waste of time"* – without really analyzing the "WHY" behind the results.

- When you can't diagnose what's causing your poor results, **you hire the wrong resources** – because you don't know exactly what skills you need.

- The vendors you hire may not recognize the real problem either. **They execute what you said you needed**, but your results don't improve. And the cycle continues . . .

You need a **step-by-step discovery of what your problem actually is**.

The basic diagnosis process in this chapter will help you identify exactly where to focus your improvement efforts.

You'll start by reviewing your website Traffic, Leads and Sales. And you'll walk through specifics of where to find the information in Google Analytics.

"To improve your return on marketing investment, focus on getting better results at every step in your marketing process."

Are you driving enough quality traffic?

Most of your marketing efforts probably drive website traffic. And your website is usually the first place prospects go to learn more (even when you ask them to call or visit your store).

Do you know how much traffic your marketing efforts are driving? Is that traffic declining, staying the same, or increasing?

Step one: Traffic trends

- In Google Analytics, in the left column, see "Audience," "Overview." At the top of the report, the drop-down shows "Users" (website visitors). In the drop-down after "vs," select "Sessions" (website visits).

- In the upper right corner, change the timeframe to the last 12 months. Below the timeframe, select "month."

- Just above the timeframe, select "Export" to download a spreadsheet of Users and Sessions by month.

- **Are your Sessions and Users steadily increasing, staying the same, or declining?**

- If your business is seasonal, review Sessions and Users for each month over the last 12 months, compared to each month for the prior 12 months. **How do Sessions and Users compare year to year?**

WHAT IT MEANS FOR IMPROVING RESULTS

If your total traffic isn't increasing or at least staying the same, you're probably also seeing lower leads and sales. So the problem to address first is TRAFFIC. *Are you doing pay-per-click advertising, email, or social media? Have you optimized your site for search?*

If your traffic is increasing, but you're still not getting the leads or sales you need, it's a problem with your specific Offer or Content.

See Chapters 4, 6, and 7 on Offers, and Chapters 8-10 for Content.

Step two: Sources of traffic

- In Google Analytics, in the left column, look at "Acquisition," "All Traffic," "Channels."

- You'll see the default channel groupings: *Organic, Referral* (traffic sent to you from a link on another site), *Social, Email* (if you're doing email campaigns), *Paid Search* (if you're using Google Ads pay-per-click advertising), and *Direct* (the visitor knew your URL and used it to go directly to your website).

- To look at traffic by channel for each month over the last 12 months: change the timeframe in upper right. Just above the data chart in Secondary Dimension, choose "Time" and "Month of the Year." Below the data chart in "Show Rows," select 5000. In upper right of the page, select Export to see Users by channel for each month.

  o Where does the majority of your traffic tend to come from each month? **Is traffic from that Channel increasing, staying the same, or declining?**

o **Is your Organic traffic steadily increasing over time?**

o Are your other Channels increasing, or at least maintaining their traffic levels each month?

WHAT IT MEANS FOR IMPROVING RESULTS

For many websites, Organic traffic makes up a significant portion of your monthly traffic.

When you have an SEO problem, you'll see it reflected in Traffic, Leads, and Sales. You should see a steady increase in Organic traffic, as your website becomes more established, you grow your Content through blog posts, and you attract more in-coming links and social shares.

If you don't see Organic traffic increasing, your SEO (Search Engine Optimization) needs to be improved. *(We'll talk about SEO in Chapter 14.)*

If your Organic traffic takes a substantial drop, you may have a specific problem. Check your Google Search Console (sign up at https://search.google.com/search-console/welcome) for any problems from Google's point-of-view.

- Google Search Console is free. If you have Admin access to Google Analytics for your website, you can add Google Search Console yourself. Just tell Google to look at your Google Analytics account to "verify" ownership of your website.

If all traffic by channel is low, you need to improve your traffic-driving efforts with better targeting, more attractive Offers, or relevant Content.

Step three: Quality of visits

What happens once visitors get to your website?

You need traffic that will become a qualified lead or a customer. So more traffic in general is not the answer. Check the "quality" of your traffic and how visitors respond to your website.

- Look at *"Bounce Rate"* which is the percentage of visits that don't go past one page. (In Google Analytics, see "Audience," "Overview.")

- Look also at *Pages/Session* (in "Audience," "Overview"). How many pages are viewed in the average visit?

WHAT IT MEANS FOR IMPROVING RESULTS

High Bounce Rate and low Pages/Session may indicate:

Visitors didn't find what they were looking for. This could be a **Navigation problem** or it could be a **Content problem**.

- *If your website has a Navigation problem*, you'll also usually see a low percentage of visitors navigating to your most important product/service pages (see "Behavior," "Site Content," "All Pages" to see traffic by page.)

- *If you have a Content problem*, it might start on Home.

  o In Google Analytics in the left column, see "Behavior," "Site Content," "All Pages," and look for "/" to see results of your Home page. If your Home page has a high Bounce Rate and/or low Average Time on Page, it could be due to lack of Content.

- You can review Bounce Rate and Average Time on Page for all of your key pages.

In Chapter 11, we'll go into more detail on website Navigation, and address website Content in Chapter 12.

Could your marketing tactics be driving more traffic?

If number of Users to your website is low, review the tactics you're using to drive traffic. Many times, it's not the tactic, but how it was executed.

Reviewing results by tactic can also reveal website problems, if you follow the traffic through to leads (created on your Lead Generation Offer page) and sales (created on your product/service pages).

- To see Lead Conversions in Google Analytics, you'll need Goals set up for each Lead Offer. *(We'll go through the steps in Chapter 3.)*
- To see Sales Conversions in Google Analytics, you'll need to have Ecommerce Tracking set up. (Ask your webmaster.)

Here's a brief introduction to analyzing each tactic. *(We'll go into detail in Chapters 15-17).*

Email

- What was the **Click-Through Rate (CTR)** for your last campaign?

- Compute Number of Leads divided by Emails Delivered to get your **Lead Conversion Rate**.

- Compute Number of Sales divided by Emails Delivered to see your **Sales Conversion Rate**.

WHAT IT MEANS FOR IMPROVING RESULTS

A low CTR, Lead Conversion, or Sales Conversion Rate could indicate the email **Offer or Content** wasn't relevant or attractive to the audience.

If you had good CTR but low Lead Conversion, that indicates a problem with your Lead Conversion page (either the **Content or the form**.)

A good CTR but low Sales Conversion *from customers* may indicate:

- The **Content** on your Landing Page was incomplete or didn't answer their objections.

A good CTR but low Sales Conversion *from opt-in leads* could mean they need more education before they're ready to buy. It could also indicate the Landing Page didn't address their objections.

We'll cover more details about email in Chapters 16 and 17.

Pay-per-click (PPC) advertising

The challenge with Search Engine PPC (like Google Ads or Microsoft Advertising®) isn't usually in driving traffic. It's attracting qualified visitors who are genuinely interested in what you're selling — and doing it cost-effectively.

What's the click-through rate for each ad?

- **Low Click-Through Rate** (CTR) is a copywriting problem. (In ads.google.com, open a "Campaign," then "Ad Group." Select "Ads" from left menu)

- Have you been able to boost ad CTR over time (with Testing)?

What's the click-through by keyword?

- In Google Ads, select "Keywords" from the left menu.

- Your keywords may be too generic if you see low CTRs (generally below 1%.)

If your PPC traffic is low and you're spending your daily budget every day, reduce your bids. If you still need more traffic, you may need to increase your daily budget.

Are you driving quality traffic?

- In Google Analytics, see "Acquisition," "All Traffic," "Channels." For "Paid Search," what's the **Bounce Rate**? How about **Average Session Duration** and **Pages/Session**?

- High Bounce, low Average Session Duration, and low Pages/Session all indicate the **traffic may not be qualified**. (*Try to better target your keywords, and write more specific ads.*)

- **What percentage of traffic converts** to Leads or Sales? (*See Chapter 15 to set up PPC Conversion tracking.*)

What is your **Cost Per Lead** or **Cost Per Sale**?

- Divide your PPC expense by Leads (or Sales) for the same period. What was your **Cost Per Lead or Cost Per Sale**? Is that acceptable?

- Have you been able to reduce your Cost Per Lead or Cost Per Sale over time? *Better targeting of both your keywords and ad Content can help.*

More on PPC strategies in Chapter 15.

Is your website generating leads effectively?

When your goal is a lead, your Offer is what drives that lead. Here's how to analyze your Lead Generation plan step by step:

Step one – Traffic to key Offer pages

In Google Analytics, in the left column, see "Behavior," "Site Content," "All Pages." Review the number of Unique Pageviews to each key Offer page.

WHAT IT MEANS FOR IMPROVING RESULTS

If traffic is strong to your key Offer pages, that means your target audience sees the Offer as attractive (and your Offer is easily visible on your website).

If number of visits is poor to your key Offer pages, you may need to either: test different Offers, improve the way you "sell" the Offer, or improve the visibility of your Offer on your website.

See Chapter 12 on Website Layout and Offers to learn more.

Step two – Conversion of traffic to leads

To determine Lead Conversion for the website: Divide the total number of lead form completions by Users for a time period.

- If you have Goals set up in Google Analytics for each Lead Offer, select the time period to review in top right.

- In left column, see "Acquisition," "All Traffic," "Channels." Above the chart under "Conversions," use the pull-down to see Goal results.

- *We'll cover how to set up Goals in Google Analytics in Chapter 3.*

To compute your Conversion Rate by Offer – take the number of **Goal completions for that Offer divided by Unique Pageviews** of the Offer page.

WHAT IT MEANS FOR IMPROVING RESULTS

- If your *site's Lead Conversion Rate is low*, that could mean your Offers aren't visible enough, they're not appealing to your audiences, or there's a problem with your Offer pages.

- If an *Offer's Conversion Rate is low*, that indicates a problem with the page. Either the **Content didn't effectively sell** and prove the value of the Offer – or the **form asks too many questions** (or both).

In Chapter 4, you'll start planning Offers for each Persona. Chapter 5 covers Lead Generation Strategy step-by-step. Chapter 6 presents Lead Generation Offer ideas.

Are you generating sales effectively?

When your goal is a sale, your website Sales Copy is usually what drives the sale. But you have to get the visitor to the product or service page first.

Step one – Traffic to key pages

In Google Analytics, see "Behavior," "Site Content," "All Pages." Locate your key **product or service pages** and review "Unique Pageviews."

- Are your product/service pages attracting significant traffic?

- Compare Unique Pageviews of your key pages with your total site visitors. (See "Audience," "Overview," and review "Users.") *Is a significant portion of your visitors getting to your key product/service pages?*

WHAT IT MEANS FOR IMPROVING RESULTS

If you have a low number of Unique Pageviews for your product/service pages (and *Unique Pageviews is a small percentage of Users*), it could indicate a **Navigation** problem (visitors couldn't find what they were looking for).

It could also indicate the **Content** on Home and other Landing Pages didn't convince visitors to stay.

See Chapter 11 for more on website Navigation. Chapter 12 discusses website Content.

Step two – Quality of page Content

- What's the Bounce Rate on your **product/service pages**?

- In "Behavior," "Site Content," "**Landing Pages**," review the pages where the majority of your visits start. What's the Bounce Rate on those pages?

WHAT IT MEANS FOR IMPROVING RESULTS

If Bounce Rate is high on your product/service pages or your most common Landing Pages, you could have a **Content** problem there. *(See Chapter 8 for Messaging Strategy.)*

Step three – Conversion to sales

What's your overall site Conversion to sales?

- In Google Analytics, select the time period in top right. In left column, see "Acquisition," "All Traffic," "Channels."

- o If you have Ecommerce Tracking set up, you'll see columns for Transactions and Revenue.
- o *Or you can set up a Sales Goal* (more on that in Chapter 3).

- Divide your *number of Transactions by total Users* ("Audience," "Overview," and see "Users.") to compute **Conversion Rate**. Is it improving or declining over time?

- To see **sales by product**, go to "Conversions," "Ecommerce," "Product Performance" to see "Unique Purchases" by product.

  - o See "Behavior," "Site Content," "All Pages." Find the particular product page and look at "Unique Pageviews."
  - o For each product, divide Unique Purchases by Unique Pageviews to compute **Sales Conversion by product.**

WHAT IT MEANS FOR IMPROVING RESULTS

Your Content drives your Sales Conversion. **Improving your Content** is where you should invest your time and money.

A promotional Sales Offer can also help drive sales.

We'll discuss Sales Offers in Chapter 7. Chapter 10 addresses the specific characteristics of copy that sells.

For better results, start with better diagnosis

Your marketing revolves around three key metrics: **Traffic, Leads, and Sales**. Focus on those metrics to analyze your progress step-by-step.

Your diagnosis in each of these three areas helps you pinpoint exactly where you need improvement, so you can focus your marketing efforts.

It helps ensure you stop wasting money on futile campaigns and inappropriate solutions that won't actually solve your problem (or improve results).

To improve your return on marketing investment, focus on getting better results at every step in your marketing process.

Results Obsession Strategy #1:
Learn How to Diagnose Your Situation Step-by-Step

Diagnose Your Opportunities to Boost Results

Not happy with Traffic, Leads, or Sales? Change the key elements that drive them, especially: Offer and Sales Copy.

TRAFFIC

- Low traffic: change the Offer, or description of your Content or Offer
- Low traffic to key pages: change Menu Navigation or Content on Home

LEADS

- Low clicks on lead-generating tactics: change your Offer or the Sales Copy promoting the Offer
- Low traffic to Offer page: highlight Offer on Home, blog, and product pages
- Low Conversion on the Offer page: change Sales Copy or simplify the form

SALES

- Low traffic to product/service pages: improve your navigation or Landing Page copy
- Low sales from product/service pages: improve your Sales Copy or add an Offer

Figure 2.1

Chapter 3

Why Customers Buy – The Key to Superior Results

Once you identify your opportunities for improvement, how should you start to improve your marketing results?

*"Start where all marketing starts —
with your customers."*

You want to understand what your customers are looking for and why they buy. Because it doesn't matter how smartly-crafted your Offer or how benefit-oriented your Sales Content, if it doesn't appeal to your particular audiences, you've wasted your efforts.

When writing Copy, developing Offers, or planning website Navigation, it's supremely helpful to have a very specific picture of your audience. You *want to know who you're writing to,* who you want to appeal to, and who will use your website.

29

You'll want to uncover the process your Buyer goes through, the Content needed to make a decision, and reasons why each type of buyer buys from you.

In this chapter, you'll start to create **"Buyer Personas" — summaries of each of your Best Customer (or target audience) types**.

Your summaries will go far beyond the traditional customer profile demographics. Buyer Personas should result in *actionable insights* to **drive Content, Offers, website experience, and tactics for reaching your audiences.**

Move beyond the customer profile with 4 main tasks

The keys to getting the most value from creating Buyer Personas are:

- **Gather information directly from your customers (where possible),** and from those who work with them — your Sales and Customer Service staff

- **Use objective analytics** about the behavior of customers

You don't want to guess who your actual customers are, and how and why they buy. You want to *understand exactly what information your prospects really need,* not what you think they need.

This chapter presents a process to help you outline the key characteristics, problems, questions, and habits of each of your target audiences, using **four main tasks**:

1. Analytics

You'll look at analytics from your website, social media pages, email campaigns, and pay-per-click advertising campaigns.

2. Information-gathering

You'll gather information from customer comments, blog comments, and comments on your social media pages. You'll look at your key competitors' blog and social media comments. And you'll review any industry research and online discussions.

3. Sales interviews

You'll interview your key Sales and Business Development staff individually. You'll want to talk to those Sales reps who brought in your Best Customers, and those who brought in new customers recently. (Listening to Sales as they speak with prospects by phone can be helpful as well.)

4. Customer interviews

You'll talk directly with your Best Customers. Ideally, you'll want to schedule 20- to 30-minute interviews, by phone or in person, with five of your Best Customers within each Persona type. (But if you can't arrange customer interviews, you can use a customer survey.)

You want to identify everyone involved in the purchase decision.

- That could include some Personas who visit your website to gather information, but *aren't involved in the final buying decision.*

- It might also include those who *don't visit your website* but are involved in the decision-making process.

If you sell B2B: For each of your Best Customers, you'll identify the most important individual(s) within each customer account, as well as others involved in the buying decision.

You'll typically end up with 3 to 5 Buyer Personas. Some may be more "primary" Personas, and some may be more "secondary" in terms of importance and their role in the buying process.

One-page summary for each Buyer Persona

You'll focus initially on six key areas to help you define your Buyer Personas. Your goal is to create a one-page summary or outline for each Persona.

PERSONA NAME: _____

1. WHO THEY ARE: Demographics, Geographics, Background, Attitudes, Device Preference, Online Activities, Buying Behavior (what they buy, quantities, and frequency)

_____

2. KEY QUESTIONS THEY HAVE: What Do They Want/ Need (goals, challenges, and objections to overcome)?

_____

3. WHY US: Why Do They Choose Us (how do we help achieve their goals, overcome challenges)?

_____

4. IMPLICATIONS: for Content, Offers, and Media

_____

5. ROLE IN PURCHASE:

_____

6. SUMMARY PHILOSOPHY (a real quote):

_____

Figure 3.1

You'll start by identifying your Best Customers, and move to the four tasks above. After you gather everything, summarize what you've learned, and complete the six elements in the one-page Persona summary in Figure 3.1 (one for each Buyer Persona).

You can usually craft effective Buyer Personas in just a few weeks. (*We'll add other elements to this outline in Chapter 4.*)

Identify and define your Best Customers

You want to *identify Best Customers by revenue.* You'll also want to identify their buying behavior.

Identifying Best Customers

Step 1: Customers by revenue

Create a list of your customers by **revenue for the last 12 months**. If you have revenue by customer for a longer period, you may want to look at the longer timeframe.

- You want a large enough sample of customers to include a number of each of your Personas.
- *If you're selling memberships or a single product or service*, you may need to look at revenue over a longer time.

Step 2: Best Customers by revenue

Sort customers from highest revenue to lowest revenue.

- *If you're selling more than one product or service*, typically a small portion of your customers will generate a majority of your revenue. To see that revenue concentration, add revenue from all customers, and compute 80% of that total revenue number.

- Look at the number of customers that account for the top 80% of your revenue. These are **typically your Best Customers. They may represent the top 10% to 30% of all customers**.

Purchase behavior among Best Customers

What can you learn about each "Best" Customer from their sales history:

- **Products:** What's the first product or service they typically buy (if you sell multiple products)? What product or service mix does each customer buy from you over time?

- **Frequency:** How frequently do they buy? How many purchases (or projects) per year?

- **Time as Customer:** How many months between their first purchase and their last? If you provide a monthly service or yearly contract, how many months or years have they been customers?

- **Volume:** Do they buy high quantities per purchase? What's the average dollar size of each purchase (or project)?

- **Multiple buyers:** If you sell to consumers, is there more than one purchaser per household? If B2B, do you work with more than one department or division in the company?

Buyer behavior by Buyer Persona

Within these Best Customers are your "Buyer Personas."

Once you define your individual Personas, you want to know:

- **What percentage of revenue does each Persona generate?**

You'll want to come back to this question once you have a clearer idea of your Buyer Personas.

You'll now go through the four main tasks of Analytics, Information-Gathering, Sales Interviews, and Customer Interviews.

Analytics and information-gathering

Website analytics

The following details are for Google Analytics (google.com/analytics**).** If you've set up **"Goals" in Google Analytics,** you can then create **"Segments"** to learn about those who completed each "Goal."

TO SET UP A GOAL

- In Google Analytics (google.com/analytics), sign in, and select "Admin" (last option in left column.) In the right column ("View"), select "Goals." Select "New Goal," and choose the type of Goal you want — Revenue or Acquisition (lead.)

- Under "Goal Description," name your Goal (Sale, White Paper, Webinar, etc.), and select type as "Destination."

- In "Goal Details," "Destination," choose "equals to" and enter the page URL of your receipt page (for a **sale**) or your "thank you" page (for a **lead**). Click "Save."

Be sure to **create separate "thank you" pages for each Goal** (white paper download, webinar sign-up, enewsletter sign-up, sale, etc.).

TO SET UP A SEGMENT

- In "Admin," in the third column, select "Segments." Click the red "New Segment" button, and **name your Segment** (Buyers, White Paper Downloads, Webinar Sign-ups, etc.).

- In the menu, select "Conditions." From the pull-down, choose "Goal Conversions," and **select the Goal you want to use to Segment your data** (Sale, White Paper, etc.).

- Select "Per Session." From the next drop-down, select ">", and then enter 0 in the last box. This indicates you want to see only those Sessions that resulted in at least one Goal completion.

Once you have Goals and Segments set up, you can use Segments in Google Analytics reports. On many reports, you'll see "Add Segment" at the top. **Add the Segment you've created** (Buyers, White Paper Requesters, etc.) **to compare to All Users**. Or remove "All Users" to look at your Segment.

Your website analytics can give you some demographic, geographic, and device usage details. You can look at "Buyers" as a Segment if you have an ecommerce website. Or look at those who complete one of your forms if you're generating **leads,** or look at "All Users."

AUDIENCE CHARACTERISTICS

Be sure to view these for each Segment you've set up.

- For **Age Group** and **Gender**: In left column under "Audience," see "Demographics."

- For **Geographic Location**: See "Audience," "Geo."

- For Device: Select "Audience," "Mobile," "Overview" to see visits and transactions from **Desktop, Tablet, or Mobile Phone**. Look at the devices used by "All Users" versus what device your "Buyer" Segment used to actually buy.

PAGES AND POSTS VISITED

- **What web pages get the most traffic**? In the left column, see "Behavior," "Site Content," "All Pages" to see "Unique Pageviews" – the number of sessions (visits) where that page was viewed at least once.

- **Your most popular blog posts** (by number of Unique Pageviews) indicate the hot topics for your audience.

- What pages do **Returning visitors** view most often? See "Audience," "Behavior," "New vs Returning." Click "Returning." From the "Secondary Dimension" (the pull-down just above the data chart), select "Behavior," "Page" to see what pages Returning visitors are viewing. (You can compare that to what "New" visitors are viewing.)

TRAFFIC SOURCES

- In left column, select "Acquisition," "All Traffic," "Channels" to see the source of your Customers, Leads, or Visitors. (Above the chart within the "Conversions" section of columns, you can select a specific goal to view by Channel.)

- Click the "Social" Channel to see sales, leads, or visits by individual social media site.

LEAD FORM COMPLETIONS

Have any of your Best Customers completed your online forms to download Content, sign up for a webinar, etc.? (Check especially for actions they took *before* they became a customer.)

If you don't have that information for Best Customers, review the characteristics of those who've filled out your online lead forms. (You can set up a Segment for those who've completed each Goal/Offer.) Compare characteristics by Content topic and Offer type.

- Depending on what data you're capturing with your online forms, you may have geographic information, (and for B2B) **titles and industries**. You can determine company size by researching company name (if you're capturing it).

- **Which Offers are most popular? Which Offers seem to attract each Buyer Persona type?**

BLOG COMMENTS

- Are your customers commenting on your blog posts? Which types of customers tend to comment?

- What blog post topics are generating the most comments and shares? If you're using social sharing buttons (from a program like AddThis® or ShareThis®), you'll have analytics to track number of shares.)

- What questions do customers and prospects ask?

- What words do your customers and prospects use when they talk about their problems or need?

CONTACT US and CHAT

Review comments from your online Contact forms and transcripts from your online chat. What do prospects ask about? Capture the words they use.

SEARCH TERMS

- In Google Search Console (search.google.com/search-console/wel-come), you'll find the search terms that drove your Organic traffic (see "Search Traffic," "Search Analytics"). What keyword phrases are your visitors using to find you?

Pay-per-click (PPC) advertising analytics

You can learn a lot about what's effective with your audiences through PPC Testing. Your tests can reveal the most attractive headlines, benefits, search phrases, and specific wording. (The details below are for Google Ads.)

Look at the ads with the strongest click-through (CTR), and those with the highest Conversion to sales or leads (*see Chapter 15 for Conversion tracking):*

- Which Offers are most effective?
- What headline and description was most effective? What specific wording and benefits work best?

If your PPC ads target specific audiences, which keywords are most effective for each audience? Under the "Keywords" tab, select "Search Terms" to *see the actual phrases your prospects searched for on google.com.*

Email analytics

Include in each email message or e-newsletter a link to "learn more," "get the (Lead Generation Offer), or "add to cart." That way, you'll be able to see exactly which topics, Offers, or products each contact is interested in.

- **Which email topics and Offers get the most clicks** from each type of audience?

- (For ecommerce:) **Which email messages and Offers actually drive sales most effectively from each type of audience?** Look at number of sales divided by delivered email messages.

- *Before they became a customer* — what email topics and Offers were most popular (in your Lead Conversion Series or enewsletter) with each Persona? Which were most popular with your Best Customers (before they became a customer)?

Social media analytics and other information

Your social media page analytics will have some **demographics** of your followers. (Although these followers may not all be your customers, it gives you some idea of the types of people who follow you.)

ACTIVITIES

Review the activity on your company page on each social media site. **Who is liking, sharing, commenting, or retweeting**? Is it your Best Customers, other customers, or non-customers?

Are your Best Customers following you? Do certain types of customers only follow you on certain sites? Are there some Personas that don't seem to participate in social media?

POST TOPICS

Each social media page also has analytics showing the **number of interactions by post**. For each of your pages, look at **what topics get the most clicks**, comments, retweets, likes, and shares.

COMMENTS

You'll want to gather and review the comments and questions you receive on your social media pages (as well as *on the social media pages of your competition*). Organize the comments by topic, and note the specific phrases the audience uses.

Note those comments received from your Best Customers and other customers. Organize them by Buyer Persona to help identify hot topics, attitudes, and questions.

FACEBOOK®

You can research a sample of your Best Customers on Facebook, to identify demographics in their profiles (where they're visible).

Review comments on your company page.

To view your analytics, go to your business page and select "Insights" from the top menu:

- From the left menu, select "People" for gender, age group, location, and language data.

- Click "Insights" in the top menu. If you have an active page with many posts, you'll see an "export data" link in the upper right. You can download detailed activity on your page, posts, or video posts.

LINKEDIN®

On LinkedIn, you can **research each of your Best (B2B) Customers** (or a sample of them) individually.

You may be able to identify **background, education level, type of degree(s), years of experience**, and **time in position**. You may find a description of their job activities.

- Take a sample of your Best Customers if you have more than 100. Try to include customers in different industries, different size companies, different departments, etc. – so you'll cover your main customer types.

For analytics, go to your business page, and select "Analytics" from the top menu.

- To see demographics, choose "Visitors" (from the pull-down) or "Followers." Scroll down to "Demographics" where Job Function is the default. Use the pull-down menu at "Data for: Job Function" to see information on **location, seniority, industry, and company size**.

- Back to the "Analytics" pull-down in the top menu, select "Updates" to see clicks, click-through, comments, shares, and engagement rate.

TWITTER

- On your Twitter page, in the left column, click "Profile." Then click "Followers" to see who your followers are.

- Go to "Notifications" to see likes and re-tweets.

From the left menu, select "More," then "Analytics":

- Click "Tweets" in the top menu to see engagement and top tweets. Select "Export Data" in upper right to download the detail by tweet.

- Go to the page of each Best Customer (if they have one) to see who they follow (under their name, click "following.") What blogs or online publications do your customers retweet? What topics do they tweet about?

- What hashtags are your Best Customers likely to use?

To see demographics data on your Twitter followers, you may want to sign up for a month of followerwonk.com for $29.

Data from your CRM

- Review the **locations** of your Best Customers to see any geographic concentrations.

- For B2B: gather the **titles** of Best Customers and any "firmographics" data you have on the company (**company size, industry**, etc.). For each contact, note the department or function, and gender.

Testimonials and customer comments

Read your customer letters. Ask your salespeople or customer service staff for positive emails they've received.

- What topics and words appear most often in the messages? Why are they satisfied? **Why do they say they buy from you?** Look for key benefits they cite.

- If they include numbers, use them. "We saved $X or cut our time by X%." (If they didn't cite numbers, you may want to contact customers and **ask if they can quantify the benefits.**)

Search for online reviews on Yelp, Amazon, or other websites (which may be industry-related). Check reviews of products/services similar to yours.

Sales calls

Sales calls can be a great way to learn more about your audiences. **Listen in** to identify questions, concerns, objections, and wording your prospects use.

When I was doing a copywriting project on-site for HNC (now part of FICO), I was sitting in a cubicle across from a Sales Manager.

I heard him on the phone with a client, explaining a key benefit of the software. And I remember writing down the specific words the Sales Manager used, because it was a great way to explain the benefits simply.

Competition

COMPETITORS' WEBSITES

Review the Content by topics – their key messages, white papers, other Offers, videos, blog posts, and case studies.

COMPETITORS' BLOGS

- What topics are getting the most comments? What are people asking or commenting about?

COMPETITORS' SOCIAL MEDIA PAGES

- How does their average number of likes, shares, and comments compare to yours? Do their posts seem to target one or more types of customers? That may indicate their Best Customer focus, and topics those types of customers are most interested in.

- Note the topics getting the most comments, likes, and shares. What are the comments?

Other research

Look for online reviews, forums, blogs, and articles related to your industry, product, or service. You're looking for key concerns and problems of your target audiences, what topics they're most interested in, how they talk about certain issues, and what phrases they use.

- *Industry Research Reports*: look for industry or professional association studies of users of your product or service, or key roles or titles in your industry. Reports may include demographics, activities, interests, attitudes, challenges, and motivations.

- You may also find *job listings* for similar positions to those of your Best Customers. They can identify key activities, typical background, and experience.

- *Industry Blogs*: Look for trade association and thought-leader blogs your audience may rely on as influencers. Which topics have the most comments? What key questions do readers ask?

- *Online Discussions*: Check discussions on Quora and other online forums where your prospects participate.

Sales interviews

You'll want the input of those who deal daily with your customers, especially with your Best Customers.

Schedule individual interviews with your key Sales reps. Individual meetings, rather than group meetings, will tend to be more productive and avoid "group think."

After completing your Analytics and Information-Gathering, you may have some potential types of customers or Personas that you'll want to ask about.

You'll want to find out:

- What questions do prospects typically ask – during the first phone call, first visit, subsequent visits? (Are the questions different depending on the industry, department, or level of individual in the company?)

- What interests them most about our products or solution?

- What goals are they trying to achieve?

- What problem(s) are they having?

- How do they handle the task now?

- What challenges (issues, barriers, fears) do they face?

- What are their objections? What are the barriers to purchasing?

- What information does the prospect need to present to the decision-maker, or to move the process to the next step? (How does that differ by type of individual?)

- Who else is involved in the purchase decision? If B2B, who does the prospect report to?

- Why did the last customer who purchased from you buy?

- What seems to close the deal with customers? What benefits or features were most critical in choosing us?

- What do customers say about why they do business with us? Do you have any "thank you" emails or letters from clients that talk about why they like doing business with you/us?

Customer research

The best way to understand your different Buyer Personas, and why they buy from you, is to ask them individually.

You want to gather direct quotes from your customers or Best Customers — to get their actual words. Be sure you include some recent or new customers, who are more likely to remember their situation before they purchased from you. You can either:

- Talk directly to your Best Customers – by scheduling one-on-one phone interviews. This is usually the best approach for high-ticket products or services. You'll want at least five interviews per Persona.

- Or, directly survey your customers. This is usually the best approach for lower-ticket ecommerce websites. You'll want to end up with about 100 responses per Persona.

You want to know:

- Why did you start looking (for a product, service, or solution)? What were you trying to achieve? Were you having a problem?

- What were you using before our product/service?

- What did you need to learn about?

- Where did you find information about us? (Ask which publications, blogs, social media sites, forums, or online groups.)

- Before you chose us, what did you think about our company or product/service?

- Why did you originally consider us?

- What kept us on the "short list" as you made your decision?

- What other options did you consider?

- Why did you choose us over your other options?

- What benefits or features are most helpful to you? What do you like about continuing to buy from (or work with) us?

- How does this compare to what you were doing before?

- Who else was involved in the decision?

If you interview customers one-on-one, keep track of what each customer said, so you can later analyze what different *types* of customers say.

If you survey customers, be sure to include some classification questions for analysis.

Role in the purchase

How does each Buyer Persona participate in the purchase decision – what's the role they play? They could be: **initiator, researcher, influencer, evaluator, decision-maker, buyer, and/or user.**

Your individual Personas could each have more than one of these roles. (With a Consumer purchase or in a very small business, a Persona could have all of these roles.)

Each Persona may not be involved in every stage of the decision. There may be "Visitor Personas" who visit your website to gather information for a decision-maker, but those "Visitor Personas" may not play a role in every stage of the Buying Process.

There also may be important Buyer Personas involved in the final buying decision who may not visit your website, because others are doing the early-stage research for them.

Persona name and summary

PERSONA NAME: You'll want to give each Buyer Persona a name (like "Tony the SVP" and "Bridget the Manager") so everyone in your organization knows exactly who you're talking about.

SUMMARY PHILOSOPHY: After you've reviewed what you've gathered about each Buyer Persona, try to encapsulate each Persona's philosophy in a one-sentence summary. Ideally, this summary sentence is an actual quote from a customer, like:

> "Bridget, the Marketing Manager" –
> *"Can we find a resource to manage this for us?"*

> "Tony, the SVP of Sales and Marketing" –
> *"Where are the qualified leads?"*

To improve your marketing, understand why your Personas buy

Starting your Buyer Persona summaries – and refining them over time – is the foundation for smarter Lead Generation strategies, marketing Offers, website Navigation, and Sales Content!

Once you focus on Personas' real concerns and objections, all of your marketing campaigns will become more effective.

Now that you've got your one-page Persona summaries drafted, we'll add to them in the coming chapters.

Results Obsession Strategy #2:
Develop a True (and Actionable) Understanding of Your Customer Types

---

Persona Name: Tony, the SVP

Role: Decisionmaker in choosing outside vendors

Summary Statement: *"We need more leads, and I'm not sure they're from the right audience."*

Who He Is: SVP, with other departments besides Marketing reporting to him. Background in Operations. Understands his industry well. Focuses on the numbers – how many leads, how many sales. He expects to see results. Tends to find other websites he likes and wants to replicate. Will be involved in phone conferences and proposal stage with potential vendors.

Key Questions: He won't visit the website. He will read the proposal.

Why Us: His marketing manager recommended

Implications: Proposal should focus on results achieved and objective analytics when possible.

Figure 3.2

Persona Name: Bridget the Manager

Role: Researcher and recommender of outside contractors and vendors to her boss, the SVP Marketing and Sales

Summary Statement: *"I can get a resource to manage this for us"*

Who She Is: A mid-level marketing manager with 10-15 years of experience, who mostly manages outside marketing services providers. She needs turnkey solutions. She identifies vendors she has heard about from others or from which she's received direct mail. She researches them on her desktop PC.

Key Questions: Who uses them? Are they qualified in Google Analytics? Can they work with our other outside resources?

Why Us: Recommended by one of her agencies. Qualified in Google Analytics. Detailed proposal proved expertise.

Implications: Client List, case studies, certifications are important.

Figure 3.3

Chapter 4

Plan More Effective Offers by Buying Stages

Y our Offer plays such a critical role in generating response. The Offer motivates your audience – it gives them a reason to take action NOW.

In Chapter 2, we talked about the role of the Offer when you're trying to diagnose problems —and plan how to improve results:

- If you're not driving enough **traffic** to your Lead Generation page(s), you need a more attractive Offer. Or you need to make it sound more attractive (in your pay-per-click ads, social media, email efforts, etc.)

- If your traffic is increasing to your Lead Generation page(s), but your **leads** are not, look at the Content on the page and the amount of information you're asking for on your response form

- If your traffic in increasing to your ecommerce website, but your **sales** are not, an attractive Offer can help get more visitors to buy now

Your Offer can:

- Identify prospects you can market to directly (because it gives prospects a reason to give you their contact information)

- Determine or drive the quality of the prospect
- Motivate prospects to take the next step
- Move prospects through your Sales Process faster
- Help you **track and measure response** to marketing efforts
- Give the prospect a reason to buy from you (sales Offer)

Too often with Lead Generation, the Offer isn't well thought-out. Or worse, there isn't any Offer at all. How many web sites do you visit that just say "contact us"?

As a result, many web sites, email messages, online ads, and social media posts are much less effective than they could be. Typically, it's either because:

- There isn't an Offer
- The Offer is what everyone else is offering
- The Offer doesn't motivate YOUR audience to take action

---

*"If you want a big change in response,
change the Offer."*

What's an Offer?

The Offer is:

1. **The special "deal"**: Why should I act or respond now? What do I get?

    - It's the reason why I'm giving you my email address
    - It's why I'm buying now, or buying 2, or spending at least $XX

2. **What drives or motivates the specific action** you want

    Your Offer should motivate your prospect to take the next step in your Sales Process.

The worst "Offers" you can make are probably "get more information" (yawn) or "contact us." Neither is motivating, and both will get less response than more attractive Offers.

3. **What will motivate YOUR audience to take action**

Will the Offer you're considering really be something that gets your particular audience to act?

- The more affluent your target, the more competition there is for their attention. Your Offer needs to be something that would motivate an affluent target to act.

- The more senior your business target, it's more likely there's a gatekeeper and lots of competition for attention. Your Offer needs to get on the boss's desk *and* get the boss to take action.

Craft your Offer to help prospects assess their (or their company's) situation, so they feel ready to take the next step.

We'll focus on identifying that next step for each of your Personas. And we'll look at what **types of Offers** could drive that action. *(The next chapters include specific Offer ideas.)*

Outlining your Buying Stages

In Chapter 3, you identified your Buyer Personas and learned why they buy. Now, you'll build on that, by focusing on **what the buying process (or "buyer journey") looks like for each Buyer Persona.**

"Buying Stages" are the specific steps your prospects take before making a purchase. When you understand them, you'll be more strategic about your Offers (as well as many other elements of your marketing).

For the portion of the process in which each Buyer Persona is involved, you want to identify the steps they take.

Looking at the one-page summary of each Buyer Persona that you developed in *Chapter 3*:

- The "Key Questions" of each Buyer Persona may happen at different Buying Stages

- If you thought of "Implications for Offers" for each Persona, we'll use those in relation to each Buying Stage

Buying Stages dictated by the "3 C's"

The "3 C's" dictate your particular Buying Stages:

1. COST: how significant is the purchase

2. COMPLEXITY: of your product or service — how much research and education will be needed to make the decision

3. CHANGE: how much your product or service changes the way your audience does things — how much research, education, and time might be needed to make the change

The *more Costly or Complex the decision*, or the *more it Changes the way your prospects do things*:

- The longer the Research and Evaluation phases in the process
- The **longer your overall sales cycle**
- The **more complex your Buying Stages**
- The greater your Buyer Personas' **need for Content**

Conversely, for less costly, less complex purchases that don't significantly change the way the Buyer Persona (or the company) does things, you might expect a faster sales cycle.

The discussion below lays out three general Buying Stages.

- Some industries (especially B2B) have a longer sales cycle and more steps in the process. Within other industries (especially B2C or less costly purchases), the steps might be compressed to just a few.

- Your particular prospects may have a more abbreviated Buying Path – or they may have more "sub-stages" within each of these three overall Buying Stages.

Prospect "paths" to become a customer

In Chapter 3, you looked at each of **your Best Customers before he/she became a customer**:

- Was he/she on your email or enewsletter list?
- Did he/she do the free trial or demo, or request a sample?
- Did he/she download a coupon before purchasing?
- What Content Offer(s) did he/she download?
- If B2B, did he/she attend a webinar before becoming a customer?
- What was the order of actions? Check the date he/she first became a prospect, and follow subsequent dates to see the order of actions taken to become a customer.
- *From your CRM*: how many times did he/she talk to, email, or meet with someone from your Sales team? Were different people involved in each meeting? What was the purpose or focus of each meeting? What questions did the prospect have?

Is the path the same for every Persona?

It's likely some *B2B Personas* prefer white papers, while others may attend a webinar. You might find some Buyer Personas are involved in many more Buying Stages than other Personas.

Some B2C Personas take longer to make a decision, while others have a much shorter Sales Cycle.

Buying Stage 1: Research and education

This "Early Buying Stage" is where many companies are missing appropriate Offers. And that's incredibly dangerous as Christopher Ryan from Fusion Marketing Partners summarizes:

- Forrester® reports 74% of B2B buyers do at least half their research online before buying offline

- SiriusDecisions found that prospects completed **70% of their research before ever contacting a company**

- Corporate Executive Board reports 57% of executives **already made their decision** before contacting sales.

Early Buying Stage Offers are critical to ensure you don't miss a huge portion of your prospects.

The Buying Process starts when one of your Buyer Personas (or someone in their company) either: recognizes they have a problem, becomes aware of a possible solution or better way of doing something, or is "inspired" to improve or change something.

That usually starts some type of "Research Stage." For *inexpensive purchases*, prospects just might want to know what's available.

For *more expensive B2C or B2B purchases*, prospects may **want to become educated** on the topic or category, understand the possibilities and options available, and try to identify what they want or need.

Early Buying Stage 1 questions might include:

WHAT TYPES OF SOLUTIONS TO CONSIDER

The prospect may not know exactly how to solve the problem. The prospect may be looking for possibilities – what are the **different types or categories of solutions** to consider? For example:

- I want to improve the look of my kitchen with new countertops. I know about granite and marble. But I discover there are quartzite and engineered stone countertops I should learn more about before I make my decision.

- I need to manage my Twitter efforts more effectively. What types of solutions exist? I discover at least two categories – solutions I have to download to each device I use, or online tools.

WHICH TYPE OF SOLUTION TO PURSUE

The prospect may need to **learn more about what each potential solution can do**. Prospects might compare features and benefits of different types of solutions, to try to select the right Category of solution.

WHAT FEATURES TO LOOK FOR

Prospects want to learn about **recommended features and benefits they should look for.**

Each of the situations in Buying Phase I presents **major Offer (and Content) opportunities.**

Offers for Buying Stage 1

If a prospect is looking for a solution to a problem, the information needs may include:

- What types of solutions exist
- Pros and cons of each type of solution
- How to evaluate or determine if each solution is appropriate or may solve the problem
- Recommended features to look for

You could turn each of these needs into an Offer. You can develop an Offer that will:

- Explain *how to solve a particular problem*
- *Compare different ways to solve the problem*
- *Help the prospect do a simple self-assessment* to determine the right solution and/or features
- Suggest the key features to look for in a solution, so *you dictate the list of criteria all options have to meet*

57

The format of your "low-commitment" Offer could be:

Educational Content: Research report, industry study, comparison report, Buying Guide, video or archived webinar, ebook, fact kit, case studies (of how a particular problem was solved)

Self-Assessment: Needs survey, planning kit, current plan analysis, "what stage are you in" analysis

Category Comparison Tool: cost or ROI comparison, features/benefits comparison, interactive selection tool

One example: virtual data sites are an online way for many companies to securely share and track the usage of large files. The first-time visitor needs to understand: what is a virtual data site, what are the benefits, what features does it typically include, and how much does it cost.

That prospect needs an Offer that makes sense for this stage in the Sales Process, such as an:

- Industry Report on *"The Top 10 Ways Real Estate Companies are Benefiting from Using Virtual Data Sites"*

Even if your website is an ecommerce site, you may still want Early Buying Stage 1 (Lead Generation) Offers. Those Offers help you capture emails when prospects first visit your website, so you can talk to them directly.

Early Buying Stage Content may help you reach your prospects before they consider your competition. If you can be the company that educates on how to solve a problem and what to look for in a solution, you set yourself up to be at the top of the prospect's "short list."

Buying Stage 2: Identify companies/brands

Stage 2 questions include:

WHO OFFERS THIS **TYPE** OF SOLUTION?

The prospect might start compiling a "short list" of companies to consider.

WHICH COMPANY/BRAND OFFERS THE **BENEFITS** I NEED?

Prospects start to identify the features and benefits they want, and may create an "initial cut" of companies or brands.

This is the Phase where most companies focus their advertising, website Content, and Offers by **selling against others in your category**.

When you focus here, you assume prospects know:

- Your product category exists and what it does. (What about prospects *who don't know what type of solution they need* to solve the problem?)

- The name of your category, so they can search for it. (What about prospects who *don't know your category exists?)*

Focusing only here misses a huge opportunity to expand your prospecting – and reach more of the market before prospects become "sold" on a different type of solution.

So be sure you have Offers to reach prospects in Buying Stage 1 and in Buying Stage 2.

Offers for Buying Stage 2

At Stage 2, prospects have chosen the **type** of solution. Now, they need to identify **products or services from specific companies**.

Your website visitors at this Stage may need guidance in how to choose exactly the right product. They may need to understand *how your particular brand of solution works, what your particular benefits are, and what "flavors" (variations, levels, packages, options) you offer.*

Offers for Buying Stage 2 (to get your company "on the list" for consideration) include:

- Case studies
- Competitive comparison reports, cost comparison guide

- Webinar
- Online demo, free trial
- White papers that illustrate your expertise
- Product selection guides, "How to choose" reports

For our virtual data site: The prospect needs help comparing options and deciding what features are most important. Logical Offers at this stage are:

- Comparison Report on leading virtual data site providers
- Special Report on *"Choosing the right virtual data site"*

Buying Stage 3: Evaluation and decision

In this stage, prospects compare and evaluate the companies/brands on their "short list." They may:

- Compare companies or brands on a specific list of criteria
- Look for reviews
- Review case studies to learn how others use the solution
- Talk to others who've used one of the companies or brands
- Look for each company's Client List to see who uses the product
- Do a test drive or trial or demo
- Request a sample or fabric swatch
- Ask for a sales presentation (or go into a retail store)
- Get a price quote, request a proposal, or send out an RFP

Offers for Buying Stage 3

When prospects are ready to select a vendor or specific brand, they may be trying to understand:

1. The more **intangible** differences between your company and the competition – such as your customer service, and how responsive you are

2. Your **credibility** — does your product/service do what you say it will do, who's a happy customer, etc.

Prospects may want to do an on-site visit to see your solution — and talk to some of your reference accounts.

Offers can demonstrate your solution or your expertise, make a more personal connection with the decision-maker(s), or guide the prospect in terms of selection criteria. Offers might include:

- Template for writing an RFP or RFQ for your industry
- Guide to evaluating products or suppliers in your industry/category
- Product/service/vendor comparisons
- Return on Investment analysis or ROI evaluator tool
- Demo, Pilot program
- Cost comparison, lifetime cost comparison
- Breakfast/lunch briefing (especially by technical staff) or technical conference call/brief (to answer objections)
- Webinar/seminar on Implementation
- Online meeting with reference accounts
- Trial Offer – special price/discount for first month (or more)
- Sales-Driving Offers – buy 1, get 1 free; free shipping on your first order; spend $XXX, take x% off your first order; Quantity discount based on number of users; % discount for pre-payment.

For situations where you have a long Sales Process, your "Stage 3" may actually be multiple Stages. In that case, you may need to use several of the Offers to move the prospect through to the next Stage.

When you understand the journey of your Buyer Personas, you can create logical Offers to move prospects through your Buying Stages.

Offers by Persona by Buying Stage

Now you're ready to put your Persona knowledge together with your particular Buying Stages.

Based on the specific steps in your Sales Process, you want to identify potential types of Offers by Persona for each Buying Stage.

That will give you every opportunity to capture prospects' contact information, and motivate them to take the next step.

You may want to create a spreadsheet like *Figure 4.1 below*, to map out the particular Buying Stages each Persona may be involved in.

	Persona A	Persona B
Stage 1: Research		
– Questions		
– Action		
– Offers		
Stage 2: Vendor ID		
– Questions		
– Action		
– Offers		
Stage 3: Decision		
– Questions		
– Action		
– Offers		

Figure 4.1

Outline these elements by Persona:

QUESTIONS: From your Buyer Persona summaries, what questions does each Buyer Persona have? Can you assign each question to a Buying Stage?

ACTION: Think about the logical next step or "Action" you want each Persona to take at each Buying Stage.

OFFERS: For each Buying Stage, what might **motivate** the prospect to take the next step?

Consider your particular Personas' interests. Will a $5 gift card for coffee motivate a C-level executive? Will your C-level executive sit through a webinar? (Or are they more likely to view a summary video?)

Those doing the research for the decision-maker are most likely to attend a webinar or read a white paper.

We'll go into more detailed Offer examples in the next few chapters.

Appealing to multiple Personas

When you know that more than one Persona is involved in the decision, do you need two separate Offers? You may be able to craft one Offer that appeals to multiple Personas. For example:

- If you need the buy-in of a C-level executive, that audience tends to be concerned about high-level issues like: ROI, improving productivity, and improving efficiency.

- If a mid-level manager is gathering the information, they may focus on operational issues specific to their department.

You might make an Offer of a white paper that presents *"How to boost your data processing efficiency, while achieving a positive long-term ROI."*

That gives the mid-level manager the benefits he or she is looking for, along with information needed to sell the boss on the ROI.

I wrote the copy for a campaign done by Rosen Brown Direct that had two targets – Marketing decision-makers and IT decision-makers. We offered a pre-recorded webinar they could view at their leisure, as well as a package of gourmet coffee and biscotti to enjoy during the presentation. It stood out among other webinar Offers and included very "low-commitment" gifts that were appealing to the two audiences.

Remember that every visitor to your website isn't ready to buy today. But if you can capture their contact information by offering useful Content, you'll build a list of leads to educate over time (and maybe before the competition).

Understanding your Buying Stages will help focus your marketing Offers

Your website may attract visitors at every Buying Stage. You'll want to include a range of Offers (and Content) to meet your prospects' needs at those different Stages.

If you can craft Offers that answer your Personas' key questions at Buying Stage 1 – when they're just starting their research – you can grab a head start over the competition.

Your Offers that drive action should:

- Identify and help generate "Early Stage" leads (Buying Stage 1)
- Drive the next step to move leads through the Sales Process
- Help you track and measure response

In the next few chapters, we'll focus on the Lead Generation Process, and then specific Offers to generate leads and sales.

Results Obsession Strategy #2:
Understand Your Personas' Specific Buying Stages

References

Ryan, C. 2018, *How Mapping the Buyer's Journey Can Lead to More Revenue.* CustomerThink. <https://customerthink.com/how-mapping-the-buyers-journey-can-lead-to-more-revenue>

Persona	Stage 1: What do I need?	Stage 2: Identify appropriate vendors	Stage 3: Compare/ Choose
Bridget the Marketing Manager	**Questions:** How can I make the company's website work better?	**Questions:** Who is qualified in Google Analytics?	**Questions:** Who uses them? What results have they achieved? What is the approach?
	Action: Gather contact information	**Action:** Gather contact information	**Action:** Request proposal
	Offer: "7 Steps to a High-Yield Lead Generation Website"	**Offer:** "How to Use Analytics to Tune-Up Your Website"	**Offer:** Website Audit
Tony, SVP of Sales and Marketing	**Questions:** How can we get more leads?	(not involved here)	**Questions:** What's the vendor's plan to get more leads?
	Action: Get contact information		**Action:** Request proposal
	Offer: "7 Steps to a High-Yield Lead Generation Website"		**Offer:** Website Audit

Figure 4.4

OFFERS BY BUYING STAGES

Chapter 5

Lead Generation Strategies to Drive the Leads You Need

Why aren't you generating more leads?

Does your website need to be redesigned? Do you need new messaging? Or are visitors not taking advantage of your Offers?

If you're struggling to generate leads, it might not be a problem caused by your website, email, or any of your other marketing tactics. It's likely a **strategy problem** with two issues:

- You need Offers on your website to meet the needs of your Buyer Personas at each Buying Stage (from *Chapter 4*)
- You need appropriate Offers in given Lead Generation efforts, to achieve the goals of your overall Lead Generation plan

"If you're not happy with the leads you're getting, change the element that drives the lead — your Offer."

It's common for about 98% of website visitors never to leave a trace (by filling out a registration, sign-up, "contact us" form, or making a purchase.)

To compute this percentage for your website, add the number of completed Lead forms, contact forms, and sales for one month. Divide that number by Users to your website for that same month.

- If you had 72 downloads of your Content Marketing Offers (and no other activity), and you had 14,237 visitors during the month, more than 99% of all visitors never left a trace.

    o   72 / 14237   =   0.51%
    o   100% − 0.51%   = 99.49%

It's time for a better Lead Generation plan.

Make the focus all about your Offer

When you're driving leads (in email, pay-per-click ads, etc.), *the copy needs to be all about the Offer* (rather than your product, service, or company).

Focusing on the Offer to drive one action at a time is the best way to get your audience to take action.

If the purpose of your website is to generate leads, *you need a Lead Generation Offer on Home, every product/service page, and every blog post*.

Too many marketers, agencies, and web developers don't think about an actual **Lead Generation strategy for websites designed to generate leads**. It's why we still have "more information" pitches (or just "Contact Us").

- The proactive approach is to **give your audience a strong reason to take action**.

Lead Generation goals drive Offers

Quantify your goals for a particular effort

Do you have a sales force that needs a steady stream of leads to call? How many reps do you have? How many calls can they make per day? These numbers help you figure out how many leads you need per week.

- You may only want Sales to call qualified leads. In this case, you'll need to increase your initial Lead Generation goal – because only a percentage of leads will be (or can be) qualified to give to Sales.

Maybe you have a revenue goal, or you want a specific number of new customers. Look at your Conversion Rate at each step in your Sales Process. Work backwards to help figure out the number of leads you need to start with, to create the number of new customers that you want.

For example:

- If you have 5000 website visitors per month, and 3% of all visitors complete one of your online forms = 150 leads per month
- 30% of those 150 leads were sent an email, and responded to the next step to request a quote = 45 qualified leads
- From those 45 qualified leads, you had 13 sales (or about 29% Conversion to sales).

Looking at your initial 5000 visitors, less than 1% became customers. So if you need more than 13 sales per month, something has to improve at one or more steps in your process. Either you need to:

- *Drive more traffic*
- *Drive more qualified traffic*
- *Get more visitors to visit your Lead Offer page*
- *Get more visitors to your Lead Offer page to complete the form*
- *Make a more attractive next-step Offer in your email*

This type of planning will help you create a realistic Lead Generation budget in relation to your goals.

Plan the role of each Offer in your Lead Generation plan

What are you trying to accomplish with a particular Lead Generation Offer? For example, your goals could be to:

- BUILD A LARGE DATABASE OF LEADS to market to.

    o This is a *"high quantity, low initial quality"* strategy. You want a high *quantity* of names that you can work over time, without regard for each name's immediate *"quality"* (i.e., their likelihood of turning into a sale.)

    o This is the goal with a website — to capture the largest number of visitors, understanding they're likely at various Buying Stages.

- IDENTIFY THE "A" LEADS – You may need to find those ready to purchase who have a budget allocated.

    o This objective means *high quality names, but it also means a low quantity.*

    o Make this type of Offer in an email campaign to your lead database, to get "A" leads to "raise their hand."

- GATHER HIGHLY QUALIFIED LEADS – You may want to focus on leads that are useful for Sales to contact, so they won't be wasting their time with follow-up.

    o You can focus on "A" (ready to buy) and "B" (actively researching) leads. This is a *good quality, fair quantity* strategy.

- TAKE THE NEXT STEP — maybe you're marketing to leads that have already responded to a previous Offer, and you're trying to get them to take the next step.

    o You'll typically make this type of Offer in email, direct mail, or by phone.

70

In each of these cases, the level of "qualified" lead you're looking for will help you decide on the type of Offer you need to make. (We'll talk more about managing Lead Quality versus Lead Quantity below.)

Plan Offers to create A, B, and C leads

You're likely driving traffic to your website from all of your other marketing efforts.

Each website visitor may visit your site during different Buying Stages. So your website needs to meet the needs of your **entire audience.** At any point in time, visitors to your website could include "A," "B," and "C" leads.

"A" leads: high quality, very low quantity

"A" leads are those visitors who are **ready to buy.** The "A" leads will do a trial, "Request a Demo," or "Contact Us." But visitors ready to talk to Sales today are the smallest quantity.

"A" leads are in Buying Stage 3 or the Decision Stage

Hopefully, your website doesn't assume all visitors are "A" leads and ready to buy now. And "Contact Us" isn't the only trackable action or "Offer" on your website, is it?

Are you capturing your "B" and "C" leads?

"B" leads are those who are "in-market," gathering information and **actively looking** for a solution. It may be too early for them to talk to a particular company, because they're still researching options and looking to see what's available. If they can't find the answers to their questions on your website, they're unlikely to contact you. They're just going to visit your competition.

Some may do a trial. If they don't, you'll need another Offer (one that's "lower commitment" than a trial) to attract their attention and capture their contact information.

**B leads could be in: Buying Stage 1 (Research Stage) or
Buying Stage 2 (Identify Vendors Stage)**

"C" leads are the "sightseers." They're interested and **want to learn more but aren't actively searching for a solution**. "C" leads are "lower quality" because they're not "in market." But you can be the company to educate them about what's possible and get them interested.

They likely won't bother contacting you if they have questions. They may become "B" and "A" leads over time – but you'll need a "lower commitment" Offer to capture them.

You want to lead **C leads into Buying Stage 1 (the Research Stage) with your Offer.**

A Leads	Ready to Buy	Buying Stage 3: Decision
B Leads	"In Market" & Looking	Buying Stage 1: Research and Buying Stage 2: Vendor ID
C Leads	Sightseers but interested	Move them into Buying Stage 1: Research

Figure 5.1

The majority of your site visitors are potentially "B" and "C" leads. Those are the 98% of visitors that never leave a trace (by filling out a form, etc.). But you've spent time and budget to drive those visitors – why not find a way to capture more of them?

Low commitment Offers

The average website misses 98% of its visitors — usually because it lacks some **"lower commitment" Offers.**

When prospects visit your site for the first time, what are the Offers they see? If your only Offer is "Request a demo" or "contact us," to a prospect that may mean "I'm ready to talk to a salesperson." Few prospects on their first visit to a website are ready for that.

A lower commitment Offer allows the prospect to provide some contact information to get the Offer (which might be an educational piece of Content.)

These types of Offers help meet the needs of a wider variety of visitors, so they **drive lead quantity**, and build a database of leads to follow-up.

Each of these Offers (similar to the Buying Stage 1 Offers we looked at in Chapter 4) could be seen as low commitment:

- White papers, proprietary studies, or reports from third parties
- Case studies showing how others use your products to solve problems. (You can go beyond written case studies and consider videos or pod-casts. There's nothing stronger than allowing a prospect to hear directly from your customers.)
- How-to articles
- "Is this solution right for you" guides, product buying guides
- On-demand, pre-recorded webinars
- Self-assessment tools ("How well does your company . . .")
- "How to choose a supplier/partner" guide

You might be concerned that if you use lower commitment Offers to boost Lead *Quantity,* you'll also reduce Lead *Quality*. But you *want* to capture "B" and "C" leads – before someone else does.

- You'll use your Email Conversion Series of messages to educate your "B" and "C" leads over time. And you'll present next-step Offers to move them through your Sales Process. (*More on this in Chapter 16.*)

- Your next-step Offers can actually help you qualify your leads – and help them become Sales-ready.

So don't be afraid of capturing lower-quality leads. Let your Email Conversion Series do its job and deliver qualified leads to your sales force.

Balance Lead Quantity with Lead Quality

You really can't consider Lead Generation Offers without considering Lead "Quality."

Lead Quality refers to how likely it is for the lead to become a customer. You want to achieve the right balance of **Lead Quality** versus **Lead Quantity**, because each tends to have *an INVERSE relationship with the other:*

High Lead QUALITY usually means low Lead QUANTITY

High Lead QUANTITY frequently means low Lead QUALITY

The level of commitment of your Offer from your prospect's point-of-view is what determines Lead Quality.

For example, the *lowest commitment Offer* you could probably make is "Enter our sweepstakes." The result is:

- *High Lead Quantity–* lots of prospects may enter.

- *Low Lead Quality* – a small percentage of those leads will actually be interested in your product or service. The majority will have a very low probability of converting to a sale.

The opposite is also true . . .

Perhaps the *highest commitment "Offer"* you could make is, "Call us" or "Contact Us." It's the same as saying, "Call to talk to a salesperson." Only the true "A" leads will usually respond. The prospect has to be *really* interested in your product or service to contact you.

The results are very predictable. You'll get:

- *Low Lead Quantity* – because very few prospects are ready to talk to a salesperson today.

- *High Lead Quality* – those few who are ready to talk today are "in market," actively searching for a solution, have the budget, and are ready to buy. You'd expect a high percentage to convert to a sale.

Modify Lead Quality and Quantity by changing Offer and Content

You can craft Offers between "high commitment" and "low commitment."

- Some elements of your Offer and copy will tend to get you *more qualified leads* – we'll call those "Lead Qualifiers."

- Other elements will tend to deliver a *higher quantity of leads* — those are "Lead Multipliers."

Improving Lead Results

"Lead Qualifiers"	"Lead Multipliers"
• Mention price	• No price
• Provide more info	• Less info
• Ask for more info	• Ask for less
• Nominal fee	• No fee
• Narrow appeal	• Broad appeal

Figure 5.2

Lead Qualifiers

If you're getting good Lead Quantity — but poor Lead Quality — for a specific Lead Generation effort, some changes will *improve Lead Quality:*

- **Mention price** or a price range for your product or service. *Especially if you sell a premium product*, be sure your prospects know the ball-park. You want to ensure that those who respond really are willing and able to spend that amount. (Note: in the next few chapters, we'll address many ways to talk about "price" that can help illustrate the true value to a prospect.)

- **Tell more about your Offer and its benefits**. More information helps prospects "qualify" themselves. They're more able to decide whether this is what they're looking for, or if the information will be helpful.

- **Ask a few more questions on the response form**. The more information you ask for (or the more required fields), *the higher the Quality (but the lower the Quantity).* Those willing to give more information or answer more questions are more genuinely interested in your Offer.

- **Charge a nominal fee**. If you're offering samples, charge a small fee. A catalog selling slipcovers offers fabric swatches, so you can see the fabric and true color before ordering. They charge $3 for up to five fabric swatches, and you'll get a $3 credit when you place an order. Those just casually interested probably won't request a swatch, but those who are genuinely considering an order will invest the $3 to insure they pick the right fabric and color.

- **Make your Offer have narrow appeal**. "Get free movie tickets just for coming into our new golf shop" is too generic. Instead, offer a free sleeve of golf balls that will only appeal to golfers. **The closer your Offer relates to your product or service, the higher the Quality** of your leads.

- **Require a credit card** to try your service.

- **Require that the prospect contact you** to arrange a demo.

What if your "Quality" problem is leads from the *wrong audience*?

If your Offer is too generic, like "download our brochure," you're not **using your Offer to target the right prospects**. Think about the specific problem(s) of your target audience (or what they want to achieve). Craft an Offer to address problems from your target Persona's point-of-view.

In B2B, for example, if you're targeting the manager level, their focus is usually on productivity. So instead of a brochure with the overall benefits of your product or service, why not create a white paper on *"X Ways to Boost Your Department's Productivity with (product or service)."*

- Design your Offer to *appeal to decision-makers at a certain level, at certain-size companies, and in certain industries, when possible.*

Lead Multipliers

To improve the *quantity* of leads: reduce the commitment level, make it easier to respond, or make a more attractive Offer.

- *Reduce the amount of required information you ask for.* (Only ask for the information you need to make your Email Conversion Series work. *Email address, name, and maybe a question to help target* your email series is likely all you really need.)

- Offer on-demand access – to the webinar or the demo. A "Request a Demo" Offer *where the prospect has to contact you* to demo your software is a high commitment Offer. Prospects will perceive anything that implies "talk to a salesperson" as high commitment.

- Allow your prospects to try your product without a credit card. A "free trial" may sound low commitment — but requiring a credit card isn't perceived as low commitment.

- Broaden the appeal of your Offer. Offer a popular gift card – something everyone can use. **The broader the appeal of the Offer, the higher the quantity** of leads.

- Make a more attractive Offer — something that might be perceived as more valuable or helpful

- Don't mention price.

- Tell them less.

- Don't charge a fee (for your catalog or for a sample).

Elements that Affect Commitment

Reduce Commitment	**Increase Commitment**
• Little info required	• More info required
• Access anytime	• Access on a schedule
• No credit card needed for trial	• Credit card required
• No contact with company needed	• Need to contact Sales for demo

---

Figure 5.3

The key to crafting the most appropriate Lead Generation Offer is to **decide where you want to be on the "Quality/Quantity Spectrum."** For example:

- An investment advisor wanted to attract consumers with considerable investable assets. In the communication, we specifically mentioned *"if you have investable assets of $250,000 or more"* to allow consumers to self-qualify themselves. In this case, the investment advisor *wanted high Lead Quality, and was willing to sacrifice high quantity.*

78

- A Midwestern bank wanted to build a list of families living near a new branch. They planned to market to the list over time. *The bank wanted high Lead Quantity and was willing to sacrifice quality.* The agency I was with at the time, Rosenfield Vinson, created a promotion that offered free "welcome" gifts and a sweepstakes drawing if residents came to a series of special Grand Opening Events. This low commitment Offer drove branch visits and built a substantial mailing list.

What if you want qualified leads and good quantity?

In this case, you might try a **low commitment Offer, tied specifically to your product**, so those who respond are genuinely interested in your product or service.

For example, if you want to promote IRAs, make your Offer a useful report on IRAs:

"Top 10 Ways to Take Advantage of the Latest IRA Tax Laws."

This low commitment Offer should have good appeal, but it will attract only those really interested in funding an IRA.

What if you were a financial planner opening an office in a new area? You send an Offer for a free consultation and ask homeowners to call you to schedule it. What would your results be?

- Although the "free consultation" might seem like a low commitment Offer, **this is really a high commitment Offer.**

  o You're essentially asking them to call to talk to a salesperson.

  o Plus, in this case, you're asking people to share sensitive financial information with someone they don't know, someone they don't yet trust, and someone whose advice they don't know if they should rely upon.

- You will get very few (if any) phone calls (low quantity).

- But if you do get a call, that person will be of *very high quality* – and more likely to convert to a customer.

What might be a better Offer in this situation? How about a **lower commitment Offer** to introduce yourself and demonstrate your expertise? How about a free report titled:

*"7 Mistakes You Might Be Making Without
Having a Financial Plan"*

This Offer will get a wider number of prospects to respond.

You should *constantly be testing Offers* to find the right combination of Lead Quality and Quantity for your situation.

How much should you spend for a lead?

It depends on how much each lead is worth to you. You can compute that based on how much new customer (or order) is "worth" to you.

First, consider your "profit per sale" and your objectives:

- **Do you have to make a profit on the initial sale?** If so, you'll need to factor that into your Lead Generation plan.

- **Can you bring in new customers at breakeven or at a loss?** That may make sense for you if you have repeat or monthly sales, where each customer can become profitable over time.

Here's a look at a simple "Breakeven Analysis":

Step one: "Gross Profit Per Sale"

Take your Purchase Price minus your **Direct Costs of completing one sale**. *In Figure 5.4 below*, the product or service sells for $790. We have $190 of direct costs (for purchasing or manufacturing, packaging, etc.), leaving us with $600 gross profit on every sale.

- If you're selling a service, and salaried staff will close the sale and deliver the service, there may not be any direct costs of closing and fulfilling one more sale. If you offer a commission per sale, that commission would be included in your direct costs.

- In this example, you may be willing to spend the entire $600 "gross profit per sale" to bring in a customer – if you expect future sales. Or you may need to add some profit into your "Direct costs."

Breakeven (BE) Analysis

Price minus	
Product Costs/Order	$790 - $190
= Gross Profit Per Sale	= $600
Total Cost divided	
by Gross Profit Per Sale	$15,000/$600
= BE Quantity	= 25 sales

Figure 5.4

Step two: "Breakeven (BE) Quantity"

Take the total cost of your proposed Lead Generation program. Divide it by your "Gross Profit Per Sale" to see how many SALES you need to cover the cost of the program. That's "Breakeven Quantity."

- In the example above, we're looking at a $15,000 program. At $600 gross profit per sale, you'd need to bring in 25 sales to cover the marketing costs.

Since you're doing Lead Generation, you need to look at your "Conversion Rate" at each step in your Sales Process. That will help you "work backwards" from the number of sales you need, to determine the number of leads you need.

In Figure 5.5 below, we need 25 sales to Breakeven (C).

- But we have to generate leads first, so we need to know our Conversion Rate. In the example, 30% of leads have converted to orders or customers in the past.

Lead Generation Offers

- Gross profit Per Sale   = $600 (A)
- Total Marketing Cost   = $15,000 (B)
- B/A = Breakeven   = 25 (C)
- C/# Delivered   = 25/5000 = 0.8%
  BE Sales Response
- C/Conversion   = 25/.30 = 83
  Leads Needed (D)
- D/# Delivered   = 83/5000 = 1.66%
  BE Lead Response

Figure 5.5

- ○ If you're new to Lead Generation, you may want to use 20% Conversion or less. Conversion Rate can vary from 1% for web Offers to 30% for well-qualified leads.

- For 25 sales divided by .30 (30% Conversion Rate) = 83 (D). We need 83 leads from the initial Lead Generation effort.

- That means our Cost/Lead = $15,000 / 83 = $180. **If we spend $180 per lead, we will just breakeven** by covering our marketing cost.

Step three: Breakeven (BE) lead response rate

Is 83 leads a reasonable number of leads to expect?

- Our Lead Generation program reached 5000 names. Take 83 leads divided by 5,000 = Breakeven LEAD response rate of 1.66%.

Have your past Lead Generation efforts come close to 1.66% response? If so, this program may make sense.

What if your Sales Process has multiple steps?

You should calculate the Conversion Rate at each step in your process. If you're driving website traffic, you might have these steps:

- Let's say you're using Google pay-per-click Ads. You're generating clicks at an average cost of $2 per click, and you drove 5000 clicks this month that cost you $10,000.

- About 3% of those website visitors filled out your form to get your Offer. So 3% of 5,000 visitors = 150 "step one" leads.

- Of the 150 leads, 30% took the next step (came in to your facility, emailed or called to talk to a rep, requested a price quote or proposal, etc.). So you have 45 "step two" leads.

- Of the 45, you closed 33% for 15 sales. So you spent $10,000 to drive 15 sales or $667 per sale.

If your gross profit per sale is $600 and you need to breakeven or make a profit on each sale, this program wouldn't be profitable for you.

To help the program become profitable, you could:

- Reduce your cost per click in Google Ads (the easiest and fastest solution to test in this case)

- Improve your "step one" Offer or Landing Page to try to improve that 3% Conversion

- Improve your "step two" process to try to improve that 30% Conversion (which might be unlikely)

- Raise your purchase price.

If your gross profit per sale is $600 and you know you'll have additional sales per customer, you may be fine with spending $667 per sale.

This is the type of financial analysis to do before you commit to a new Lead Generation program. This will help you determine what types of Offers – and Lead Generation programs — make financial sense.

If generating leads is key, your team should live and breathe Lead Generation

If the main objective of your website is to generate leads, you're in the Lead Generation business. It's time for you and your marketing team to become experts in Lead Generation.

Everyone on your team should understand the inverse relationship between Lead Quality and Lead Quantity – and how to use lead multipliers and lead qualifiers to improve results.

In the next chapter, we'll address specific Lead Generation Offers and how to "merchandise" them so they sound irresistible.

Results Obsession Skill #1:
Understand Everything About Lead Generation

Chapter 6

Lead Generation Offers

You want to create an arsenal of irresistible Offers to attract each of your Buyer Personas.

Before you craft an effective Offer, consider:

- What Offers does the competition use – and *how can yours stand out?*

- What are *your unique benefits or areas of exp*ertise (if selling services) – and how could an Offer emphasize them?

- Does your audience know anything about your category of solution? Could you use an Offer to educate them?

Your Lead Generation Offer should give prospects some value in exchange for providing contact information.

Types of Lead Generation Offers

If you're generating leads, your Offer is usually composed of *something free* with or without a deadline. The challenge is to make "something free" sound particularly appealing to get *immediate* action.

*"Create Offers that motivate
your particular audience(s) to
take the action you want."*

Some categories of lead Offers are:

Try it free

This could include free trials, test drives, demos, free month, or a free single copy (if you're selling site-licensed software).

A "Try it Free" Offer can be *low commitment*, like: "Register and download the demo at your convenience."

Or Try it Free can be *medium commitment*: "Register to see an upcoming demo" (in a webinar setting at a defined date and time). When you click "Demo," you get a listing of all the upcoming webinar dates, each of which has a registration form.

Try it Free can also be *high commitment* if the prospect has to "Request a Demo." That implies that a salesperson will be doing an individual demo.

If you're offering a free trial, *you might find shorter trial periods convert better*. Some online services that started with a 30-day trial have tested their way down to much shorter trials, typically 7 days.

Implying some urgency with the trial – rather than giving a leisurely 30 days – may get prospects to start working with the software, service, tool, etc.

Free sample Offers

Your Offer can give your audience a "taste" of what your full product might be like, with a sampling Offer:

- Free sample size
- Free swatches
- Free book chapter or first part of a course
- Free 2-minute clip from your video
- Free results summary from a study

Free information (Content Marketing) Offers

Create unique Content in a useful format

Packaging your "more information" into useful Content can create great low commitment Offers to bring in "B" and "C" leads at Early Buying Stages. Your free information Offer can:

- Show your specific audience how to solve a problem.
- Show prospects how to gain a key advantage.
- Explain pros and cons to compare solutions
- Outline key features and benefits to look for when choosing your type of solution.
- Present case studies of how your company solved a problem or created an advantage for a client.

As you show your audience how to solve the problem, gain the advantage, compare, or choose, you'll also be demonstrating your company's expertise.

And actually proving your expertise is much more powerful than just talking about your services.

Consider interesting formats that might be appropriate for your audience and their problem. How about . . .

Checklist	*Workbook*
Resource Guide	*Video*
Quiz	*eBook*
Podcast	*Mini-Course*
Performance Report	*Idea Kit*

Re-use Content to create Offers

If you review all the Content you've created – presentations, articles, blog posts – you might be able to re-use and re-purpose that Content into some attractive Offers.

If you've prepared slides for a trade show (or other presentation), you could add your commentary in the Notes section to create an eBook.

Could you take all of your blog posts on one topic and re-package them into a special guide?

You could re-organize some of your website Content into checklists, special reports, white papers, eBooks, etc. Few, if any, visitors to your website read everything. Why not highlight some of your Content in a special Offer?

Give your Offer a title that will attract your audience

In Lead Generation, you want to sell the Offer. The best way to sell the Offer is to give it an intriguing title that makes it sound so valuable and useful that your audience thinks, *"I've got to get it."*

For example:

- We could offer a brochure (yawn) on our Lead Generation services. But few visitors are going to provide contact information to get a services brochure.

- Or we could offer a white paper on the *"5 Missing Pieces of Your Lead Generation Puzzle"* (an Offer on our website). This topic sounds valuable and interesting.

Free assessment

Assessments can help prospects:

- Analyze their situation
- See how well your product or service fits their needs
- Determine what they might need to get started

- Choose specs to get a price quote

A free analysis or assessment Offer could be a: needs survey, portfolio or current plan analysis, talent test, assessment quiz, "grader" (how do you score), or planning guide.

Sometimes you'll need to talk to or meet with the lead and gather more information before you can move them to the next step. A free analysis or assessment Offer can get your salespeople "in the door."

Free class

Your free class Offer could be a: video or archived webinar, interactive Zoom® class, podcast (for download through Apple Music or Google Play), or breakfast/lunch briefing. Any of these events can demonstrate your expertise and make a more personal connection with a group of prospects.

HubSpot® has an online academy with online video courses. Register for the academy, and you can access as many courses as you'd like.

Free online tools

Your Offer could be access to calculators, analysis tools, ROI tools – anything that helps the prospect learn something, analyze something, or move them closer to finding a solution.

Consider access to:

- Problem/solution recommender
- Tool to design a system

Integrity HR, a company that provides outsourced HR services, offers a *"Cost of Hiring Worksheet and Turnover Calculator."*

You can also make your publicly-available online tools into Offers. Just give prospects the option to "enter your email to get your final recommendation (or an estimate) in writing."

Free gift

For higher dollar sales, offer a free gift along with your "free information" (or a 2-step gift, where the salesperson delivers the second piece of the gift).

Merant Corporation Lead Generation Offer:
free report + gift

The objective for Merant Corporation (now Serena Software) was to educate IT and Marketing audiences about web CMS systems. The Offer was a free report on the solution category – plus something more fun to "sweeten" the Offer:

- Access to a special video from industry analysts, Gartner®
- Plus, designer coffee and biscotti (to enjoy while you watch the video)

In this case, the Offer included a product-related gift to improve Lead Quality, plus a fun gift to boost the Offer's appeal (for Lead Quantity).

Series of gifts

Perhaps one of the most famous Series-of-gifts Offers was created for a financial services company. The company wanted to encourage targeted company presidents to meet with its Account Reps. They mailed a series of three prospecting packages to the company presidents:

- Each of the three packages included a baseball, autographed by a famous player.
- In the third mailer with the final baseball, the Offer was:

    "Schedule a meeting with an Account Rep to receive your baseball display case."

This Offer gave company presidents a strong reason to meet with an Account Rep — to get an attractive gift that "completed" the set of the three autographed baseballs.

Enter to win

A free entry into a sweepstakes or drawing is the lowest-commitment Lead Generation Offer you can make.

If you're trying to *build a database* of "suspects," consider:

- Stop by our booth (or store) and enter to win

- Visit our site and enter to win

- Enter and choose your enewsletters:
  o The entry form for a $50,000 DIYnetwork sweepstakes included a sign up option for dozens of enewsletters.

- Take advantage of magazines at special prices and enter:
  o The Publisher's Clearinghouse online sweepstakes entry process takes you through almost a dozen pages of special Offers for magazines.

Bank grand opening mailer builds consumer database

When I was Director of Client Services at Rosenfield/Vinson, we created a campaign mailer to announce the Grand Opening of a new bank branch. The objective was to build a database of young families living in the area.

The mailer included three "Winner's Tickets," each to be returned to the branch during one of three Grand Opening weekends. Each completed ticket earned a free gift plus a sweepstakes entry. Both the free gifts and the sweepstakes prizes were chosen to appeal to kids and their parents:

- *On the first weekend,* each completed Winner's Ticket earned a free T-shirt, plus an entry into the sweepstakes
- *The second weekend's free gift* was a baseball cap, plus another sweepstakes entry
- *The third weekend's giveaway* was a fanny pack, plus another sweepstakes entry
- *The sweepstakes prizes* included a TV, computer, a basketball arcade game, and a grand prize trip to Walt Disney World® Resort

As an additional incentive to return each Winner's Ticket, the bank donated $1.00 for each completed Ticket to the Say No to Drugs Foundation, a group chosen for its appeal to parents of young children.

For any accounts opened during the Grand Opening, the bank donated $5.00 per account to the Foundation. This Grand Opening was a great success in terms of visitors and new accounts opened.

APC Lead Generation uses business-to-business sweepstakes

To drive visitors to their web site, APC® offered a "register to win" sweepstakes, with one of their products as the prize.

When the visitor entered a "Key Code" from the ad, a second Landing Page opened with sweepstakes specifics – plus product information.

The sweepstakes entry form didn't even appear above the fold on the Landing Page. You had to scroll down past the product information to get to the entry form – so every visitor saw the product information.

Offers to identify A, B, C leads

Scotia Howard Weil builds a lead database, then identifies "A" leads

Brokerage firms tend to make Offers for free information, and then follow-up by phone to those prospects. But that could mean making phone calls to a lot of unqualified leads – which may not be the best use of the brokers' time.

Rosenfield/Vinson designed a campaign to build a large database of leads the brokerage firm could market to over time. The first Offer was:

- Get your free guide, *"Tax Reform Strategies for Investors."*

When leads received the "Tax Reform Strategies" guide, they also received a second Offer. That second Offer got the "A" leads to raise their hand, so brokers could focus their follow-up only on those leads:

- *Free six-month subscription to Investment Outlook if you talk to a broker by (date).*

Presenting multiple Offer options in a single effort

You can identify the "A" leads, as well as address key questions of visitors at earlier Buying Stages, by directing prospects to an Offer most appropriate for them.

We were selling e-Content Management Systems. We believed our targets could be at four main points in the Sales Process:

- They weren't sure if e-publishing made sense for them. (the not-really-looking "C" leads)
- They might be interested in e-publishing but needed to learn more. ("C" leads)
- They might be sold on e-publishing, but are unsure as to the best way to implement a solution. ("B" leads)
- They might be ready to review the company's particular solution. ("A" leads)

Offers for Each Buying Stage

- I'm not convinced of the value of e-publishing
- How does e-publishing work?
- Why do I need a systems integrator?
- I'm ready for a proposal

Figure 6.1

We presented the four options in *Figure 6.1 (above)* on the Landing Page. When prospects clicked on an option, they were taken directly to a page with an Offer appropriate for that situation, either:

a. White paper on the benefits of e-publishing

b.   Video on how e-publishing works
c.   Comparison report on ways to implement an e-CMS solution
d.   Interactive form where they could input specific requirements to cus-
     tomize a proposal

Merchandise your Offer to illustrate the value

Once you've crafted the idea for your Offer, you need to make it *sound* irresistible to the audience.

Decide to ban "more information" or "free information" non-Offers. Be creative. Re-package your "more information" into a useful piece of Content your prospects will value.

Create a title for your Content (special report, white paper, video, online course, etc.) that will intrigue your audience — and make them really want the Content. How about:

"How to Create a Qualified List of Prospects in 3 ½ easy steps"
or
"The Ultimate Small Business Guide to Driving Retail Traffic"

Craft some bullet points of **what prospects will learn** from your Content. Make those bullet points as specific as possible to convince your audience of the value of your Content.

Figure 6.2 below lists the bullet points of what you'll learn from our Lead Generation Offer, *"5 Missing Pieces of Your Lead Generation Puzzle."*

When you focus on the great benefits of your Offer, you'll leave the visitor thinking, *"I have to get that"* – and you'll drive more responses.

Learn how to build a smarter Lead Generation System

- Discover how to generate more Leads from your SEO efforts

- Make your Social Media efforts completely trackable — and Lead-Generating!

- Craft Early Stage Offers — to reach 43% of your market before your competition

- Create a plan for capturing "A," "B," and "C" leads

- Learn secrets of driving Lead Quantity — from designing to promoting a High Quantity Offer

---

Figure 6.2

Realtor® Lead Generation: special seller-focused report stands out among the competition

You don't have to be a large company to do a smart Lead Generation campaign. I received a great and timely Offer from two local real estate agents, looking to generate a list of homeowners who might be considering selling their homes:

A New Special Report:
How to Sell Your Home in a Buyer's Market
(And Get the Best Price Faster than Anyone)

What a great title! These agents could have done what every other agent does – send a postcard with a picture of their latest listing on one side, with listing details and their contact information on the other.

Instead, they created an **Offer that focused on a particular goal – that of identifying potential new listings**.

They used this Offer in direct mail and in local newspaper ads. They stood out, because they were the only Realtors® *focused on potential sellers.*

How to use the Offer

How should you use your Lead Generation Offer?

In Lead Generation efforts, your copy should sell the Offer (rather than your product or service) to drive the first step – the gathering of contact information from prospects.

How to Use the Offer

SALES

• Sell the product

• Offer is something extra to motivate the sale now

LEADS

• Sell the Offer to drive the next step in the sale

Figure 6.3

The common error in Lead Generation is to pitch the product too early – and that makes for wasted money on prospecting.

• If you're pitching a webinar, *focus your copy on selling the webinar.* Tell attendees what they'll learn at the webinar, rather than pitching your product or service.

You want to **motivate one action at a time**. Focus on getting the lead first – by selling the Offer.

Free trial from UPS®

I received a well thought-out Offer from UPS.

- The headline: *"A free offer engineered (and guaranteed) for speed"*

- I see it's from UPS, I see something is "free," we ship packages, so I'm likely to open it.

The Lead Generation Offer is to *try the service for free*. **The entire effort is built around the Offer** as it should be:

- When I open it, the headline is: *"Get ready. You've been chosen to take UPS on a high-speed test drive."*

- I see details on how to enjoy a free UPS shipment.

I'm not distracted by a lot of information about their service. Instead, everything focuses on driving that free trial.

To generate more leads, start being more creative with your Offers

To get prospects to take action, you need to work harder to make your Offer really sound like your audience can't pass it up.

In most cases, *your chance to get the lead will never be stronger than when prospects first see your web page, email message, or online ad.*

So motivate them – give them a strong reason to act IMMEDIATELY – with a great Offer.

Start testing different Lead Generation Offers – and give each one an irresistible name and fabulous list of *"what's in it for me?"* benefits.

97

Results Obsession Skill #2:
Become an Expert at (Lead Generation) Offer Construction

References

Kobs, J. (1991). *Profitable Direct Marketing, second edition.* McGraw-Hill

Chapter 7

Sales Offers for Every Objective

When you're driving a purchase, the Offer can be the "something extra" that motivates the visitor to buy now. As you craft your sales Offer, think about how your Offer can:

1. Differentiate you from what the competition is offering
2. Give your Buyer Personas a strong reason to act now
3. Reduce common objections (e.g., it's too expensive, etc.)

To choose the right sales Offer, start with your objectives.

"There are at least 22 different types of Sales Offers. How many have you tested?"

Objectives of a sales Offer

If you want to drive an immediate order, what's your goal?

- **Drive new orders:** Bring in new customers.

- **Get repeat orders:** Motivate past or existing customers to buy again.

- **Upgrade customers:** Encourage purchasers of your basic model or service to upgrade to your premium version.

- **Increase average order size:** Make each order more profitable by encouraging larger order sizes.

- **Take your customers "out of the market":** Get customers to stock up on your product, so they're less likely to buy from a competitor.

Each of these objectives may require a different type of Offer.

Components of sales Offers

If your objective is an immediate order, there are (at least) four components you can use in your Offer:

- **Pricing, quantity, and payment terms**. There are many options beyond a sale price that will motivate the sale.

- **Guarantee.** Everyone wants to know they can get their money back if they're not satisfied. Writing a strong – and unique – guarantee (or extending the warranty period) can boost results.

- **Deadline or expiration date**. Create a sense of urgency by offering something for a limited time, to get the prospect to take action *now*.

- **Bonus gift or something extra**. Something free with purchase can be a strong motivator. Cosmetics companies use the "free gift with purchase" Offer frequently.

Your Offer can be a pricing/terms Offer with a deadline, a bonus gift Offer with a deadline, or some combination of these elements. But a guarantee should always be part of your sales Offer.

Carbite Golf Polar Balanced Putter promotion

Carbite Golf used an Offer that effectively *combined the four components of price/terms, guarantee, deadline, and special bonus*:

- 3 easy payments of $49.97
- Full 90-day risk-free trial and guarantee — receive a full refund if you're not sinking more putts

- And receive the *Putting Secrets of the PGA® Pros video* plus head cover (a $39.95 value) as a free bonus when you order by xx/xx/xx. Keep the free gifts no matter what!

The elements of this Offer combine to **address all of the most common objections** to the order:

- *"I can't afford a $150 putter."* No problem, we'll bill your credit card over 3 months, just $49.97 a month.

- *"What if I don't like the putter after I get it?"* No problem, just return it for a full refund. But you can try it out for a full 90 days.

- *"Why should I try this putter?"* Completely risk-free trial that could improve your game, and you get a free video to keep no matter what.

Here are some ideas for Offers that drive an **immediate order**, and how to improve Offers that miss the mark.

Price/quantity/terms Offers

Customer-only sale

Give your customers special pricing or access to sale pricing or new merchandise before the general public. This Offer drives sales (and loyalty) without alerting your competition to your reduced prices.

Introductory or limited-time Offers

Consider: introductory or "charter member" Offer, early-bird discount (frequently used to drive seminar registrations), "first 50" to purchase get something extra, buy before the price goes up, seasonal sale. All of these Offers have a **time limit** as an integral part of the Offer.

If you need to drive orders for a **new** product or service, you might offer it at a special "trial" price.

I saw an ad that seemed to be introducing a new website, with the headline *"Introducing (nameofsite.com)"*. Presumably, the objective of the ad was to drive web traffic.

The Offer should have supported that objective, by helping to drive online sales. But the ad contained a curious Offer: *Call to save 10%.*

Huh? *Isn't the whole purpose of the ad to drive sales on the web site?*

This Offer should have been something to motivate the web visit, like:

Enter bonus code XXX to save 10% on your first order at (nameofsite.com)

Bundled or unbundled product/service Offers

You could package two or more products together at a bonus price and call it a *"bonus pack."*

Or package a sample size with the regular size of another product for a *"Free sample with order"* Offer. (Cosmetics retailers know that customers can purchase name-brand cosmetics from many websites. To differentiate them-selves and keep customers buying, the smart ones include free samples with every order.)

You could bundle some of your premium services together to drive the purchase of the upgraded services.

To drive trials, you could also consider an "unbundled" Offer. You might strip off some features to offer a cheaper (limited functionality) version as an "entry level" product (or service).

DMA/ANA bundled product Offer

Why not take two or more of your products, put them together, and give the package an interesting name? That's what the Direct Marketing Associa-tion (now part of the Association of National Advertisers) did when it bundled a copywriting report with another creative-focused report called:

"Getting Creative Bundle"

That's much more interesting than saying, "When you buy book A plus book B, you save."

But they missed the opportunity to emphasize the savings, by showing me the price of each report separately. I see the bundled price, but I can't tell whether the "Getting Creative Bundle" is a great deal or not.

It would've been more effective to say:

Save $XX with our special "Getting Creative Bundle"

What if you were offering the Harry Potter® series of books as a bundle at $XXX? Why not tell me **I'll save $X over buying each book individually**?

You could also allow customers to create their own "bundle," with **special pricing on logical add-ons.** They could add a carrying case (with a laptop), other accessories, printer ink (with a printer), etc.

Good, better, best Offers

If you have three levels of service, you can present "basic, mid-level, premium" or "good, better, best" options. Frequently, this Offer causes more buyers to upgrade from the basic or lowest-cost option to the intermediate one.

- Basic product/service without X, X, and X $ 49
- Intermediate product with X, X, and X $ 79
- Deluxe product with X,X,X, and X $ 99

It also identifies those willing to pay a premium price for additional features or a higher level of service.

Series, subscription, or membership discount

Get a reduced price if you subscribe to the whole series or pre-pay for a full year. Or get a reduced price on the first month when you sign-up for the subscription or membership.

You'll also see the "good, better, best" Offer used for subscriptions, where the "Better" and "Best" options reduce the per-issue cost for a longer term:

Good option: Get 12 months for $2.00/issue   ($24)
Better option: Get 18 months for $1.78/issue   ($32)
Best option: Get 24 months for $1.50/issue   ($36)

Trade-in Offers

This can be a brilliant Offer for motivating laggards to move up to a more current model.

Carbite Golf wedge promotion

Carbite Golf offered a *"trade in discount"* on a new wedge. Buyers could ship their old wedge back to Carbite in the new wedge's box, and Carbite donated all the old wedges to a local junior golf program.

Synthetic lawn ad creates questions

"Never Mow Again" is the headline I saw in an ad. There's a guy pushing a lawnmower in the background, and a big red circle with a slash over the whole photo. It's a good attention-getter. The ad includes a unique Offer as a clever tie-in with a synthetic lawn:

- *"Purchase a Synthetic Lawn before April 15, and We'll Buy Your Old Lawnmower!"*

Then I wondered about the second Offer in the ad — a "20% off coupon." Do I get 20% off AND you'll buy back my mower?

It's always best to spell out the details, so your prospect doesn't have any unanswered questions *(objections)*. Maybe it should have been:

"Save 20% on your Synthetic Lawn before April 15 – and we'll even buy your old lawnmower"

Rebate

Rebates cost you less than the value of all rebates that customers qualify for, because only a portion of buyers will claim a rebate. You avoid discounting your product and maintain more margin than if you offered a "sale" price.

Quantity limit

Including quantity limits actually encourages customers to buy more. For example, if you add a restriction of "limit 2 per customer," it will actually encourage more customers to consider buying two. It plants a seed in the buyer's mind – like, "maybe I should get two."

Quantity discount

Get a particular discount if you buy a certain amount or quantity.

It can be a *"stepped" discount by dollar amount purchased* (save $20 if you spend $100, save $15 if you spend $75, etc.).

Or you can offer a *volume discount* for a certain quantity purchased.

Quantity discounts can help drive up your average order size. You can also use them to keep your customers from buying from the competition for a period of time.

JC Penney mailer

To motivate a higher average sale, consider a graduated Offer, where I save more as I spend more.

When I was at Rosenfield Vinson, the agency created a birthday mailer for JCPenney® credit card holders. The mailer featured a graduated Offer to encourage larger purchases:

It's time to celebrate!
- *$10 off $ 50 or more*
- *$15 off $ 75 or more*
- *$20 off $100 or more*

This is actually a straight 20% off Offer– but it's more effective to talk about actual dollar savings (than percentages).

Quantity discount for loyalty

At my local car wash, if I prepay for 10 car washes, I get each one at a discount. This quantity discount helps ensure I'll keep going there to get my car washed.

Series of payments or delayed billing

There's another category of Offers that get the product in the customer's hands without requiring payment (or complete payment) upfront. Some options include:

- **Bill me** – commonly used with magazine subscriptions.

- **Terms or extended payments** – makes the purchase seem more affordable by spreading out the payments: *"3 easy payments of $29.95"*

- **Delayed payments or interest** – frequently used by furniture retailers. You may see Offers of "no payments for 6 months"," no interest until the following year," etc.

Something free Offers

Something free with purchase Offers

Buy one and get one free, buy 2 and get 1 free, free gift with purchase, multiple free gifts with purchase, or free service with purchase.

If you're selling a subscription service, consider "13 months for the price of 12" (one month free). Or get a free service or gift when you sign-up or pay for a subscription.

Two for one Offer

I received an email that suggested a great way to "spend a day" would be to go wine tasting at a particular winery.

Two Offers were included, both appropriate with the objective:

- *2 for 1 Wine Tasting Tickets* (reinforced by a photo of a couple)

- *$10 off at the winery's restaurant* (to potentially increase the per-couple revenue)

The "dollars off" Offer is clear in its value – much more effective than a "percentage off" deal.

Buy one, get one free

I saw a local ad that was driving non-group traffic to an indoor go-cart raceway Monday through Friday. Their smartly-crafted Offer was:

- *Get 1 Free Race with the purchase of 1 race. Valid for up to 4 people*

That Offer makes people think "maybe I should bring 3 of my friends!"

Gift with purchase

Qualcomm® Eudora® Email Software Test Offers

While I was consulting for the Eudora division of Qualcomm, we spent 6 months testing Offers to drive paid upgrades from their free email software. We tested a number of "something free with purchase" Offers, including:

Purchase the upgrade for only $29
- *Receive a free 60-day subscription to an online service*

Purchase the upgrade for only $69
- *Get 30% off at Amazon.com*
  (Depending on what you ordered with Amazon, that 30% discount might cover the cost of your $69 upgrade.)

Texas Nurses Association (TNA) test Offers

We tested many different Offers for the American Nurses Association to sell a one-year membership. These two were for their Texas affiliate, the Texas Nurses Association or TNA.

For the first Offer, we paid to purchase a booklet of "Smart Travelers' Checks" for a vacation-oriented bonus for nurses:

Get *15 Smart Travelers' Checks,* each good for $20 to $200 off on airfare and cruises (for a total of up to $2200 savings!), when you join TNA today. *(The savings on just a single vacation can pay for your TNA membership!)*

The second Offer didn't cost us anything. I contacted JCPenney® and offered to promote their nurse's uniforms in our campaign, if they'd give us a discount Offer. They were happy to have us mention:

Save 20% on your next purchase of uniforms from JCPenney

Gift with minimum order

Free gift Offer from SK&A Lists (part of OneKey™)

How can you motivate a marketer to spend money on mailing lists during a down economy – plus drive orders of a particular size? How about an attractive gift with a minimum order size?

SK&A offered a *"FREE iPod Shuffle® with your mailing list order of $3,000 or more."*

If you're considering a "bonus gift with order" as your Offer, you might also consider:

- **Multiple gifts** with the order. These types of Offers are common in infomercials, catalogs, or other mail-order efforts.

- **Gifts with a total value that equals or exceeds the cost of the purchase** – popular for membership and subscription promotions:

    "Subscribe to our investment newsletter for just $99 and get 5 special reports – each with a cover price of $20. That's $100 worth of reports, so your newsletter is essentially free."

- **Two-step gift** – you get part one of the gift (or the first gift) just for ordering, and then you might receive a more valuable gift (or the second part of the gift) when you pay the invoice. This can be highly effective, especially when you can't really enjoy the gift until you receive both pieces, or if the gift is more useful in a pair.

Free additional service

If you're selling services, why not expose customers to more of your services? Let them try one service free when they purchase another. A mailing house might promote:

FREE Postcard Design — with the printing of your postcard

Free upgrade

Consider offering a deluxe edition of your product or service for the regular price. Add technical support, a carrying case, or some other benefit to create your "Deluxe" edition:

109

- Now through xx/xx/xx, *get the "gold" version for the price of the regular version*

Or offer a free service with purchase (free monogram, free second color of printing, etc.)

If you're selling consumable products or repeat services, this is a great way to *expose customers to your more expensive (and higher margin) versions.*

The power of free shipping

When you offer free shipping for purchases over a certain amount, you'll usually increase your average order size (as well as orders). Or offer a free upgrade to rush shipping to differentiate your offering.

- We added an Offer of *"free shipping over $75"* to a golf client's ecommerce website. The average order size almost immediately jumped up as a result.

Loyalty freebies

Offer points in a loyalty program to encourage repeat purchases (miles, cash back, get 1 free after your 10th purchase, special pricing, discounts, etc.).

Yogurt and ice cream stores, coffee shops and sandwich shops, gas stations, drug stores, and supermarkets have all used this type of Offer.

For example, Subway® and Starbucks® have frequent customer cards or apps. You earn points for each purchase and get a free sandwich or drink after you accumulate enough points.

Deadline Offers

Pre-release Offer from Broadway San Diego

On the website of Broadway San Diego (an entertainment portal), this Lead Generation Offer gets prospective ticket buyers to submit their email address:

Sign up for our "E-Lert" messages to gain access to the best seats before they go on sale to the general public

After I signed up, I got an email that delivered a "Pre-Public Release" Sales Offer. The headline is "Phantom of the Opera Pre-Sale Begins Today."

You'll have access to the best seats, when you purchase before tickets are available to the general public

In this case, they used the "before available to the general public" Offer to motivate the sale – without giving up any margin!

Guarantee/warranty Offers

You can use a smartly crafted guarantee to motivate the purchase by removing common objections like:

- What if I don't like it, it doesn't fit, it doesn't work, etc.
- What if I have to pay to ship it back
- What if I find it cheaper elsewhere

The Guarantee can be a strong Offer in itself (especially if you're offering an extended Guarantee), or it can enhance other components of your Offer.

Extended guarantee

If the competition is all offering 30 days, consider 60 or 90 days, or even a 6-month guarantee.

Carbite Golf had great success with a **90-day trial**. It was different, it implied the company's great faith in its products, and it gave golfers a significant amount of time to try out the club. (The longer golfers played with the club, the more likely they were to keep it.)

Make the guarantee really convince me of the value

Here's an extended guarantee from a company that sells personal organizers. The headline screams, *"6-Month Money-Back Guarantee":*

*"If you're not 100% **convinced this organizer gives you at least an extra hour of productive time each day**, just return it within 6 months (and still keep the 2 free gifts)"*

In this case, the smart guarantee reinforces *the product benefit*.

Lowest price and price match

If you compete on price, you may want to offer a lowest price guarantee.

- I called FedEx® Office recently to ask about volume pricing for color copies. The manager gave me a price quote *and* a price-match guarantee. **If I found a lower price, he would match it.** It was a great Offer that kept me from shopping around.

Lowest price with double the difference

To give the buyer confidence to buy from you, offer to pay double the difference, should they buy and then find the product at a lower price elsewhere.

Return shipping

You can offer to make returns easy by paying for return shipping. Many ecommerce websites (including Chanel®.com, Nordstrom.com, and Zappos®.com) include a return shipping label with every shipment. It's another way to remove a common objection to ordering, and motivate the sale!

Of all of these different sales Offer options, how may have you tested? If you're stuck in the dollars-off or percent-off "perpetual sale" rut, why not test something new?

"If you're looking for a big change in response, change the Offer."

"Merchandising" the Offer

How can you make every sales Offer irresistible?

When you're trying to drive an immediate order, focus on the benefits of the product, but:

- **Add an attractive Offer as something extra that motivates the audience to buy now.** It's the *"but wait, there's more."* "If you order by (date), we'll throw in this bonus (price, something free, or guarantee)."

The key is to make the Offer sound as irresistible as possible. In fact, the way you state your Offer can be as important as the Offer itself:

- Focus on what the prospect will get or enjoy (the benefit of the Offer)

- If it's a price offer, use a price that sounds like a special offer. $49 sounds like a special deal — and it sounds cheaper than $50.

- If you want to offer a discount, **offer dollars off instead of a percent discount**. Most people can't easily calculate what they'll save with 15% off – but when you say, *"save $10,"* the benefit is clear. (In fact, most people can only figure out a 50% discount. But when 50% off is tested against a dollars-off Offer, dollars off still tends to do better.)

- **Something free** always sounds good. Compared to "half price" or "50% off," "buy one, get one free" tends to do better.

Not the way to do it . . .

I received a mailer with no company name on the outside, just the headline:

"Limited-Time Offer: Save 20% off the New Edition!"

The company is trying to get the envelope opened, and they apparently believe they'll have a better chance without the company or product name. Let's think about this:

- They believe if I see the product or company name on the envelope, the 20% savings won't motivate me to open it. Then, *why would I be motivated to buy once I see that information inside the envelope?*

When you're selling, promote the benefits of your product or service first, with the Offer as the "something extra." In this case, the focus should have been on the product, for example:

"Get 50% more contact names in the latest edition of the Guide to National Advertisers – and save $50 if you order by (date)."

Packaging and Promoting Your Offer

Selling memberships

When you're selling memberships, it can be very effective to show the actual dollar value of everything included in the membership. The prospect can see that if you add up the benefits included, the **value more than equals the cost of the membership**.

The San Diego Zoo® used to do that in their mail efforts for membership renewals (and at least one of their efforts won a DMA ECHO® Award because of its great results).

Now on their website, when you click the Membership tab, you just see a list of membership options. You have to keep toggling back to the Tickets page to compute the true value of the annual Membership.

Wouldn't it be more helpful for potential new members to see how Memberships compare to purchasing individual tickets?

How to use numbers

Numbers that mean the same thing — or that are very close to each other — can be *perceive*d very differently. For example:

- **If you want something to sound LONGER, use the bigger unit of measure**. One month sounds longer than 30 days. One hour sounds longer than 60 minutes. A "three month" guarantee sounds better than "90 days" — *"Use it for 3 full months."*

- **When you want something to sound SMALLER** — break the cost down to a smaller timeframe (month, day, etc.), or compare its cost to something everyone can relate to. If your service sells for $216, it could be $18/month – or *"less than $.60 a day . . ."*

    o *Get one year of coverage for $100 – just 27 cents a day*

Merchandising the Offer

Price Breaks:	$49.99	vs	$50.00
Odd vs Even:	$ 7.97	vs	$ 7.90
Perception:	$ 7.32	vs	$ 7.99

Figure 7.1

- **If you want a number to look BIGGER, include zeroes**.
    o 5 million versus 5,000,000 (all the zeroes make the number look bigger)
    o 25k versus 25,000

- **$49 sounds MORE AFFORDABLE than $50,** as does $99 compared to $100.

- **Ending a price with an odd number – especially a 7** – works better than ending a price with an even number. Tests have found that $7.99 is better than $7.94. Some tests also revealed that $7.97 worked better than $7.99.

To be sure, run your own pricing tests.

- **Don't leave money on the table**, by setting a lower price when a slightly higher price might seem similar. $69 and $79 may both sound similar to prospects, but $79 will make you more money. (Obviously, this works when you're selling a unique product or service that isn't available from multiple companies.)

Financial implications of your Offer

When you're driving sales and considering a price Offer, the cost of that Offer may reduce your purchase price.

A free gift Offer could add an additional cost.

If you're offering a free service, there may be no additional cost if the service is delivered by a salaried employee or online.

So the Offer may reduce your "gross profit per sale" — it **may give you less margin to use to cover your marketing costs**. But an attractive Offer can improve your response rate.

Breakeven Analysis of Offers

- Gross Profit Per Sale = Price minus Product Costs Per Order minus Offer cost

- Re-run Breakeven: what response do you need to cover the cost of the Offer?

Figure 7.2

You can use a Breakeven Analysis *(from Chapter 5)* to determine how much additional response is needed to still breakeven when your margin is lower. Here are the calculations:

Gross Profit Per Sale = Purchase price minus direct out-of-pocket costs of one order

Services or memberships may not have any actual direct or out-of-pocket costs of delivering one more service or membership.

- If you're selling multiple products from your effort: take the total revenue generated from your last effort, minus the out-of-pocket costs of fulfilling all the orders from that effort, and divide by the total number of orders. That will give you "average gross profit per sale."

Breakeven Quantity = Marketing cost divided by Gross Profit Per Sale

Breakeven Response Rate = Breakeven Quantity divided by number reached (mailed, etc.)

Evaluating "something free" or a discount

In the example in Figure 7.3 below, we're considering an Offer that will reduce our margin by $5 (such as a free gift-with-order Offer).

- When we compute Gross Profit per Sale, direct product costs per order are $5 higher to cover the gift. (With a discount, the purchase price would be lower.)

- The cost of the promotion might be $15,000. Dividing $15,000 by Gross Profit per Sale of $55 gives us a Breakeven Quantity of 273.

- Breakeven Quantity of 273 divided by the mail quantity of 15,000 = Breakeven Response Rate of 1.82%.

Has the sales response rate been in the ballpark of 1.82% from past efforts? Or do you think the addition of the free gift (or a discount) can boost response to this level? If so, this Offer and marketing program has a good chance of at least breaking even.

If you can't just breakeven on the sale and need to make a profit, this Offer may not be appropriate, and/or you may need to consider a less costly marketing effort.

Breakeven (BE) Analysis: Free Gift

- Gross Profit Per Sale = price $79 - $24
  minus product costs per order   = $55

- Total cost divided by
  Gross Profit Per Sale = $15,000/$55
  BE Quantity   = $273

- BE Quantity divided by
  delivered quantity =   273/15,000
  BE Response Rate   = 1.82%

Figure 7.3

What if you don't have prior response rates?

- For email to an outside list, assume 0.2% SALES response.
- For email to your own opt-in list, assume 1% SALES response.

All of these response rates are a conservative place to start. Your own response rate may vary substantially (either higher or lower), depending on your market, product, Offer, and copy.

What if the Breakeven Response Rate isn't likely?

The most controllable items in the Breakeven Analysis are:

- Your sales price
- The amount of any discount Offer you're considering
- The cost of any gift Offer you're considering
- How much you plan to spend on marketing

If you ran the Breakeven Analysis and determined you needed too high of a response rate just to break even, you can consider changes to these elements.

You always want to run a Breakeven Analysis on any new marketing effort before you spend a dime. Include your proposed Offers in the Analysis to help you choose the best options for Testing.

To drive more sales, get more creative with your sales Offers

You want to entice your audience with a unique sales Offer that stands out from the competition.

- There are at least 22 different types of sales Offers you could use. How many have you tested?

Don't just flip a coin and say, *"what should we offer this month?"* Start by defining a specific objective for the Offer. Then consider the four components of sales Offers that you could use. And be sure to evaluate the financial impact of your Offer before you make it.

When you've created a sales Offer that makes economic sense, "merchandise" it to make it sound irresistible.

Be sure your team builds expertise in crafting sales Offers that cost-effectively drive sales.

Results Obsession Skill #2:
Become an Expert at (Sales) Offer Construction

References

Kobs, J. (1991). *Profitable Direct Marketing, second edition.* McGraw-Hill

Chapter 8

Messaging Strategy for Copy that Sells

W hy isn't your copy as effective as it could be? How can some copy be 2 or 3 times more effective than other copy? The key is having a better messaging *strategy*.

It's tempting to "jump in" and start writing or editing (or call your agency or freelancer and tell them to get started). But, your copy will get significantly better results when it follows a well thought-out strategy.

"The right plan can help ensure your copy sells — with the right Persona-focused emotion, and unique 'why us' message."

In Part I below, we'll talk about how to plan Messaging Strategy for copy that drives a lead or sale, as well as educational Content. You should *do this strategic prep work whether you're doing the copywriting or giving the project to a copywriter.*

Part II focuses on copy that drives a lead or sale. We'll cover three Creative Strategy elements – the first of which you'll think about as either *the copywriter or the marketing manager.* The second and third elements are *part of a copywriter's planning process*, and you'll want to see those elements in a copywriting plan or proposal.

I. What to gather before you start writing (or before you hire a copywriter)

Here's how to craft a Messaging Strategy to *boost your copy from average to exceptional.*

Know your Personas' hot topics (in detail)

The most effective copy speaks directly to each target Persona. So, you'll want to have as much in-depth knowledge about each Buyer Persona (that you're targeting) as possible.

If you're not writing the copy, be sure to give your copywriter your **Buyer Persona one-page summaries**.

"If you can't turn yourself into your customer, you probably shouldn't be in the ad writing business at all." Leo Burnett

From your one-page Buyer Persona Summaries:

- **Who are they in terms of Attitudes**: What does your audience think about your company/products/services – or your *category* of product/service?

- **What's most important to your audience?** What are their key questions? What are the hottest topics they're interested in? *What problem keeps your prospects up at night?*

- **Why do your customers buy your product over the competition?**

Be sure to consider how familiar each particular Persona is with you and your offering:

- *For prospects* -- Are they aware of your **type** of solution? If not, you may need more educational Content (and Offers) to introduce the solution category.

- Does the audience know your company? What are their current perceptions? Your *copy may need to change those perceptions*.

- *If you're writing to customers* — Have you kept in touch regularly so they'll remember you? If not, your copy may need to remind them of their last purchase with you and the benefits.

Writing for your website audience(s)

If you're writing copy for your website:

- Have you directed the copy to a single Persona (on an educational page or blog post)? Or do you **need different pages that address each Persona's key issues**?

- If you're creating copy for a Product or Service page, you may be able to address the "hot buttons" of multiple Personas on the page. Or you might include links to related pages tailored for each Persona, like: "The CIO Perspective on an XYZ System."

- If you're writing copy for the Home page or About Us, you'll need copy that addresses multiple Personas.

Message format by audience type

Your particular Personas may each want certain types of information in certain formats. (You may have thought about the format issue as you planned your Offers in the last few chapters.)

Sample Personas

Here are two sample Personas for a small agency that sells marketing services to small businesses:

1. **"Michael" is the founder of the business.** Michael may not have a marketing background. He doesn't subscribe to "best practices" marketing industry enewsletters. He doesn't have an in-depth knowledge of any single marketing area. But he does read publications specifically directed at small business owners – and **is always looking for marketing ideas that can help his business.** He frequently handles marketing tasks himself. And he always needs to generate more sales.

2. **"Bridget" is a mid-level marketing manager who has a general marketing degree.** She is usually in the role of managing and coordinating, rather than actually working on her website or preparing copy. She relies on the expertise of the agency or freelancers, whether they're the right resource for her or not. She tends to be the entire in-house Marketing department. Finding the right resource to handle the project is her focus.

Each Persona is likely interested in different benefits of your services. The level of detail I might go into for Bridget would be very different than what I might create for Michael.

Figure 8.1

- If you're marketing to engineers or scientists – they want the facts and the specific numbers. They want to see the spec sheet. You'll want to provide proof of your claims and quantify benefits where possible.

- Some prospects are more visual – and prefer to watch a video. Other prospects are more time-sensitive, and just want the information fast — so include a video transcript for them.

What have you tried and what were the results?

For a promotional effort, be sure to review results from past efforts to see what you can learn.

Before you develop **new website Content**, review what your audience thinks of your existing Content. Look at the pages and topics that are most popular in terms of website visits, blog visits, and social media engagement. *(In Google Analytics, see "Behavior," "Site Content," "All Pages" to see traffic by individual page.)*

- The number of "Unique Pageviews" for a page tells you **how popular the page or topic is.**

- Review Bounce Rate to determine the **quality of the Content** on a particular page. A high Bounce on a Landing Page (especially product page or blog posts) indicates *a high percentage of your visitors didn't visit the Offer page or Contact Us.*

From Testing (in pay-per-click advertising, email, etc.), you may have discovered some headlines, benefits, message elements, and Offers that were more effective than others.

- If you've tested any **Landing Pages** against each other, identify what changed in the winning page.

- Have you tested different **email** Subject Lines, Offers, or messages? Review what's been done before to see what you can learn (and what you can pass on to your copywriter or agency)

- o For the email messages that had the **highest click-through**, what Subject Line, overall message, and Offer did they use? (What about the email messages with the poorest CTR?)

- o If you're selling via ecommerce, what email messages had the **highest Conversion to sales**? *Look at number of sales divided by number of delivered emails.*

  (You may find that emails with high click-through don't always have the highest sales Conversion Rate. So follow results through to sales.)

- Are you running **pay-per-click advertising** and testing different ads? Look at winning headlines and descriptions. Note what headlines and descriptions didn't do as well.

  - o Look at **Click-through Rate (CTR)** to see how attractive your ad copy was to your audience. Look at **Conversions** to see which ads drove leads or sales most cost-effectively. *(See Chapter 15 for more on Conversion Tracking)*

  - o Even if you aren't doing pay-per-click advertising regularly, you can use it to run a short test. You can test different headlines (or different descriptions) in a PPC ad to find the winner. Just set a daily budget limit to control the costs of your test. Once you've completed your test, turn off the Campaign.

- Check clicks on each **social media** post to review your most popular topics. *(See Chapter 2 for analytics for each social media site.)*

What is the competition saying?

To help you craft your own "why we're different" message, be sure to look at your competition and their messaging:

- **What's their "why should you buy ours" positioning**? Check their Home page, About Us page, product/service pages you're competing with, and press releases.

- **What products or services do they emphasize?**

- **What key benefits do they focus on?**

- Do they *talk negatively about any lack of features, or ways of doing things that your company or product does?* (This may indicate an area where you'll need to re-educate your audience about your benefits.)

- What Offers are they using to capture leads or drive sales?

- What educational topics are they talking about on their blog and social media pages? Which are the most popular in terms of comments, likes, and shares?

What next step do you want prospects to take?

Plan the Offer before you start writing.

You should think about the specific Offer you're going to use – and the action you want your audience to take – before copywriting begins.

- *If you're generating leads*, **your entire copywriting effort should focus on the OFFER.** (That's true for a Lead-Generation web page, or for a separate promotional effort like PPC ads or email.)

- *If you're driving sales*, your effort should focus on the unique benefits of your product or service – with the Offer as the something extra to drive the sale now.

If you're creating educational content like a blog post, every blog post page should have an Offer to help capture visitors' information and give them more information on the topic.

Assemble your strategic foundation

Understand:

The hot topics of your target Persona(s)
Your past results

How you compare to your competition
What you want the Offer to do

Then you're ready to start structuring your message.

Don't leave out a review of any of these areas – your writing will be less effective if you do.

II. Messaging strategy

Focus the message on driving leads or sales

When you're driving a sale, you want to create a unique message that answers the question, *"why should I buy yours"?*

And when driving a lead, your unique message should focus on *"why should I request or sign up for this?"*

Too many websites talk about benefits that are TRUE OF EVERY PRODUCT OR SERVICE in an industry or category.

Few websites really do a good job of **answering** *"why should I buy yours?"* (also called the "Unique Selling Proposition.")

To answer that question effectively, review the "why do they buy?" section of your Persona summaries:

1. **Write down the reasons your Personas buy from you.**
2. **Cross out anything that's also true of your competition.**

With the message elements that remain, **answer these questions:**

- Most of our competition (does this), but our company (or product or service) is different because _____.

- What is it about our business that's **better for the customer** than dealing with the competition?

- What makes our product/service **more valuable** than that of the competition?

- What's the **advantage (or key combination of benefits) that only we offer?**

Decide what you want your audience to **remember** about your company (or product or service) *after they've read your copy.*

Try to **encapsulate the big payoff** the customer will enjoy *in one or two sentences.* You want to craft a memorable statement that will:

- Deliver a distinctive benefit -- or unique combination of benefits – significantly different from the competition. (Your key message should **not be something your competition can say.**)

- **Not be easily imitated** by the competition.

- Focus on **meaningful benefits most important to your buyers**

- **Prove** your difference or benefit. Quantifiable benefits are the most compare-able and powerful.

- **Be memorable** (usually the more specifics, the more memorable it is).

- Include a "promise" you can deliver, that customers will clearly see.

Your key benefits statement is complete when it helps your target Persona(s) answer the basic question, *"Why should I do business with you"* versus the competition.

This *"why we're different"* message is the foundation of your story.

It's something you'll want to make clear throughout your website (no matter where the visitor starts), in every email and other promotional effort, and on your social media pages.

Strategic copy approaches

Now that you've created a main message, let's talk about *ways to structure your message.*

Tell a story

- This could be a **problem/solution case study** of what your product or service has helped a customer achieve. Show how others solved a problem -- what they struggled with, what they tried, and what was the result.

- This is a great way to PROVE or illustrate your unique benefits.

- The key is to make it a **compelling** story -- that will really engage the reader and keep him or her reading. If you can be compelling, you can generate very high readership.

- Use the Offer at the end to drive the next step.

- **Appropriate for**: case studies, or a unique email approach

Early benefit

FOR LEAD GENERATION

- **Pitch your great Offer** (maybe a Content Marketing or other educational Offer) in your headline or email Subject Line. Introduce the problem and your Offer in the first paragraph. Then, outline the Offer's *"what's in it for me"* benefits in bullet points.

- **Appropriate for**: Lead Generation website pages, emails.

When you're considering agencies or copywriters to develop a Lead Generation campaign – in email, online ads, or other media channels – ask them how they'll structure the campaign.

From any potential vendors, you should hear, *"it'll be all about the Lead Generation OFFER."*

If you don't hear that, run in the other direction. Your resources MUST be experts in crafting and **testing** Offers.

FOR ECOMMERCE

- If you've got a great sales-driving Offer or a unique product benefit, lead with that at the beginning of your message (Offer-focused or product benefit-focused approach)
- **Appropriate for:** Home, About Us, product/service pages and website Landing Pages -- and all promotional efforts

Early empathy

- Relate to the specific challenge(s) of your Buyer Persona(s). Especially logical for those Early Buying Stage 1 visitors who *need help figuring out how to solve their problem.*

- This approach starts with more of a *"we understand your situation"* warm-up. If a strong emotion frequently drives your purchase, this is a smart way to use that emotion in your message.

- This is the traditional sales approach, with a relationship-building warm-up to build rapport.

- **Appropriate for:** Home, About Us, product/service pages, Landing Pages, and all promotional efforts.

Beyond these three main approaches, there are *more specific sub-approaches.* I first saw some of these in Joan Throckmorton's book *("Winning Direct Response Advertising"),* including:

- Invitation
- Secret
- Testimonial (Carbite Golf sent out a successful appeal that was almost entirely a testimonial from a customer)

- Question
- Problem/Solution

These copy sub-approaches give you a more specific way to write your main headline or lead-in sentence. Realistically, you could **start with any of these five sub-approaches – and write a "story", "early benefit," or "early empathy" approach**.

It's when you think beyond the obvious directions that some really great ideas can happen.

Emotional drivers

What about emotion? Great copy should weave emotion throughout, to motivate your audience to take the action you want.

Bob Hacker (of The Hacker Group) was the first person I heard speak about the emotional drivers that drive response. He cited these seven:

1. Anger -- *"don't allow this to happen"* (for political fundraising)
2. Flattery
3. Fear -- *"are you missing out"* or *"what would happen if . . ."*
4. Guilt -- frequently used in insurance marketing (*"What if they were left without . . . when you could have protected them"*) and fundraising (*"could you say no to this child"*)
5. Greed
6. Exclusivity
7. Salvation -- *"finally, there's a solution . . ."*

I've used most of these – they're great for idea-starters, and a smart area for Testing.

For the Eudora® Division of Qualcomm®, for example, we tested a *Fear approach versus Exclusivity*. We discovered that Exclusivity was far more effective for their "early adopter" audience – even though both messages cited the same product benefits.

For most copy efforts, at least one of these emotions will make sense. Pick one or two to consider — that fit your key message and the problems, attitudes, and concerns of your Buyer Personas. For example:

- What keeps each of your Personas up at night? Could be: *fear or guilt*

- What motivates each Persona? Could be: *anger, fear, guilt, greed, flattery, exclusivity, salvation*

Use only one emotional driver in each version of your copy. (But *if more than one emotion may make sense, write more than one version. Then, test* the versions against each other to find the winner.)

For Texas Nurses Association, we tested an Anger approach versus Exclusivity versus Salvation:

Anger: *". . . some days, the way health care is run can literally make your blood boil – can't it?"*

Exclusivity: *"An invitation to make a difference for your patients, for nursing, for yourself."*

Salvation: *"You're one voice – is anyone listening to your concerns? Do you wonder how – as a lone nurse, you can ever have an impact . . . Join the Texas Nurses Association . . . the biggest, most powerful network of nurses to make your voice heard loud and clear . . ."*

For Eudora®:

Fear: *"Do you make these five embarrassing mistakes with email?"*

Exclusivity: *"If you pride yourself on always having the best . . . on always being the first . . ."*

There are additional lists of "wants." Vic Schwab created perhaps the first often-cited list of desires that others have added to, including:

- Health

- Money (coincides with the "greed" emotional driver) – make money, save money
- Security
- Popularity, Praise, Appearance ("flattery" emotional driver)
- Comfort, Leisure, Enjoyment ("salvation" emotional driver)
- Advancement, Accomplishment
- Save time ("salvation" emotional driver)
- Prevent worry, doubts, risks, embarrassment, criticism, pain ("fear" emotional driver)

Combining one of these basic wants with one of the 7 emotional drivers can help you create a strong appeal.

The Corporate Executive Board found that it's important for emotional appeals to be used throughout the Conversion process – through all of the emails in your Conversion series. Liz O'Neill Dennison suggested that in B2B buying, emotions matter more than logic and reason or a rational argument.

Be sure to ask agencies or copywriters you're considering: what emotions would they use in your project – and why. **If they don't address emotional appeals** in their proposal, **they may not understand how to write copy that really sells.**

In Chapter 10, we'll talk about how to use an emotional driver to get started with your message.

The right plan can help ensure your copy really sells

"Why should I buy yours?" is the most critical question to answer in your marketing. Everyone on your Marketing team – especially those drafting and reviewing copy – should know the clear answer.

Learn how to build emotion into your copy – and be sure your copywriters **plan the emotional driver before they start writing.**

Once you have a Key Message, Copy Approach, and one or two Emotional Drivers to consider, then your team is ready to start writing.

Results Obsession Skill #3:
Learn how to create a strong foundation for copy that sells

References

Throckmorton, J. (1997) *Winning Direct Response Advertising.* NTC Business Books.

From Promotion to Emotion (2013) The Corporate Executive Board Company. <https://plan2brand.com/wp-content/uploads/2015/07/CEB_Promotion_to_Emotion_whitepaper.pdf>

Burnett, L. (1995) *100 LEO'S: Wit & Wisdom from Leo Burnett.* The McGraw-Hill Companies.

Schwab, V. (1956) *Mail Order Strategy.* Hoke Communications.

Dennison, L. O. (2014) *Content Marketing for Business Service.* Kapost. <kapost.com/b/content-marketing-for-business-services/>

MESSAGING STRATEGY

Chapter 9

GREAT COPY: How to Recognize, Write, & Refine It

Whether you write copy yourself, or review another writer's copy, you should know how to recognize copy that really SELLS. (And you should recognize **engaging** educational Content, as well).

In this chapter, you'll learn the secrets to great writing that apply to every element of copy. We'll also talk specifically about how to craft fabulous headlines, engaging lead paragraphs, helpful subheads, and stellar body copy.

"When you learn to recognize copy that sells, you boost opportunities to drive superior results"

Secrets to writing fabulous headlines

David Ogilvy says:

"On the average, 5 times as many people read the headline as read the body copy. When you have written your headline, you have spent 80 cents out of your dollar."

(And for Sales Copy) *". . . unless your headline sells your product, you have wasted 80% of your money"*

The headline has some critical roles:

- Draw the eye of your target Personas
- Drive the click (in online ads)
- Get your message opened (in email)
- Grab attention to make the reader want to learn more
- Draw your reader in to the copy
- Tell readers what they'll learn by reading more
- Build and enhance your brand image

How long should your headline be?

Longer headlines tend to be more effective – because they allow you to be more specific about the benefit.

But your headline should still look like a headline. Don't overdo it and write a paragraph.

Some headline ideas

Here are some great ways to craft a headline, along with the emotional drivers *(from Chapter 8)* you could use:

- Big benefit *(with salvation, greed, fear, exclusivity, or flattery)*
- Great Offer *(with salvation, greed, fear, exclusivity, or flattery)*
- Something free
- Something of value

- Discount or special
- Invitation *(with flattery or exclusivity)*
- Secret *(with exclusivity, fear, greed, flattery, or salvation)*
- Solve a problem *(with anger, fear, greed, or salvation)*
- News
- How to
- Question (why, what) — focus on a problem, or be intriguing or curious. Be careful of writing a headline to which "no" would be a fast answer *(with anger, fear, guilt, greed, or salvation)*
- Command
- Useful Info — "how to" . . .
- Inside Info
- Testimonial *(with fear, guilt, greed, exclusivity, or salvation)*
- Flag the audience — "Are you more than 10 pounds overweight?"
- Numbered ways

Writing headlines step by step

Why are some headlines less than effective — while others totally grab the audience? Great headlines:

1. Present the most important benefit, and make it crystal clear "What's in it for me"?

Your headline is the most important copy on the page – use it to deliver the most important information.

In both your sales and educational Content, the headline should tell your audience what they're going to learn by clicking or reading more.

You want to give your Personas the **strongest possible reason to read more.** Because if your Buyer Personas don't see a benefit in your headline, *they're not likely to read your copy to look for it.*

Your audience doesn't really care about your company or your product – they only care about what it does for them. *Don't assume your audience will figure out why they should care about what you're selling.*

Avoid the feature-based and "our"-focused headline:

- *"Our CRM software includes an email campaign manager"*

Craft a benefit-based and "you-focused" headline instead:

- *"Create, send, and track email campaigns directly from your CRM system"*

Dr. Henry Durant studied direct headlines (that immediately offered a benefit to the reader) versus indirect headlines (that used teasers, puns, plays on words, or something unrelated to the product or its benefits). He found that *direct headlines were 400% more effective.* We've found direct headlines at least doubled response over indirect headlines.

2. Position your company, product, or service uniquely

Your headline should help build and enhance your overall brand image. It should sound uniquely like your company – and not similar to what anyone else is saying.

Your headline should showcase the significant benefit (or unique collection of benefits) that differentiate you:

"You'll enjoy 24/7/365 live US-based support plus 30% more memory"

Lexus once ran a 2-page magazine ad with the headline,

"Does your car fall apart this well?"

Huh? Is that an appropriate image for a luxury brand? (I saw the ad only once, and perhaps that's the only time it ran . . .)

3. Be as SPECIFIC as possible about the benefit

Generalities – that don't *immediately paint a picture in the prospect's mind* (like "quality," "value," "innovation," etc.) – aren't memorable or believable. And they won't differentiate you from the competition.

If you're using generalities, you haven't done enough competitive (or customer) research to know what your unique benefits really are.

What do "specifics" mean? Include specific numbers or other details to add credibility. Don't say "you'll save thousands" if you can say, "our average customer saved $12,373 last year." That's **more memorable and believable**.

And numbers catch the eye and stand out – especially uneven numbers.

> *"Removes 53% more metals from your water"* vs
> *"Removes more metals from your water"*

The specificity of 53% looks like a result from an actual study.

For Carbite Golf:

- *The putter that helps you make 99 out of 100 putts from 10 feet!*

Does your website use generic headlines like "Solutions," "Products," or "About Us"? Which page headline below is more appealing?

> *Courses*
> or
> *All the Required Hours to Renew Your License Tomorrow*

4. Talk directly to your audience with "you" and "your"

Or, start with an action verb, where the "you" is implied:

> *"You'll boost your response"*
> *or*
> *"Boost your response"*

I worked with Richard Rosen's agency on a Merant™ (now Serena® Software) copywriting project. We used "you-oriented" headlines that each addressed a Persona:

> (To marketers:) *"Finally, you can depend on IT without being dependent on IT."*

(To IT:) *"Finally, a way to keep Marketing off your back and have more time to do the fun stuff."*

5. Use the strongest action verb possible

You could say:

XY software *includes* the best CRM features from 10 years of experience
or
XY software *teems* with the best CRM features from 10 years of experience

Even better, turn it around to get the prospect doing the action and lead with the action verb:

Turbocharge your CRM with the best features from 10 years of experience

6. Use the strongest words possible

You want to present a clear, unique picture to the reader:

Your company's logo will appear prominently on this clear glass mug
or
Showcase your company's logo in vibrant full color on this clear glass mug

7. Lead with emotion

Your headline should introduce the emotional driver you're using. Here are three we created for the ANA (American Nurses Association):

Exclusivity:
"An invitation to make a difference – for your patients, for nursing, for yourself"

Salvation:
"Feeling overworked and under-appreciated? Here's what you can do to change things"

Anger:
"Who knows what's best for your patient – you or some politician?"

Do your headlines need to be "creative"?

Your headline needs to speak to your audience. Be careful with puns, plays on words, or other attempts to be funny or clever.

Readers are quickly scanning. If they don't get your point, can't understand the benefit, or can't tell what you're selling, **they're not going to read further**. And that means *you've just wasted your budget.*

Jerry Della Femina said,

"Nobody has the time to figure out what you're trying to say. So you need to be direct. Most great advertising is direct. That's how people talk. That's the style they read. That's what sells products or services or ideas."

Use the "so what?" test

If you read a headline and think, "so what," the headline is weak. You may have a "so what" headline if it's:

- **Too general**
- **Less benefit-oriented**
- Not hitting the emotional hot buttons of the target audience
- "Talking to the company" rather than your audience, by using "we" or "our"
- Something your competitors could say

Typically, **the more specific and targeted to your audience**, the more effective your headline.

Crafting a Compelling Lead-In

Headline: *Build and Run Web Apps Faster*

First Sentence: *Do your developers have superpowers?*

(What a lead-in sentence!)

The first few sentences are your lead-in or "lede." They're especially important because they determine whether your reader will go any further. (And that's true with educational writing as well as Sales Copy.)

To write a "LEAD-IN" that grabs, put **the most important thing you could say to the prospect (after the headline) in the first line**.

Your lede should be:

- "You"-oriented – talking directly to the prospect
- Involving and compelling – a strong statement to draw the reader in
- Written exactly the way you'd say it face-to-face
- Short so it looks inviting to get the reader started

How should you start the message? For Sales Copy, **think of what you'd say to a prospect either face-to-face or on the phone.**

Sales Copy: remind of pain, hint of pleasure

A good salesperson would never start their pitch with "Since 1999, we've been serving the needs . . ." Yet, how many web pages and email messages start this way? (Way too many . . .)

An **effective lead-in typically uses the pain/pleasure combination**:

- Remind-of-pain: *"Do you struggle with . . ."* or *"Are you having trouble with . . ."*
- Or hint-of-pleasure: *"Wouldn't it be great if you could . . ."* or *"What if you could . . ."*
- Or both

This effective lead-in IS what you'd say to me if I was in your office. And it's absolutely the best way to draw readers into your copy – whether you're selling to consumers or businesses.

The lede is where you develop one of the seven emotional drivers.

Examples to improve sales ledes

"I am a full-time professional, enjoy my work, and am determined to give you the finest real estate service possible."

So what? Why does the prospect *care*? How about:

"When you're ready to sell your home, be sure you select a full-time listing agent with a proven-effective marketing plan."

Consider this lead-in that includes unnecessary words and isn't written the way you'd say it out loud:

"I have contacted you in regard to your pension assets being managed by someone other than (company name)."

How about promising a "what's in it for me" benefit, and introducing a **salvation** emotional appeal:

"What could it mean to have your pension assets safely in the hands of the #1 manager?"

A university extension website (targeting those working full-time) has this lead-in for its Business program:

"The rapid and complex changes in business continue to place increasing demands on all levels of an organization."

How about specifics and a lede that prospects might actually care about:

Choose from 15 certificate programs to help prepare you for the next step in your career in just 12 months.

The lead-in sentence for a Singing class hits the spot. It's conversational – exactly the way you'd say it. And it shows a clear understanding of the Persona they're targeting:

"Do you sing in the shower?"

Here's a specifics-laden lede for a Marketing Certificate:

"Learn everything you need to know to quickly enhance your career and earning capacity in marketing, advertising, public relations, or media."

See how well this conversational copy builds emotion — and gets the audience to say, "yep, that's me" — for a Difficult People in the Workplace class:

"Do you grind your teeth in frustration each time you have to work closely with someone who drives you nuts?"

Lead-in, copy approach, and headlines work together

How does your lead-in relate to copy approaches *(from Chapter 8)* and headline options? Your lede can:

- **Introduce a story** (if that's what your copy plan is)

- **Promise an early benefit**: If you have a great Offer, you might want to put it up front.
    - That lede would work with these headline options: *how to, question (what, why), numbered ways*

- **Early empathy**: The "remind of pain, hint of pleasure" lede helps you build some empathy, and imply "we know your pain."

    > Example from John Deere®: *"You know what an ordeal the purchase of grounds care equipment can be ... "*

Educational ledes: tell me something I don't know

Some writers seem to think that because it's a blog post, they should make a lot of "small talk" at the beginning. But for educational Content, **your lede paragraph decides whether readers will keep reading**.

Say something intriguing, challenge them with an involving question, or give your audience some useful statistics **they might not know**. *Don't waste your reader's time with a first paragraph that doesn't really say anything.*

What about this lede:

"If you're like many companies, you send a monthly email newsletter to your customers and others on your mailing list."

That's not a bad lede, it's just not very engaging. Why not hint at what they'll learn from your blog post:

> *"If you're relying on an e-newsletter or other promotional emails to nurture your prospects and retain your customers, do you know if those emails are being read?"*

The lede should make your audience want to keep reading. Does the lede below tell you anything useful?

"As you know very well, the advertising and marketing business changes rapidly and frequently."

This is a "so what" lede. If I "know very well," why are you telling me? Instead, think about what the Persona is looking for:

> *"What's the best way to stay up-to-date on all the latest marketing test results?"*

Body copy: what to include in what order

Now it's time to craft the rest of your sales message. The main area of copy is your "body copy." For Sales Content (driving a lead or sale), your body copy needs to *get your target Persona(s) to take action.*

For educational Content, the body copy needs to *keep your readers engaged and tell them something they didn't know* to deliver value.

Sales Content

What makes the difference between copy that effectively drives prospects to register, buyers to buy, or visitors to visit or call – and copy that doesn't?

Good Sales Copy uses the words of your most effective salesperson to sell in writing.

To write copy that sells, *you have to know how to sell.*

Look to those who are best at selling – your best salespeople. What are the specific words your best salespeople say face-to-face or over the phone to engage prospects? Those words are likely the same words that will be effective in your online marketing efforts.

Selling is selling: Process doesn't change by channel

If I make a sales call (either in person or by phone) to try to sell you my product, I'll likely follow some particular steps.

When generating sales with words, your copy handles one or more of those steps in your Sales Process.

And that Sales Process doesn't change just because you're selling with words. Nor does it change with the media channel.

> *The same steps you follow to sell in person or by phone are the same steps (and the same words!) you should use to sell effectively in email and web.*

So what are the steps in the Sales Process?

Copy that really sells follows the Sales Process

Step 1: Build early rapport using a "pain/pleasure" lead-in

You may be creating a need that prospects didn't know they had. For example: *"Are you 100% happy with . . ., do you wish you could . . .?"*

Appropriate for Sales and Lead Generation Copy. Some blog posts and educational Content can also start this way.

Step 2:   Introduce your product or your Lead Generation Offer

Once you've reminded of the pain your product or service solves, and/or hinted at the major benefit it delivers, introduce your solution (or Lead Generation Offer): **We have the answer.**

Step 3:   Reveal benefits of your solution or Lead Generation Offer

Introduce the major reasons why your audience should buy (or take advantage of your Lead Generation Offer). These are the *"what's in it for me"* points or your key benefits.

This is a great place for bulleted copy. You want to **"sizzle" your benefits** — make them sound irresistible to the prospect.

Step 4:   Pitch your Sales Offer — tell the prospect why to act now

Introduce your special *Sales Offer* with a time limit to motivate an immediate sale.

Some *Lead Generation Offers* use time limits to motivate the response. Or you can tell prospects what they might miss *every day* by not taking advantage of your Lead Generation Offer.

Step 5:   Close with a clear call to action

Tell prospects **how to take the next step.** If you want to drive leads or sales to your website or 800 number, mention the Landing Page or 800 number *prominently*. If you want prospects to come to a retail location, tell them where, how to get there, and during what hours.

Remind your audience of the "lost opportunity" – what they'll lose if they don't act now.

Step 6: (If selling) Answer objections and build credibility

This is the single most commonly overlooked point in copy. If I was selling face-to-face or over the phone, I'd have the opportunity to ask you if you had any additional questions — like what might prevent you from following through immediately, what concerns you have, etc.

Your copy needs to anticipate the most common objections and address them. If you don't, you leave unanswered questions in the prospect's mind:

"Gee, I wonder if that means"   or   "I wonder if it includes"

As soon as unanswered questions remain in a prospect's mind, the prospect is unlikely to act. That means you've just wasted your marketing dollars and reduced your Conversion Rate.

- With a website, there's no excuse for leaving unanswered questions. You've got room to provide the answers — **you can link to more information, provide FAQs, etc.**

- You also have room to **prove your benefits and build credibility**. You can link to *testimonials, case studies, and reviews.*

  Proof and specifics help address the "how do I know this will work" or "are your claims really true?" objections.

Step 7: (if selling) Reiterate the Offer and how to get it

This is the Sales Process. Follow the steps and write your thoughts *exactly as you would say them* face-to-face (and look for these steps in copy you may be reviewing).

Read your Sales Copy out loud. If something doesn't read exactly the way you'd say it, revise it.

Sales and educational Content: how much copy?

There's a simple way to decide how much copy you need:

For LEAD GENERATION or SALES efforts:

- Have you discussed every benefit that's likely to be important to the Buyer Persona(s) you're targeting? (If Lead Generation, focus on the benefits of the Offer. If selling, focus on the benefits of your solution.)

For SALES efforts:

- Have you answered every potential **question** the Buyer Persona(s) could have?
- Have you addressed every potential **objection**?

For EDUCATIONAL efforts:

- Have you told your audience something they didn't know?
- Have you tied your message into your solutions or expertise?

Once you have your Content written, take the time to make it as reader-friendly as possible. The challenge with long copy is how the visitor perceives it. You can make long copy NOT look like long copy by:

- Writing frequent and very specific subheads (which act like an outline of the key benefits or points)

- Breaking up long paragraphs and long sentences

- Using bullet points and/or numbered points

- Organizing it into multiple web pages, and linking to more information from your Landing or product/service page. Keep in mind **usability on a mobile phone and don't make pages too long**. A very low percentage of website visitors will scroll to the bottom of the page.

- *(If selling a single product or on a Landing Page:)* Include frequent calls to action, somewhat like an infomercial (tell a little, then go for the sale, tell a little more, include an "Add to Cart" link, etc.).

Several times during the many decades that I've been writing copy, various individuals have predicted the death of long copy. *The problem with that philosophy is that it's not a matter of "long copy" versus any other length of copy. It's a matter of SELLING.*

If I need to cover four different key benefits to get the product or service sold, and I have to answer multiple key questions for each Persona, as well as address multiple key objections, then I need copy to address all of this.

Your sales message is incomplete if you're not talking to each of your Personas, or you've missed a way to sell against a competitor.

Learn how to recognize components of great writing to boost results

Selling in copy is a critical skill.

When you learn how to recognize a superior headline, a smartly-crafted lede with an appropriate emotional driver, and copy that follows the Sales Process, you'll boost opportunities to drive superior results.

We'll talk more about fine-tuning and editing copy in *Chapter 10*.

Results Obsession Skill #3:
Learn how to really sell with words

How to Identify High-Quality Writers

When you review a writer's portfolio, do you know what to look for?

Strong Content that will attract and keep an audience reading tends to have these qualities:

1. ENGAGING HEADLINES

You should see *benefit-laden headlines that give you a strong reason to stay on the page*. When you read the headline, do you want to read more? Or are the headlines short and generic, and don't communicate anything useful? Does the headline try to be too "cute" or "creative" — rather than communicate key benefits?

2. THE WRITING DRAWS YOU IN

The "lead" or first paragraph should make you want to keep reading. If you read the first sentence and say, "so what?" -- that writer may not be the right choice for you.

3. EASILY SCANABLE

If you just read the headlines and subheads, do they outline the entire story for you? Do you learn all of the key points on the page? That's important because 85% - 90% of your audience SCANS first. Be sure you hire a writer that understands how to write scanable copy (with subheads, bullets, numbered points, call outs, etc.). Frequently, subheads are missing entirely, or they may be too short and generic.

4. LEAN WRITING WITHOUT USELESS WORDS

Is the writing easy to read? Are there words, phrases, or sentences that don't need to be there? *(There are writers that take too long to get to the point*. If you can remove entire sentences or phrases -- and not change the value of the Content or its ability to sell -- the writing isn't as effective as it could be.)

5. FOLLOWS THE SALES PROCESS

If you want your Content to generate an immediate response (sign up, register, buy, etc.), it should follow the Sales Process. For example: a) The lead sentence will "remind of some pain" and/or "promise some pleasure"; b) Then, you present the solution (if ecommerce) or introduce your Lead Generation Offer; c) Then, outline the benefits of your solution or Lead Generation Offer; d) Then, tell them how to get these benefits and why to do it now.

6. ENHANCES THE COMPANY'S IMAGE

Ask yourself: a) What image of the company does the Content portray? b) Do I think more highly of the company after reading the Content?

The best way to learn to identify quality writers is to become educated in what makes quality Content. **Each element of the writing should make you want to read more.**

References

Ogilvy, D. (1963) *Confessions of an Advertising Man.* Atheneum Books

Durant, Dr. H., *Research in Advertising*

Della Femina, J. (1971) *From those wonderful folks who gave you Pearl Harbor.* Simon & Schuster

Chapter 10

Crafting Great Copy: Part 2

In this chapter, you'll learn the secrets of writing great copy that apply to every element of your writing. *(You may remember some of these points from writing headlines in Chapter 9.)*

Copy that's most effective at getting a lead or sale has *certain characteristics*. And they *apply across media* -- to websites, email, online ads, and social media (as well as offline media).

"Selling is selling. Why would I use different words for a different media channel?"

Here are the keys to great marketing copy organized by: Message Characteristics, Writing Style, and Visual Issues.

Message characteristics (sales or lead copy)

Answers "Why should I buy from you?"

Effective copy clearly proves what your product, service, or company can *uniquely* do for me. *Every* marketing effort should articulate why your offering is different.

A large seminar company called us recently. They were about to launch a promotion, and asked *"Can you look it over, and let us know what you think?"*

I scanned the page -- as most website visitors or email recipients are going to do. I read the headline. I looked for subheads (but there weren't any). I by-passed the three chunky paragraphs of copy at the top, *looking for the "why should I attend YOUR seminar" bullets*. I called the marketing director back after about 15 seconds and asked one question:

"Why should I attend your seminar?"

"Gee, you're really putting me on the spot, aren't you?" was the marketer's reply (yikes.) Yet, we expect prospects to figure out why they should buy from us, when even *we* don't know!

The *"why should I buy yours"* question should be the **first** one answered as you plan any marketing effort *(see Chapter 8.)*

After the marketer thought about my question, she came up with four great reasons why I should attend her seminar over the others. So I told her to **re-focus her page on those four great reasons**, and be sure those points stand out to the scanning reader. (She might summarize the reasons in the headline, and maybe add subheads or bullet points.)

"Why should I buy yours" -- on every page

Those four reasons for choosing that particular seminar provider belong on every page of their website. Why? The search engines' **organic results could list any page of the site**, depending on what someone is searching for. Because you can't control which page might be the "entry page," the "why should I buy yours" message *must be* on every page.

156

It's just too easy for visitors to hit the "back" button, if you don't convince them why they should stay. You want to *take full advantage of every visitor* – because you've spent time and money to drive that traffic.

Here's a discussion of an Engineering degree on a university website that never gets around to answering "what's unique about yours":

> *"Build a better future with (university). We offer programs and courses in a wide range of engineering fields . . ."*

(Well, who doesn't?) That **generic copy** doesn't engage or keep prospects reading, and it doesn't sell. If this isn't what you'd say to a prospective engineering student face-to-face, don't say it in your copy.

Benefit-focused: "what's in it for me?"

Great copy focuses on the *benefits* — the "what am I going to get from this" — rather than the features (which are facts about your product or service).

How to create stronger benefits

Think about what your product is going to do for your target audience. You might think of each feature this way:

Step 1: Your product/service is **(feature)** . . .

Example: *Search Engine Optimization. It optimizes your web copy with the words your audience uses when they search*

Step 2: Which means **(advantage)** . . .

You'll improve your visibility on search engines

Step 3: So you'll **(benefit)** . . .

You'll maximize your organic traffic.

Features tend to be the facts about your service – the size, weight, color, and what it includes.

Benefits are the "why the Buyer Persona cares."

FEATURE: "Decaffeinated by Swiss water process"

BENEFIT: *"You'll avoid dangerous chemicals in your coffee"*

Full of specifics

Does your copy rely on generalities and useless "fluff" that doesn't say anything? A lot of business-to-business websites – and consumer and B2B blog posts -- tend to suffer from that.

Instead, your copy should be laden with specifics -- because **specifics sell**. They sell because they:

- **Differentiate** you
- Make your offering **memorable**
- Build **credibility because they're believable**
- **Prove** your benefits, convince your audience, and build value
- **Answer objections**
- Help make **every word count**

Specifics include **the numbers, the test results, and the vivid detail**. When you include product specifics in your ads, you tend to generate more traffic to your website or retail store.

On one particular high-traffic corner in my community, there used to be a store called "The Healthy Back." They hired a sign-spinner to display a sign **in front of the store** that said "The Healthy Back."

But their problem wasn't visibility. Waiting at the stop light at this intersection every day, I can clearly see the name of the store. *What I can't see is exactly what they sell.*

If the store had correctly diagnosed the problem – that people don't know what they sell – they might have chosen a different marketing solution.

Why not do a print ad in the local paper, with *specifics* of what I might find in the store. That might give me a reason to come in.

Use numbers and benefit details for a stronger sell

The Data & Marketing Association (DMA) reports that using numbers and statistics to support your claims improves response by an average of **32.9%**.

- **Use uneven numbers** to build credibility. Compare *"Users saved an average of 20%"* versus *"Users saved an average of 17%."* Using 17% sounds more exact, like you actually measured it. (If your actual savings *were* an average of 20%, take the number out a few decimal places, for example, *"Users saved an average of 20.3%."*)

- **Paint a picture in the audience's mind.** *"Every company says their system is easy to use. We actually proved it – we brought in 12 new users and gave them five common tasks. It took them an average of 48 seconds to figure out how to complete each task – without guidance."*

Compare: *You'll save time with this CRM software*
                         versus
             Save an average of 22.3 hours every month in staff time with this CRM system

Which is more powerful?

You can also use very specific product details. When McDonald's launched the Big Mac in the 1970s, they used a very specific jingle in their ads. McDonald's could've launched the product by saying, "our biggest burger ever" or "loaded with more toppings than any other burger." Instead, they used memorable specifics that most Baby Boomers still remember word-for-word:

> *"Two all-beef patties, special sauce, lettuce, cheese, pickles, onions on a sesame seed bun"*

Even in educational Content, using specifics will deliver more value to your reader.

Writing Style for all copy

You-focused: get the "you" in your copy

"You"-oriented copy talks directly to your reader.

Both sales and educational copy are more effective when you:

- Address your audience by using "you" and "your."
  - *"Are you having trouble with your . . ."*

- Or lead with a verb where "you" is implied: *"Save . . . "*

- Get the audience involved in doing the action. You want to "humanize" your product by putting the prospect into the situation.
  - *"If you could gain an extra 30 minutes every day, how much more productive could you be?"*

Revise anything that isn't "you-oriented"

You want to use more "you" and "your" in your copy -- rather than "I," "we,", "us," "our," or your company or product names.

Review your writing for too much of your company "talking to itself" (also known as "we-we-ing all over yourself"). It's just normal to talk about "our (product)" and "our company prides itself . . ." But you want to turn those sentences around to focus on the customer.

> *"We manufacture our product to the most exacting specifications."* (So what?)

How about focusing on the benefits to the buyer:

> *"You'll enjoy high reliability with products manufactured to the most exacting specifications."*

(And even better if you can add specifics of those specs.)

Consider these phrases:

"Since 1987, we've been . . . we offer different models . . . our products can simplify . . ."

How about:

"You'll work with a partner with 24 years' experience . . . choose from 7 different models . . . simplify your internal workflow"

The reality is that **your audience doesn't care about you**, your company, or what you do. They care about **why it's good for them**.

You want to move away from:

- "Who we are, what we do, we can deliver," etc.

You want to turn around the copy to **talk to** your audience:
"You will enjoy" or "you will save" or "you will improve."

Compare a fact/feature-based approach using "our" with a benefits-to-prospect approach using "you":

"Our directory has changed so dramatically that up to 80% of listings are different than the information in last year's editions."
versus
"You'll get updates to almost 80% of the listings you're probably using now to help you reach more prospects . . ."

Active voice versus passive voice

In "Active" voice, **the subject** (ideally referred to as "you") **is actively doing the action**. Instead of saying "it is," "there is," "there are," or implying that "something will be done," put the prospect in the action.

Passive:	*It's a new golf swing trainer that helps develop smoothness in your swing.*
Active:	*You'll discover a new smoothness in your golf swing with this new swing trainer.*

Passive: *There's never a worry about backing up the computer.*
Active: *You'll never worry about backing up your computer.*

Passive: *Your portfolio will be reviewed and analyzed*
Active: *You'll receive a full analysis of . . . including . . .*

Second person versus first or third person

Writing in "first person" means the speaker is writing the copy:

"I can help improve your SEO Copy — by focusing on building organic traffic AND site Conversion."

When selling a service, you do want to **sell the expertise** of those providing the service. If you're sending an email message, writing in first person *may* make sense to introduce yourself.

If you are the one actually providing the service to clients, you might write in first person on the About Us page – and on your services Landing Pages

But realistically, **potential customers care more about their own situation.** It's usually best to address prospects using "you" or "your" (which is writing in "second person"):

"Do you need to build Organic traffic AND improve site Conversion? You need an SEO Copywriter who knows how to SELL!"

Writing in "third person" is typically used for story telling, where **neither the writer nor the reader are involved.** "Third person" writing tells stories by having "he" or "she" or "the customer" do the action.

You might use third person when using the Story approach or in a case study. But *third person writing can be cold and non-engaging* when you fill it with references to "the customer . . ." For most web pages, email messages, and online ads, **write to the audience – by addressing them as "you" in second person.**

Conversational – the way you'd say it out loud

Write your copy exactly the way you'd say it if you were face-to-face with the prospect.

If you're generating leads or selling by ecommerce, write your copy as a personal conversation with one individual.

- Most *testimonials get such high readership* because they use simple, easy-to-read language — just the way the person would say it.

The greatest test of good copy is to **read it out loud**. When you read copy out loud, you might notice a few key things to improve:

Words you'd never actually say in conversation

- When you read your copy out loud, are those the words you'd actually use? (Someone sent me copy today with the word "thus" in it. Really, would you ever say the word "thus" out loud? Same with "thereby" – don't use it.)

- A lot of "it is" or "you will" can make your writing sound stiff. **Use contractions** (isn't, doesn't, it's, you'll, etc.) – because that's how people speak.

- **Use simpler, shorter words** your audience actually uses.

- Don't use words your audience may not understand (like "bespoke.") They may not get the benefit.

Sentences and paragraphs that are too long

If your sentences are too long, you'll notice it when you read your copy out loud. *You may run out of breath before you finish reading a sentence.* Or you won't comprehend what you've read.

The mind actually needs to take "comprehension breaths" – to give yourself a chance to understand what you've read.

So break up your sentences into smaller, more easily comprehensible bites by:

- Separating long sentences into two shorter ones.
- **Using commas, ellipses . . . and em dashes — to help your audience "take a breath"** while reading.

The bottom line: break things up when it helps the reader.

The way people speak: grammatically correct?

Do you know when to bend the rules of grammar in Sales Copy? *Use correct grammar when that's the way most people would say it.*

But you can ignore some grammar rules, including:

- Sentences starting with "and," "or," "but," "because," or "so." Although these types of sentences aren't grammatically correct, they sound more natural. These words act as connectors. They help the copy "flow" to keep your audience reading.

Simple language that's easy to read

You want your writing to be friendly, but audience-appropriate. Too many marketing efforts (especially blog posts and websites) **sound like the copywriter was trying too hard to be "professional."** Lots of perfectly constructed, complete — and somewhat stiff — sentences.

Unfortunately, that style of copy doesn't keep your audience reading — and it doesn't SELL. That's one reason why a lot of Sales Copy generates very poor results.

- **The average American reads comfortably at an eighth-grade level** (or about a 14-year-old level).

Even if your target is a highly technical audience, you should still write conversationally to those geeks. Here's why:

When an engineer is speaking, he (or she) may be using words and discussing concepts that most of us wouldn't use. But he's likely speaking in the same STYLE as we would:

- **He's likely speaking in short sentences** — because he needs to stop and breathe.

It's the same when an engineer is reading. His brain needs places to stop and "breathe" (so he can comprehend what he read).

So, no matter how technical your audience, they still read the same way as you and I do. The eyes and brain prefer short sentences and short paragraphs -- they just look easier to read.

Every word as strong as it can be

You want to choose every word carefully, because a difference in word choice can have a significant effect on results. Think about the differences in perception between these words:

- "Evaluation" versus "test drive." Evaluation has somewhat of a negative connotation. Test drive sounds easier, friendlier, and more fun.

- "Apply" versus "Sign Up." ("Apply" implies you could be turned down, which nobody wants.)

- "If" versus "when."
    o Use "if" for things your prospect doesn't want to happen. "If you should need service . . ."
    o Use "when" for positive outcomes. "When you see the savings to your bottom line . . ."

Use **"power" words** that paint a picture in prospects' minds or draw on their emotions.

Try to avoid useless and general introductory clauses like "As you may know." (Well if I already know, why are you wasting words by telling me?)

You don't want to make your audience wade through copy that's too general, full of fluff, or that says the same thing every competitor says.

> *"We make creative products designed by professionals to meet the specific needs of clients"* (Huh? So what?)

Just about any company could say this. That makes it useless.

Verbs are the action words that bring your copy to life. **Inject** strong action verbs into your writing, so every verb paints as specific a picture as possible (like the verb **"inject"** in this sentence.)

A copywriter could "write" your copy – or I could "craft" your copy. One is ordinary, but the other implies special skill and a better outcome.

"Lean" – no useless words or phrases

You should carefully edit your copy, so *every word is there for a reason*. You want to get to the point with no extra wordiness to slow the reader down. The test of doing this right is:

If you can remove a word, phrase, sentence, paragraph, or page – and not affect the sell (i.e., no key information is lost), then you don't need that copy.

Consider these types of sentences you'll frequently see in websites, email, and online ads (as well as offline media):

- *With competitive rates, a wide range of programs, and an eager friendly staff*
- *We can serve your needs*
- *We provide a range of services to meet your needs*
- *I would like to take this opportunity to tell you*

After you read these lines, *do you know anything more?* **Couldn't you delete each of these phrases and not lose anything?**

Be ruthless in your editing. You frequently hear people say, "no one reads long copy." The fact is **no one reads long, boring copy that doesn't say anything, or that doesn't get to the point.** Unnecessary words may turn off your audience before they get to your key benefits.

Don't waste your audience's time – use only the words that absolutely need to be there.

Visual issues all writers should know

Key points just by scanning

Your copy should be easily scanable – because 71% - 85% (or more) of your audience will scan copy first.

Multiple studies have confirmed that people view web pages in exactly the same manner they review email, direct mail, and print ads. People scan, rather than read line-by-line, word-for-word.

"Scanable" means ensuring your audience doesn't miss your key points by putting them in:

- Headlines and subheads
- Captions, bullet points, and bolds

When your make your copy scanable, you're essentially creating an "outline" of your key messages.

Scanable copy looks easier to get through. It helps your audience find the information they're looking for. And they quickly see the key benefits of your product or service.

You should be able to read just the headlines and subheads and get all the key points of your message:

- What's in it for me? (the benefits)
- Why should I buy yours? (over the competition)
- What do I have to do to get it? (next step)

- Why should I do it now? (your Offer)

A website we wrote targeted those concerned about preventing heart disease. If you read the headline and subheads, you get the entire story:

"Heart disease will claim 500,000 lives this year — but you can reduce your risk by 30% to 50%"

"Heart disease is diet-related — but it's virtually impossible to reduce your risk by changing your eating habits alone!"

"Antioxidants in the right amount and right combination can help prevent heart disease"

"To reduce your risk, choose the optimal formula"

"When you order by xx/xx/xx, you'll get a free . . ."

I think it was Jacob Weisberg who first told us a huge portion of our audience scans – and **those who only scan account for 50% - 75% of those who take action!**

Looks easy to get through

When visitors arrive on a page of your website (or open your email), you want them to instantly find a reason to stick around.

Don't present your audience with long paragraphs. Visually break things up. When should you create a new paragraph?

- **When the subject changes.**

- **If things would be clearer**.

- **When you have a key point** you don't want the scanning reader to miss. There's nothing wrong with a one-line paragraph, a one-sentence paragraph, or a paragraph with three words -- if that gives the emphasis you need. (This isn't your sixth grade essay.)

168

- **To make it look easy to get through.** Lots of long paragraphs look daunting and uninviting. Break things up, so copy looks easy to read.

To sell effectively, you have to answer all of your Buyer Personas' key questions and address their objections. How do you make all that copy look easy to get through?

1. Use bullet points and numbered lists.

Bullets help emphasize your key points and are easy to scan. Numbered lists get high readership.

2. Use specific subheads.

Make every subhead useful to the reader – by t*elling the scanning reader what the paragraph or section is about.*

3. Re-organize your content into more interesting formats.

Consider checklists, charts, case studies, or Question-and-Answer (like FAQs). Visitors may read an entire page of question-and-answer and not realize they've read an entire page of copy. That's because question-and-answer reads more like a conversation — the way someone would really ask and answer the question.

4. Use on-page tabs (common on ecommerce websites).

Tabs are like subheads. Only the copy under one tab appears at any one time, so it simplifies the page. To see additional copy, just click one of the other tabs.

This is especially useful on a mobile device. You can make the detail available without the visitor having to scroll through all of it.

From an SEO perspective, search engines see the copy in ALL of the tabs as being on the same page. (And Google likes pages with enough quality Content.) So tabs can help you put enough Content on a page to help with SEO.

In general, many improvements that make a website's copy more "usable" and friendly to the visitor tend to be good for SEO as well.

Evaluating and polishing your writing

Have a copy draft to evaluate? Here's how to evaluate effectiveness:

For All Types of Copy – Educational, Lead Generation, Sales Copy

- Is the *Headline* compelling? Will it STOP your audience and draw them in?

- Are your *Subheads* specific?

- Does your copy help your readers *learn something new*? Is it interesting to read? Does it make you want to read more?

- Does it *get to the point quickly* to keep the reader engaged?

- Is it *scanable*? Could you add bullets or numbered points — to make it look easier to get through, or help organize your points so the prospect won't miss them?

- Is it *conversational*? Read it out loud. Does it read exactly the way you'd say it in-person or over the phone?

- Are there long sentences? Or long paragraphs? Is it easy to read?

- Does it positively reflect your brand image?

Lead Generation and Sales Copy

- Are the *key benefits* (of your Lead Generation Offer, product, or service) crystal clear? Can I tell *"what's in it for me?"*

- Is it complete? Are any benefits missing? Have you left out any key information? Can I tell *"why should I buy yours?"*

- Is the emotional appeal clear?

Sales Copy

- Does it **prove** the benefits (of your product or service) or your expertise (for services)?

- Could you add facts, specifics, cases, testimonials, third-party mentions for **credibility**?

Great copy that sells has specific characteristics, style, and look

When you review copy (your own or someone else's), you should know what to look for to identify **really good copy**.

And when you make (or request) changes, you should know exactly why you've made the change.

Once you internalize the points in this chapter, every piece of Content you create, edit, or review will drive better results. The elements of "copy that sells" are universal.

Results Obsession Skill #3:
Learn how to sell with words to create effective Sales Content

References

Lewis, H.G. (1989) *On the Art of Writing Copy, Second Edition.* Prentice-Hall.

Weisberg, J. (1994) *Does Anybody Listen, Does Anybody Care?* Medical Group Management Association

Chapter 11

Do You Need a New Website – or Just a Tune-up?

I s your website as effective as it could be?

Are you **continuously testing** to see if you can improve results? The most effective websites are constantly making incremental improvements – rather than waiting for a big redesign.

If you haven't been actively testing and improving, your website likely has a LOT of areas that need attention. Where should you start?

You want to know exactly what IS working – so you don't change the successful elements. And you want to identify exactly where your website needs improvement, so your revisions (or a whole new website) actually address those areas.

"Understand the characteristics of a great website, and how to measure them."

173

In this chapter, we'll talk about the overall characteristics of a great website, and you'll evaluate how your website scores. Then we'll talk about how to improve your Navigation.

In *Chapter 12*, we'll move on to improving your plan for Design and Page Layout, Content, and Offers. *Chapter 13* will help you improve your website copy. Finally, *Chapter 14* tackles the key elements you should know about Search Engine Optimization (SEO).

Characteristics of a great website

A great website should:

- **Be built for your audiences**
- Be continuously **improved through analysis and testing**
- **Enhance the experience with your brand**
- Help **achieve your objectives** cost-effectively

Is the focus of your website on these four areas? The result should be a website that is:

Traffic driving, specifically:

- **FIND-able**: your SEO efforts should drive strong Organic search engine traffic.
- **LINK-able**: your Content and Offers should be attractive to bloggers and other websites, so they want to give their audiences a link to your site (good for SEO and traffic)
- **SHARE-able**: your Content and Offers should be so interesting, unique, and valuable that your audiences want to share them (which helps drive even more traffic)

When you craft your Content and Offers: are you trying to create something so interesting that your audience will **share** them? And other websites will want to **link** to them?

Leads and sales driving, specifically:

- **NAVIG-able**: each Buyer Persona is looking for something specific when they come to your website. They should easily be able to find it in your menu.
- **VALUE-able**: your Content and Offers should be attractive, unique, and useful to your particular Buyer Personas.
- **ACTION-able**: your Offers (especially Early Stage Offers) should help motivate every Persona to take the next step. Your Sales Content should answer key questions – and objections – so visitors can be confident to take action.

Have you *focused your website on the actions you want your Personas to take*? (Or is more like a brochure? Are your Lead Generation Offers hidden?)

Your website should make your *"brand image"* (how you want to be seen) and *"brand promise"* (why you're different) come alive through the overall look, tone, and message. Is it clear to visitors why you're different? *(If not, see Chapter 8.)*

How do you measure each of these elements?

You can analyze most of these with your website analytics.

Traffic-driving elements

"FIND-able" -- Check your Organic traffic for the most recent 12 months.

- In Google Analytics, see "Acquisition," "All Traffic," "Channels." In the Search box (just above the table), search "Organic" to get just the Organic numbers.
- In the top right corner, set the date range you want to review.
- Then add a Secondary Dimension (just above the chart) of "Time," "Month of the Year" to see monthly Organic traffic. Click the "Month of the Year" column to sort. Is your Organic traffic steadily growing? *(We'll talk about SEO in Chapter 14.)*

How **SHARE-able** are your blog posts and Offers?

- Check the traffic to your blog posts and Offer pages. See "Behavior," "Site Content," "All Pages." The amount of traffic to your individual blog posts and Offer pages indicates how attractive your topics are.
- If you use a social sharing plug-in like "AddThis®," you can count your shares on social media, by email, and how many printed the page.

How **LINK-able** is your Content?

- Check "Acquisition," "Referrals" to see which websites are sending you traffic. Do you find key bloggers and other industry websites?
- From Google Search Console (search.google.com/search-console), select "Links" from the left menu to see which websites link to yours.

Your website should be a magnet to attract visitors. **To drive more traffic:**

- *Improve Your Content* – make it more intriguing, valuable, and unique to drive more links and shares (and clicks from your social media posts and search engine listings)
- *Create New Content* – for more listings on search engines, and to attract more shares and links
- *Optimize Your Content for Search* – to be more visible on search engines and drive clicks

Lead and sales driving elements

How **NAVIG-able** is your website for each Buyer Persona?

- Think about the key questions your Buyer Personas have *(from Chapter 3)*. Looking at your Main Menu, can each Persona instantly find what he or she is looking for?
- *Are your Main Menu topics clickable*? (They should link to a summary or comparison page to help visitors who don't know what they need.)
- *Do you have breadcrumbs*, so visitors know where they came from (and can find their way back)?

- *Do you have site search*? Can visitors easily find it?

How **VALUE-able** is your website (to your Personas)?

- Check your overall Bounce Rate and Pages/Session. In Google Analytics, see "Audience," "Overview."
- Look at Bounce Rate by your key pages (see "Behavior," "Site Content," "All Pages").
- High Bounce and low Pages/Session are indicators that your Personas are not perceiving your Content as valuable.

How **ACTION-able** is your Content? You can follow visitor actions step-by-step on your website in a number of ways . . .

Landing Pages

- What are your most common Landing Pages where visitors start on your website? (In Google Analytics, see "Behavior," "Site Content," "Landing Pages.") Bounce Rate and Pages/Session give you an idea of how many users visit additional pages.

  o How effective is each Landing Page at keeping visitors on the site? What is the Average Session Duration?

- **Add a Secondary Dimension** (just above the table) of "Users," "User Type" to see New Users for each Landing Page.

  o Among New Users, what's Bounce Rate, Pages/Session, and Average Session Duration for each Landing Page?

Key pages: products, services, Offers

What percentage of your New Users visits your key product/service, or Offer pages?

If the percentage is low, it could be that your Landing Pages don't give visitors a strong reason to stay and learn more.

- See "Audience," "Behavior," "New vs Returning" to see *how many New Visitors* you have in a period.

- Then under "Behavior," "Site Content," "All Pages," **add a Secondary Dimension** of "Users," "User Type" to see *how many New Visitors got to each of your key pages*.

  - For example, if your key Services page got 25 Unique Pageviews from New Users and you had 111 total New Users, that indicates that *less than 23% of New visitors got to your key Services page.* (So the Landing Page **Content didn't make them want to stay** and learn more, or they couldn't find your key Services page.)

- **What percentage of New Users got to your key Offer pages?** If the percentage is low, *your Offers may not be visible enough.* Or the Content promoting them needs to be more benefit-focused and relevant to your Personas.

Conversion

Your **"Conversion Rate" (to leads or sales)** is the final key measure of how effective (or Action-able) your website is.

- If you have Goals set up, Google Analytics will calculate "Conversion Rate" per Goal *for the site and each Landing Page.*
- *See "Behavior," "Site Content," "Landing Pages."* Above the chart, use the Conversions pull-down to select the Goal.

To convert more visitors:

1. *Craft More Compelling and Unique Offers* -- Are your Offers the same as those of your competition?

2. *Create More Targeted Lead Generation Offers* (by Persona by Buying Stage.) Do you have only one Lead Generation Offer? You'll motivate more visitors to respond if you create appropriate Offers for each Buyer Persona.

3. *Develop better ecommerce Product/Service Content* to drive sales.

Of course, there are many other elements that affect Conversion, including: how much information you ask for on your Lead Generation form, the design of your Landing Page, and the copy that promotes your Lead Generation Offer.

But the right Lead Generation Offer -- and Sales Content that actually sells -- are the **first steps to stronger Conversion**. *We'll plan Offers and Content in Chapter 12.*

Does your website enhance your brand image?

- Does your website have a unique **look** compared to your competition? What impression does it give about your company?

- Read your Home page and About Us copy out loud. *Is that what you'd say to a prospect face-to-face?* Is the copy stiff, or is it friendly? Does your Home page copy talk TO the visitor – or is it a lot of "we," "our," and your company name?

- What's your key *"why I should buy yours"* **message?** Compare this to the competition. Is it something others can say, or **is it something only you can say?**

You might need a website redesign if . . .

If your website isn't mobile-responsive, you'll likely need a redesign. If using WordPress, your web designer can choose a mobile-friendly theme or design template.

If you can't regularly update the theme for your WordPress website, you'll need a redesign. (WordPress software, design themes, and plug-ins issue periodic updates. You need to update all areas regularly to keep your website secure and running well.)

If your website is having technical issues, you may need a redesign.

But you can test many other improvements right on your existing website. So why not see if you can improve results?

Making incremental changes allows you to see what effect each specific change has.

Compared to creating a new website, you'll save a lot of time and money — and **improve results much quicker**.

If your WordPress website doesn't deliver some functionality, there may be a plug-in you can add. (A "plug-in" is software you can load into your website to add a particular function without having to create programming code.)

Try not to rush into a redesign just because *"you're tired of your website."* You and your employees may be the only ones who will tire of your website.

And that cool design you'd like to replicate might not be working well for the company you're copying it from! (And it may not be the right fit for your company. See the *"Websites Gone Wrong"* article at the end of Chapter 12.)

If you do choose to create a new website, be sure you plan these elements **before** you choose a design or WordPress theme:

- Navigation for your Personas (below)
- Content (pages) and Offers by Persona (*Chapter 12*)
- Home Page Layout *(Chapter 12)*
- SEO *(Chapter 14)*

Don't just hire a web designer and let them get started. Bring your knowledge of your Personas to the table, to *help plan Navigation, Content, and Offers (as well as what needs to be on your Home Page.)*

- **All of these elements affect the design or theme your web designer will choose**. *See the Web Development Steps at the end of this chapter.*

Navigation to direct your Buyer Personas

Your Main Menu is a key way that your Buyer Personas find the Content they're looking for.

Many pages of your site could appear in Organic search engine listings and be "Landing Pages" (the first page the Persona visits).

So your Personas need to be able to find answers from your Main Menu, rather than relying on your Home page Content.

For most websites, *a significant percentage of visits (from 25% - 50%) don't start on Home.*

- See "Behavior," "Site Content," "Landing Pages." Look for "/" to see what percentage of Sessions start on Home.

In *Chapter 3*, you identified the key questions of each Persona. Use those key questions when evaluating your Navigation.

- Can each Persona **instantly** find what they're looking for in your Main Menu? If it's not clear to each Persona where to go, you have Navigation problems.

Diagnosis

If your visitors don't spend much time on your site or visit a low number of pages, they may not be finding what they're looking for (or anything they're interested in.)

Do you see a low percentage of visitors navigating to your most important pages? In Google Analytics:

- See "Behavior," "Site Content," "All Pages." Divide Unique Pageviews for a page by all Sessions (see "Audience," "Overview.")

Ideas for improvement

Focus your Main Menu on your Buyer Personas:

- Make a list of the things each Buyer Persona is looking for when visiting your website. Pay special attention to the questions they want answered EARLY in the Sales Process, which is the Content most websites are missing (the *"How do I solve this problem, choose the right solution," etc. questions.*)

- Create Main Menu topics that clearly and instantly tell visitors where to find these items.

  o You don't want visitors to think, *"I wonder if that means . . ." Or to have to search through different sections or "learn" how your website works.* Most won't stick around that long.

	CEO	CFO	CMO
Key Questions	What results have they gotten for others? Who are their clients?	What's the ROI?	How can they improve our results?
Menu Topics	Case Studies, Client List	ROI Calculator	Find a Solution, Case Studies

Figure 11.1

182

For example, in Figure 11.1 above, a B2B services company has three Personas, each with different "Key Questions" they want answered. Based on those questions, we can create our Menu Topics.

On some websites, you may want a *list of Services or Products by the problems they solve.* For a digital agency, some of their Buyer Personas might not know exactly what they need. One Main Menu topic might be, "Find a Solution." and the drop-down menu might include:

- Drive Organic Traffic
- Build Website Traffic
- Attract Qualified Leads
- Boost Ecommerce Sales
- Improve Lifetime Value

The agency might have a second Main Menu topic called "Services" for those Personas who know what service they need.

This is how to ensure you create Menus based on what your Personas are looking for – rather than what your company thinks should be included.

There's a fitness company based in San Diego, which specializes in fast personal workouts at less cost than using a personal trainer at a gym. Among their consumer Personas, they may have:

- Prior gym members who've always wanted a personal trainer but couldn't afford one
- Prior gym members who are pressed for time and looking for a quick workout
- Those who may not have been gym members before but now are ready to address a particular problem

Each of these audiences is looking to answer different questions, like:

- Will these personal trainers be effective?
- How effective will the 20-minute workout be?

- Is this right for me if I'm not a regular gym person?

On theperfectworkout.com (The Perfect Workout™), the site Menu includes "Results" and "Beginners" to direct each Persona to the answers they're looking for.

Your menu names should be crystal clear

Create menu names that are:

- Familiar to your audience
- Specific
- More focused on benefits or function

Avoid "marketing names," and company-specific names for products and services (unless your brands are very well known).

"Find a Solution" is much more specific than "Solutions" and implies help – exactly what Early Stage visitors are looking for. "Why Response FX®" is much more specific (and compelling) than "About Us."

There's no reason to restrict yourself to single-word menu names. If you need to use more than one word, your designer should be able to accommodate that. For pull-down menus, multiple word topics should fit most designs.

Keep in mind that large menus — either many Main Menu choices and/or lots of pull-downs — work less well on mobile phones.

Order of menu items

The "hot spots" where the eye tends to go in a top Main Menu (on a computer) **are usually the topics at the far left and right ends.** Don't use "About Us" as the far left topic unless that's really where you want visitors to start (yawn. I'm guessing it isn't).

- But on a mobile phone, your menu options appear vertically. *Be sure the most important item is first (or far left on a computer.)*

Put your Early Stage Content – the "How to Solve Your Problem" options – in your far left menu position, so those most unfamiliar with your overall category see that section first.

On nextecgroup.com, we made the first menu choice *"Find a Solution" to be the clear place to start.* We have "Contact" and the phone number at the top of the masthead. So we put "Why NexTec" at far right in the Main Menu.

For an ecommerce site, you might **put your most profitable products or best sellers** in your far left Main Menu position.

Clickable Main Menu pages

Each Main Menu topic should be clickable to a summary page for all the topics in that section. The summary page might outline the benefits of each product or service, compare options, indicate the best uses of each, and **direct visitors to the right choice.**

Navigation and usability

Visitors should always know where they are within your website and how they got there.

- Use **an indicator within your menu that shows visitors the section they're in.** (The current section can be highlighted or appear in a different color.)

- Add "breadcrumbs" just below your Main Menu, so visitors can see what page they're on and how they got there.

  Home >> About >> What Customers Say

Masthead usability

In addition to your Main Menu Navigation, what other items need to be in your masthead on every page? Consider:

1. *Site Search* function – especially **important for mobile users** and sites with more Content. Even if you have a relatively small website and have never had Site Search before, **include it in your redesign.**

2. *Help functions like FAQs*. FAQs are a friendly way to answer common questions and handle objections. Some websites put Help functions, Support, FAQs, etc. in the bottom menu.

That may (or may not) work for desktop users. **But mobile users may not be willing to scroll all day to get to the bottom.**

By hiding Help, you may lose a sale needlessly, even though you actually had the answers to those objections on your website.

3. *"Utility menu"* – a separate menu that might appear at the top of your masthead. It might include topics like Contact, Help/Support/Customer Service, FAQs, Search, My Account or Login, About, etc.

If you have an ecommerce website, the theme or design template will likely place a Cart icon and a Checkout button in the masthead as well.

Jump into the mobile era and put your Help functions at the top where every user can find them.

- Zappos has their phone number and Customer Service link (with a drop-down that includes FAQs) in their masthead.
- Amazon™ has "Help" in their top utility menu.

Resist your designer's suggestion that they "clutter" the masthead.

When potential customers are looking for Help, put those functions where they can easily find them, no matter what device they're using.

"Maybe we should add instructions"

If you ever hear yourself suggesting instructions, that's a sure sign you have a usability problem. Always try to eliminate the need for instructions by making your process crystal clear to *every* visitor.

The Navigation and usability "bible" by Steve Krug is entitled *"Don't Make Me Think"* – for a reason.

Diagnose your website to focus your improvement efforts

Step one to improving your website is to understand the characteristics of a great website – and **how to measure them**.

Your team should know how to evaluate your website – and identify opportunities for improvement.

Results Obsession Strategy #1:
Diagnose your website step-by-step to see what's working

If your website struggles to generate leads or sales, you may need a better plan. Let your Buyer Personas' questions guide your Main Menu Navigation.

Results Obsession Strategy #2:
Let Personas' needs – not the company's -- drive everything

In Chapter 12, you'll evaluate Page Layouts, and plan Content and Offers by Persona. *Chapter 13* will help you polish your website copy to really sell. *Chapter 14* gives you keys to Search Engine Optimization.

Steps to a Successful
Website Development Project

INITIAL PLANNING
(covered in Chapter 11, 12, and 14)

- Determine key **Content and Offers** that answer Buyer Personas' questions

- Organize key Content into a **Navigation Menu**. For ecommerce, organize a Product Menu.

- Determine elements to be included in **masthead, Home page, key page layouts (Product page, Offer page, blog)**, and response forms

- Begin keyword research for SEO to work key topics into the Content plan *(Chapter 12 and 14)*

COPY AND DESIGN DEVELOPMENT
(Chapter 12, 13 and 14)

- If using WordPress: select a mobile-responsive theme that will accommodate the elements planned for masthead, Home, and key pages – and that will give you the look you want

- Begin Content development/editing

- Continue keyword research for SEO *(Chapter 14)*

- Develop sitemap (specify URL for each page)

- SEO consultant to give each image an optimized filename BEFORE images are loaded onto the site *(Chapter 14)*

Figure 11.2

Successful Website Development Project (continued)

SITE DEVELOPMENT (*Chapters 12, 13, 14*)

- WordPress theme loaded into WordPress *(in parent/ child configuration to allow your webmaster to update the theme when needed)*

- Final Sitemap (from SEO consultant) with page URLs to be used to create site pages *(Chapter 14)*

- Develop graphic design look for Home and main types of interior pages — Content page, Offer page, Product page, Blog, etc. *(Chapter 12)*

- Copy loaded. Optimized (by SEO copywriter), H1 headlines and H2 sub-heads coded, text links created. (Product pages created for Ecommerce.)

- Photos and graphics loaded into site, SEO consultant to load alt tags and descriptions for each. *(Chapter 14)*

- Forms created for Lead Generation Offers (downloads, sign-ups, etc.) Upload PDFs for your Content Offers

Figure 11.3

References

Krug, S. (2005) *Don't Make Me Think: A Common Sense Approach to Web Usability.* New Riders.

Websites Gone Wrong: Doesn't Anybody Know What Drives Leads?

A services company has a website that needs to generate leads. They recognize they're not getting the leads they need, and decide they need a new site.

Mistake #1: when you have a Lead Generation problem, you have an Offer problem. First step is to test new Offers and their visibility on your website.

If you don't solve your Offer problem, a new website isn't going to solve your Lead Generation problem.

The company hires a web developer who "has done lots of Lead Generation websites." The web developers bring in branding consultants to create a new positioning for the company — believing that to solve the Lead Generation problem, they just need a new positioning.

Mistake #2: Neither the web developer nor the consultants are talking about Offers.

The original Mistake keeps compounding itself with more time and money being spent, but *never addressing the original cause of the Lead Generation problem.*

Moral of the story: know what drives Traffic, Leads, and Sales, so you'll know where to focus when you need improvement. You want to be sure your improvement efforts (and any vendors you hire) actually address your particular problem.

Figure 11.4

Chapter 12

Website Design, Offers, and Content Strategy

The overall look of your website can help differentiate you from the competition. Your look can also build or enhance your brand image (as cool, friendly, luxurious, trustworthy, etc.).

And the usability of your website can help differentiate the whole experience with your company.

The topics in this chapter can help you evaluate your current website. And they're elements you should plan **before** you start a redesign.

Design and page layout

Does the layout focus on important elements?

What do you want the visitor to see first on each page? *What's the Key Action you want to encourage the visitor to take?* (Are action buttons in a prominent place?)

191

Putting the most important information first on each page is especially critical for prospects using a mobile device.

The layout of each page should also *emphasize key elements throughout the page*. Placement of visuals can draw the eye to a particular element or section (like the Offer).

What gets noticed on web pages

The eye is drawn to:

- **Any photo containing people**
- Secondly, to any other photo or prominent graphic

Photos attract more attention than illustrations. Photos showing your product in use are especially effective.

Watch the placement of photos on your web page. If the placement pulls the eye away from important elements, move or remove the photo.

If there's a person in the photo, be sure that individual is facing *into* your copy, rather than drawing the eye off the page.

Color can draw the eye to your response buttons, highlight your Lead Generation Offer, or emphasize a special sales promotion. Be sure that areas that use color actually highlight elements you want highlighted.

If you're considering any "special effects" like movement, be sure you want attention there (rather than to other elements).

It can be helpful to create a simple **"wireframe"** for each page – just a simple draft of where everything might go and what links need to be on the page. Wireframes can help you identify the most important elements on each page, and plan the "paths" (needed links, etc.) to lead visitors to related pages.

- With a WordPress site, you'll likely choose a design template or "theme." Then you'll decide how you'll use each area on the page.

"When you evaluate Content by Persona,
you see what's missing and
what should be more prominent."

Home page layout

Your Home page should "direct" each of your Buyer Personas to the appropriate Content.

- Can your Personas instantly locate the key things they're looking for? Feature those topics on Home.

- Be sure any images or graphics *add* to your message or Navigation. Too many competing graphic elements (or messages) won't draw the eye to your highest-priority items.

- Big images will make your page load slower (a problem for usability and SEO), and they push important elements down on a mobile screen.

For a Lead Generation site, the priority items are your main headline with *"why should I buy from you"* messaging, your key Offer(s), and key Content for each Buyer Persona.

For ecommerce, you might showcase your new products/services, your best sellers, or key categories that you sell.

Try not to rely on "rotating banners" to deliver key messages and Offers. Most rotating banners go by too fast for visitors to read them. That's one reason why *rotating banners score very poorly in usability* tests – and those with action buttons get few (if any) clicks after the second image.

Put your key messages in static Content that your visitors (and search engines) can easily read.

Ecommerce design elements to increase sales

The actual wording of your "take action" copy and buttons can have a huge impact on results.

Studies of web site "action buttons" have found that "add to cart" can be more effective than "buy now." "Add to cart" implies less of a commitment. And visitors prefer to add interesting things to their shopping cart as they browse (and then decide at checkout if they really want to buy everything).

As you plan or evaluate your page features for an ecommerce website (which are usually part of your WordPress theme), consider:

- Options for **sorting and filtering** products – by price, brand/manufacturer, ratings, best sellers, style, color, size, etc.

- *Video of the item in use.* I've become rather spoiled by looking at shoes on Zappos.com. They're one of the few sites that show the shoes on a model from the front and side – the next best thing to trying them on yourself.

- *In-stock/out-of-stock* – why frustrate customers by having them order and then getting an out-of-stock email? Indicate out-of-stock items on the website.

If you're offering any promotions to drive the sale, be sure that Offer appears at the top of each Product page.

You might also consider including customer reviews, related products and upgrade opportunities on each Product page.

Ecommerce checkout usability

If you're going to **require a particular format** for a field – such as phone number, credit card expiration date, etc. – show the format you want the visitor to use right in the field.

As the visitor completes each field, the cursor should move automatically to the next box.

If your password requires a number, special character, capital letters, etc., *tell the visitor before* they try to create a password without these elements.

When customers login and struggle to remember their password, why not remind them of your requirements for passwords (capital letters, numbers, etc.), which might help them recall the password they created.

Always have a "billing address same as shipping address" box.

If you want shoppers to register, ask for that just before completion of the order. Tell shoppers the benefits of registration – free shipping, faster checkout in the future, etc. And give shoppers the option to checkout as a guest – **don't force me to go to extra steps to buy.**

Plan Content tailored for each Persona

You want an overall Content plan that delivers the answers each Buyer Persona needs.

Step 1: Content gaps – what's missing?

In *Chapter 11*, you used your Buyer Persona one-page summaries to list each Persona's key questions, to help plan Navigation.

- Under your Main Menu items, outline the potential **topic** pages and types of Content you might want. (*Don't limit yourself to your existing Content pages.* Focus on topics that need to be covered.)

Once you have your outline of topics, review your existing website Content. *What topics are you missing? Which Personas haven't you adequately addressed?* Which Content can be re-used or revised?

Topics that need Content are your "Content gaps."

Persona	Search for	Content	Offer
Ann the Assistant	How does it work, what can it do, cost	Case: How emarketing is selling RE faster	
Dane the Decision Maker	How much does it cost, how easy to use, results from users	Case: How emarketing is selling RE faster	Free Demo Video
Ivan the IT/Tech	IT Specs, Support Details	Getting Started Guide, 24-hour support	
Bryon the Broker	How does it work, what can it do, cost	Case: How can emarketing help you sell faster	Free Demo Video

Figure 12.1

For a Lead Generation website, we developed the chart in Figure 12.1 above. We listed the information each Persona is searching for and translated that into a list of potential Content. (Then, we specified Offers for those Personas who will actually visit the website).

Step 2: Content by Stages

As we discussed in *Chapter 4*, most companies don't have enough Content for Early Buying Stages. If you're missing Early Stage Content, you could be missing up to 70% of prospects who won't contact a company until they've done their research.

"Early Stage" or Research Phase key questions include:

- How can I solve this problem? What types of solutions are available? How do they work?
- Possible Content Options: blog posts, videos, case studies

You might create *customer stories by topic, industry, or problem*. Customer stories usually get high readership.

Vendor or Product Identification Phase key questions include:

- Who offers the type of solution that will meet my needs
- Possible Content Options: Product Selector Tool, competitive comparison chart

Vendor Evaluation Phase key questions include:

- How does each vendor's product/service compare? Who are their clients? What do their clients say about them?
- Possible Content Options: Testimonials, Client List, Product Reviews, ROI Calculator

Once you understand the information needs for each Persona at each Buying Stage, you can plan your specific Content.

In Figure 12.2 below for one Persona, we listed the information needs at each Stage. Then, we translated those information needs into potential Content we need to create (as well as Lead Generation Offers).

Stage of Sales Process	Info Needs	Content	Offer
Solution Searching	Pros and Cons, How to Evaluate, possible ROI	Articles, videos	White paper, webinar, podcast
Vendor Searching	How does it work, specs and options, case studies	Product commenders, competitive comparisons, case studies, ROI evaluators	Product selection guide, competitive comparison report, webinar
Vendor Evaluation	Reference accounts, site visits, technical conference calls	Testimonials, how to write an RFP, how to evaluate suppliers, ROI tool	Pilot program, how to evaluate suppliers or products guide, ROI tool, Q&A webinar with customers

Figure 12.2

Step 3: New Content Audit

Identify all new Content you've created over the last 12 months (the majority is probably blog posts.)

Make a list of the key topics each Persona is interested in. For each topic, list **blog posts that covered that topic and the publish date**.

Where has your concentration been? Which topics could use additional blog posts?

Did you cover at least one topic that's important to each Buyer Persona *every month?*

Step 4: Engaging formats for visitors, shares, links

As you plan your Content, don't limit yourself to paragraphs on a page. Can you create unique formats (the competition isn't using) — that your prospects, customers, and influencers will want to *share or link* to?

- For example, can you give the prospect a 360-degree view?

Would a piece of Content be more useful or effective in a different format? What format might engage each of your Buyer Personas?

Could you re-purpose and re-organize some of your Content – to make it more interesting or compelling?

Comparison Chart	Worksheet
Quiz	Comics
Checklist	Infographic
Video	Buying Guide

Figure 12.3

There are many engaging formats in Figure 12.3 above that you could use.

- Can you inject more interest into your copy by creating some short video clips or a quiz?
- Why not re-organize some of your Content into Checklists?
- Can I read Case Studies or comments from customers?
- Can you create a comparison checklist, Product Selector Tool?

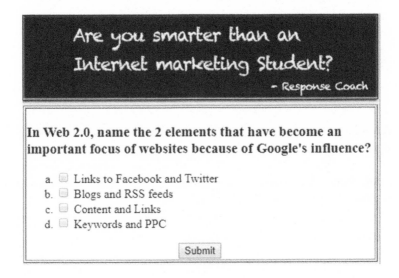

Above is one of our "Are you smarter than an Internet Marketing student?" quiz questions (from our Response Coach® Facebook® page.)

- Once you answer the question, you see what percentage of people chose each answer.

- We briefly explain the correct answer and link to a blog post that covers the topic. It's a unique way to engage prospects and drive blog traffic.

I was recently looking at Spanish courses online. The first site I visited listed four points of differentiation with a paragraph on each one. It was the perfect opportunity to allow me to click on each of the four points to *prove* their value. But there was no demo (of this ONLINE course!) in sight.

I did what most visitors will do. I hit the "back" button, returned to the search results, and clicked on another website. It was a site with *a large video screen, which showed me how the product worked.* Sold!

Offers and tools speed up your Sales Process

The key questions and concerns of your Buyer Personas will help you plan the types of Lead Generation Offers you'll need *(see Chapter 4)*. You want an attractive "next step" for each Persona to take.

But before you change Lead Generation and Sales Offers, check results of your current Offers.

Attractiveness and effectiveness of Offers

You've likely promoted both your Lead Generation and Sales Offers by email and pay-per-click ads. And you're promoting Offers on your website.

For email

- What's the Click-Through Rate *(Unique Clicks/Delivered)*?
- What's your lead response rate *(Leads/Delivered)?*
- What about sales response (*Sales/Delivered)?*
- Maybe you've tested multiple Offers in email. How did each Offer compare in terms of the metrics above?

For pay-per-click ads

- What's the Click-Through? How did the clicks convert? (leads/clicks, sales/clicks)
- If you've tested Offers, how do results compare among Offers?

For the website in general

- What percentage of Users get to your key Lead Generation Offer pages? See "Behavior," "Site Content," "All pages" for Unique Pageviews of each Offer page, and divide by Users ("Audience," "Overview") for a period.
- If your Lead Offer appears prominently on Home, every blog post, and every product/service page, but leads are low, it could indicate *low interest in the Offer.*

If you have an ecommerce website, you're likely changing your sales Offers frequently. Your reporting should tell you what percentage of buyers used each "Bonus Code" (to take advantage of a sales Offer.)

Or if an Offer didn't require a Bonus Code: check the increase in sales before and after the promotion (and last year's numbers as well, if your traffic is seasonal) to assess the impact of each Offer.

Improve your Lead Generation Offers

- **Do you have Offers targeted to each Buyer Persona**? (If not, add an Early Stage Offer that will appeal to each Buyer Persona.)

- **Does your Offer have a benefit-laden name?** Create a name that implies a valuable benefit, like *"7 Secrets to Reduce Your Taxes that Even Most CPAs Don't Know."*

How can you make your Offer different from the competition? Can you create something more interesting?

- Could you take all of your blog posts on one topic and re-package them into an *"Ultimate Guide to (a topic)"* eBook?
- If you're running a health club, just about everyone offers some type of "free visit." What if this month, that "free visit" focused on building upper body strength – you might attract visitors you normally wouldn't with this specific initial workout plan.

Don't rely on "Contact Us" (which is a high commitment choice that few visitors will be ready for).

You're spending money to drive traffic. Use a low-commitment Offer to capture contact information from as many visitors as possible. (*See Chapter 5 for Lead Generation Strategies and Chapter 6 for Lead Generation Offers.*)

Lead Generation paths

For an Offer page, if Unique Pageviews divided by Users is low, **your Offer may not be visible enough on your site.**

Where is your Lead Generation Offer on your website?

Visitors to your website won't search around for your Offer(s), it's not what they're there for. *If you hide your Offers,* it's likely that 98% of your traffic (or more) won't leave a trace.

Your Offer strategy can't be passive.

With effective Search Engine Optimization, *any page on your website could appear in the Organic search listings* as a Landing Page.

You need to make your Offers part of your proactive Lead Generation "offense" by presenting Offers to visitors wherever they go.

- Encourage Organic traffic to convert — by *including an appropriate Offer on virtually EVERY page of your website* (especially every product and service page, Home, and blog pages).

- Whenever you post a social media update that links to a page on your website or blog, **be sure there's always a Lead Generation Offer on the page you're linking to**.

On our blog, we feature our Website Rehab℠ White Paper (below) after each related Blog post (and our Lead Generation Puzzle White Paper appears after each Lead Generation blog post).

Get the White Paper: **Web Site Rehab**^{SM} --
A 12-Step Program to Turn Visitors into
Customers
Help your website become more FIND-able, LINK-able, SHARE-able,
ENGAGE-able, VALUE-able, and SCAN-able in 12 Steps.

GET THE WHITE PAPER!

- Your Offer could simply be, *"Get these Posts by Email."* You could invite visitors on each Blog post to opt in to your email list. (Many websites have found that a pop-up greatly improves opt-ins.)

Improve the Lead Generation Offer page and form

To improve Conversion from your Lead Generation Offer page, consider modifying some of the elements to improve Conversion. *(We'll talk about copy in Chapter 13.)*

- **Response button size:** If your button isn't prominent on the page, consider making it larger or a different color to stand out.

- **Button copy:** If your button says "Submit," it's time to test something more benefit-oriented, like: *"Send me your cost-saving report!"*

- **Response Page Layout:** Be sure either the button or the form begins high up on the page. Be sure to look at it on a mobile device.

The *more required fields* the prospect has to complete in your response form, typically *the lower the response. (In Chapter 5,* we said that requiring more information would reduce Lead Quantity.)

Do you really need all the information you're asking for? (For example, do you need mailing address if the requestor wants to download your white paper or sign up for your enewsletter?)

There's nothing worse than having to provide 15 elements of data to download a white paper. (And the more fields you use, the more likely visitors are to give you *junk information -- and select the first option when there are pull-down choices.)*

Pare down to just what you need — name, email address, and any **specifics that will help you target your Conversion series**. Watch the number — and length — of any pull-downs in your answer fields.

If you ask only for the information you really need, you'll generate more completed requests.

These are all key areas for Testing, which we'll cover in *Chapter 18*.

Speed up the Sales Process with online tools

What's the next logical step in your Sales Process? Once your prospects have located the right products, their next step might be to get a price quote.

- Visitors might click "Contact Us', and then wait for a sales rep to contact them.
- Once the rep determines what specific products visitors need, the sales rep may have to get back to them a second time with a price quote.

Could you speed up the process with an online tool to help "find the right product" or "design your own system"? Could the website capture prospects' contact information -- and then deliver an estimate, ROI analysis, or list of items or materials needed?

In many cases, you can replicate your "find a solution" and "price quote" process online. The benefit is the potential customer gets an immediate response — and moves through your Sales Process faster.

Improve placement and visibility of Sales Offers

Where is your sales Offer on your website?

Is it on Home and every product page?

Do you add the latest product promotion on related blog posts? *If your sales Offer applies to all products, does it appear on all blog posts?*

To boost website leads and sales, create smarter Content and Offers

When you start evaluating every piece of website Content in terms of your Personas, you'll see what's missing, and what should be more prominent.

You'll better organize each page to maximize your website real estate (especially important on a mobile phone).

Be sure that Offers for key Buying Stages for each Persona appear prominently on your high-traffic pages.

Create logical paths from your traffic-driving activities, where every potential Landing Page has an Offer that either drives a lead or a sale.

Results Obsession Strategy #3:
Design systems for continuous Traffic, Leads, and Sales

Websites Gone Wrong: When Copying a "Showroom" Design Doesn't Make Sense

The client told the web designers they wanted a website design *similar to a particular luxury clothing site.*

Websites in the luxury clothing category can be "showrooms" – because the look of the item is likely what's going to sell it. This is probably true if you're selling *furniture, fabrics, clothing, jewelry, artwork, etc.*

If you're not selling something that's sold visually, creating a "showroom website" might not make sense for you. And you'll likely *need more copy than luxury clothing websites – especially if you're not a known brand.*

The project began, without thinking about whether the overall "show-room" approach made sense for the client. The website designers were experienced in creating sites in the client's industry. **What could go wrong**?

The client was an unknown company with premium products that don't have a visual focus. But they asked the web designers to create a showroom website. The copy on the resulting site was too sparse to keep the visitor engaged. And there wasn't enough to explain "why we're different" or convince the visitor the product was worth a premium price.

The company needed to create an ecommerce website where product copy SELLS. Instead, they created a website that relied on arresting visuals to sell their product. The website didn't answer the most basic question on the mind of every visitor to the site: **why should I buy yours**?

Moral of the story: Copying someone else's site and trying to make it fit your situation can result in wasted time and money. Understand what the goal of your website needs to be — whether it's leads or sales. Your resources should understand and create a logical plan for HOW the website will achieve your goal.

Figure 12.4

Chapter 13

Website Copy that SELLS!

The key characteristics of great copy from *Chapter 10* apply to every media channel. You want to write website copy:

1. With a particular *Buyer Persona* in mind
2. With a particular *Buying Stage* in mind (i.e., what's the role of this Content for the Persona?)
3. Using a particular *Emotional Driver* (*see Chapter 8*)
4. With a particular *Conversion strategy* in mind (i.e., what's the job of this page in our Conversion funnel?)

Some argue that website copy is different from other types of copy. They don't believe you should write it the same way you'd write an email marketing message or a direct mail piece. Really?

"What's in it for me?"
"Why should I buy yours?"
"Why should I do it now?"

When you're visiting websites, do you find yourself saying, *"Okay, it's the web. I'm going to make my purchase decisions differently here than if I was looking at direct mail or email"*?

Of course not.

People are not persuaded differently just because the media channel is a website versus direct mail, email, a magazine or newspaper ad, or a TV or radio ad. You're still persuaded by things that are relevant and attractive to you, no matter what the media channel.

People don't make decisions differently because it's a website.

And **the Sales Process isn't different** with a different media channel.

It's true that every medium has its nuances. Television can demonstrate, and radio can make creative use of sounds. Direct mail can be highly personal, while email can include a link to a Landing Page. And your website can make as much in-depth information available as the visitor wants.

But the same principles that make email, direct mail, print ads, TV ads, and radio ads effective also apply to effective web pages. People want to know:

1. *What's in it for me?*
2. *Why should I buy yours?*
3. *Why should I do it now?*

It's also true that visitors to your web site (or recipients of your direct mail or email) won't read *poorly-written* copy — or copy that *looks* difficult to get through.

Effective website copy will:

1. **Tell the reader "what's in it for me"**– the benefits.
2. **Solve the reader's problem**: Tell readers about the pain you're going to solve, or the pleasure they're going to enjoy with your product.
3. **Point out the unique benefits** or combination of benefits your product or service delivers *("why should I buy yours")*

4. **Give the reader a strong reason to take action now** (a great Offer)
5. **Be scanable,** so visitors can quickly get the main points

In this chapter, we'll go into more detail on creating copy for various types of web pages.

The single most important element of your website messaging

Different types of pages on your website may require different types of Content. But there are elements that are universal across the pages you'll be writing or reviewing.

"Why should I buy yours" on every page

Your key differentiation message needs to appear throughout your website, especially on Home, About Us, your Product/Service pages, and FAQs. *Why do you need to repeat it?* There are at least four reasons:

1. Every page could be a "Landing Page"

Search Engine Land reports that 71% of consumers begin the buying process on a search engine. Every page on your site with useful Content could become a "Landing Page" and appear in the search engine listings.

That means *any page could be the first — and only — page a visitor sees.* Be sure visitors are motivated to stay.

Tell them why you're different and why they should buy yours, no matter where they land.

Does it seem like over-kill? It's not.

2. Most visitors only visit a few pages on your site

The only people who will visit all your web pages work at your company.

WEBSITE COPY THAT SELLS

Think of it this way: when you review a document, you typically read the copy from first page to last. When you create your website copy, those who need to approve that copy will read pages in order from page one to the end (*like they're reading a book*). And they'll read line-by-line, word-for-word.

But your visitors don't read your website like a document or a book. *They visit only a few pages and scan* to find what they're looking for.

3. You can't predict the path of visitors

- Visitors can enter on (virtually) any page
- Few (if any) will click on each menu option in order
- Few (if any) will visit every page on your site
- It's highly likely your visitors are reading only a tiny fraction of the information on the pages they visit.

That's because different Buyer Personas visit your website, each with different needs – and they may visit at different Buying Stages.

If you include your key points of differentiation only on Home — or you bury them on your "About Us" page — this may happen:

- **A huge percentage of your visitors will never learn the answer to the key question, "why should I buy from you?"** That means you'll waste a large percentage of the money you've spent driving traffic, leads, and potential customers to your site.

How much business could you be missing? Prove it to yourself based on your visitor actions:

- What percentage of visits starts on Home?

  - In Google Analytics, see "Behavior," "Site Content," "Landing Pages."

  - Look at the number of sessions that start on Home (shown in Google Analytics as "/") versus the total number of sessions.

- o You could find as few as **20% or as high as 70% of sessions start on Home.** (*If you only have points of differentiation on Home, 30% to 80% of your market may never see them.*)

- Look at the number of Unique Pageviews to your "About Us" page compared to total Visitors (Users) to your site.

  - o What if only 20% of visitors ever see About Us?

  - o If you only have points of differentiation on About Us, 80% of your potential customers won't see them. You could be wasting 80% of your prospecting budget.

  The single page a visitor starts on may be the only chance you'll have of capturing that lead or sale.

4. Repetition is how you build a "brand"

When advertisers run brand-building campaigns in major offline media (TV, radio, magazine, newspaper, etc.), one of their key strategies is **repetition.** They repeat their overall campaign message frequently — to help associate the company or product name with the message.

Repetition of your key points of differentiation is not overkill. You're likely one of the few who will ever read your web site page-by-page, word-for-word. *You can't assume your visitors will "get it" if your key messaging only appears on a few pages.*

Implementing "Why should I buy yours"?

How should you incorporate your key points of differentiation in your website copy? And if 85% of visitors are only going to scan, how will they ever learn what you're all about?

> **Feature your key points of differentiation in headlines, subheads, and bullet points.**

Weave them into your educational Content pages, Content Marketing Offers, and blog posts – in other words, throughout your entire website.

This helps to reinforce your positioning. And it gives each visitor maximum exposure to the answer to *"why should I buy yours?"*

Messaging for introductory or support pages

When you're developing copy for your website, each type of page will have its own copy plan:

Home page

Your home page should introduce the great benefits your company offers — the *"why should I buy yours"* message. It's your "store window." You want to **give your visitor a reason to stay** on your website and learn more.

- Be sure your Home page has a main headline that introduces your unique benefits

Your Home page should also "direct traffic." It should funnel your Buyer Personas to the Content that addresses their challenges and questions — to start each on a logical path to Conversion.

For Lead Generation

If you have a Lead Generation website, showcase your Lead Generation Offers and your most important Early Buying Stage Content. Home is the place to start meeting the Early Buying Stage needs of each Buyer Personas.

For ecommerce

Your home page should introduce your products and services.

- If you sell different types of products, you may want to feature key categories that appeal to each Buyer Persona.

- Showcase new products or services, price reductions, special Offers, and best sellers (all the great reasons to buy today). Be sure your special Offer appears in a prominent location.

About us

Your About Us page should deliver points that make your products and solutions especially and uniquely helpful to your audiences.

To build credibility, you might include information on who started the company, and how long you've been in business. Consider a company history timeline, with key dates to *highlight achievements, innovations*, or the launch of particular products and services.

For a Services business, you want to **prove the expertise** of those delivering the service, or highlight the philosophy of the company and/or its founder.

- This page can *offer real proof to help answer the "why should I buy yours?"* question.
- You may want to highlight results you've helped clients achieve.

For Product or Services businesses, list awards and third-party endorsements. Include customer testimonials if you have them.

It may make sense to map out the elements of your "About Us" story, and then decide if you need multiple pages within the "About Us" section.

If you have enough Content for "About Us" page, and you have other "credibility-building" Content, you might have multiple sub-pages under your "About Us" Main Menu page, such as:

- What Clients Say *(to highlight customer testimonials)*
- Case Studies
- Awards and Endorsements
- Press Mentions

FAQs

Frequently Asked Questions make sense for just about every organization. Use the most common questions your prospects have about working with or buying from you (from your Persona summaries).

Not only can FAQs garner strong readership, they can help answer objections – and may be useful from an SEO standpoint.

Link to appropriate pages from your FAQs, especially to your Product/Service pages.

- Don't just present a long list of questions. Be sure to ORGANIZE your FAQs into categories by topic (and in a logical order). *Help scanning readers easily find what they're looking for.*

Response pages use the Sales Process

Wherever you're trying to drive a response (on the Lead Generation Offer page or individual product/service ecommerce pages), *you're persuading – and selling.*

These are the pages where you'll use the Sales Process to present your sales message. You want to focus on the benefits each product or service delivers to answer, *"what's in it for me."*

Your sales pitch usually begins with a "pain/pleasure" statement or question *(from Chapter 9.)*

"Are you having trouble with . . . wouldn't it be great if you could"

Decide what you would say to me if we were face-to-face or talking by phone. How would you begin? It's likely you would either remind me of some pain I'm having, or hint at some pleasure I could have.

- You can introduce this in your headline, and then develop it in your lead paragraph
- Don't forget to incorporate one of the 7 emotional drivers

Present your solution, then "Sizzle your solution"

Pitch all the key benefits of your solution, product/service, or Lead Generation Offer, to answer the question, *"Why should I buy (or respond to) yours?"*

- On your product/service ecommerce pages, each key benefit could be a subhead or bullet point.
- For a Lead Generation Offer page, use bulleted benefits.

Build credibility and answer objections

For Lead Generation websites, your prospects may look for this information at later Buying Stages. Be sure your Navigation addresses these topics so visitors can find them.

From your Product/Service pages, you can link to your:

- Testimonials (you might weave them throughout your site, as well as organize them by topic on a separate page called *"What Clients Say"*)
- Case studies
- FAQs
- Appropriate blog posts that address common objections

Your headlines and subheads on Product/Service pages may also address key objections, to help scanning readers locate issues they're concerned about.

"Go for the close"

Tell me what I have to do to get your solution (or Offer) and why I should do it now. Tell me what I'll miss by not taking action.

In a face-to-face or phone selling situation, the salesperson usually will know when to wrap up and ask for the order. On your website, that function is handled by:

- "Add to Cart" button
- Request your FREE (whatever) button or text link
- SIGN UP button (for the webinar, free trial, etc.)

For ecommerce websites selling a single product or service, or on a Landing Page, you may want to include your Call to Action button periodically in your copy (the "infomercial" approach).

- In a face-to-face or telephone selling situation, the salesperson will periodically go for the close.

- Your copy can do the same – illustrate some benefits, then include an "Add to Cart" link. Then deliver some additional benefits, and repeat your response link(s).

Landing Pages

Do you have a landing page for each Buyer Persona?

Think about where you're sending traffic in your latest promotional email or pay-per-click ad. If you're just driving visitors to your Home page, you're probably not converting as many visitors as you could be.

Create promotion-specific Landing Pages that are self-contained sales stories. Follow the Sales Process on those pages. Each Landing Page should give visitors everything they need to know to take advantage of your Lead Generation or sales Offer.

The headline and first few lines should refer to what you promised in your email or PPC ad.

Personal "Sales Letter" for an ecommerce Landing Page

If you're selling one product or service, you might use the personal "Sales Letter" approach.

Landing Pages written like a Sales Letter are some of the most profitable Landing Pages today.

The Sales Letter acts as your "salesperson" — and people want to buy from other people. You write it as a one-to-one conversation with the recipient and tell your complete selling story.

Your page can follow the "Story Approach" with Offer at the end. Or you can use the "Empathy with Early Benefit" to build some rapport before the close. Or deliver the "Upfront Benefit." *(See Chapter 8 for Copy Approaches.)*

You may need different Sales Letters (Landing Pages) for different titles in a company or your different Buyer Personas.

How much Content do you need?

How disappointed are you when you click on a link promising information about a particular topic, only to find very basic or too little information?

When you promise valuable Content, be sure you deliver. Don't short-change your audience by not delivering on your intriguing headline or link. Be sure to give them enough information to **make the click worth their while**

For a Lead Generation Offer page, use a benefit headline, pain/pleasure statement, bulleted benefits, and an action button.

For an ecommerce page, don't be afraid of "too much Content." Focus first on answering your Personas' key questions.

If you had to sell the product to someone in person, think of how many sentences you'd say. *You need each of those sentences in your copy.*

What is "enough" copy?

It's when you provide enough information to **answer each Persona's questions at each Buying Stage.**

Some visitors to your website may come with a specific list of requirements they're looking for.

- So "all that copy" is there to answer questions and provide specifics — because **specifics sell.**
- And it's there to meet the needs of the range of visitors coming to your website.

Before you start to rewrite your existing website, start by analyzing the effectiveness of the current copy. You want to be sure any changes actually improve results (and don't change things that are working well).

How well does your current Content engage the visitor?

- In Google Analytics, look at "Behavior," "Site Content," "All Pages." For Home and Product/Service pages, how much time are visitors spending on those pages? What is the Bounce Rate?

- *A long time on the page indicates the page may be doing its job* – and keeping the audience engaged. Low time on page could indicate the visitor didn't or couldn't find what they were looking for.

- *A high Bounce Rate indicates a Content problem* with the page.

How effective is your Lead and Sales Copy?

What percentage of visitors to your Lead Generation Offer page completes your form to get the Offer?

If it's a low percentage (less than 3%), it could be because the copy on the page doesn't convince your prospects of the value of your Offer – or it could be that your form asks for too much information.

What percentage of visits to each product page results in an ecommerce sale? For a given time period, compare Unique Pageviews for each product page with number of sales of each product. That will give you some idea of *how effective each product page is at actually selling the product.*

"But I don't want large volumes of Content"

A team was starting a website redesign, and their manager *stated he wanted to avoid "large volumes" of Content and wanted a more "minimalistic" look.*

Is this individual saying **he doesn't care whether the site's Content sells or not** – he just wants to be sure it looks a certain way?

The fastest way to create a website that won't sell is to tell your copywriter, "I only want this much copy."

That's like telling your salesperson, *"You can only spend 10 minutes with each prospect."*

Having a vision for an overall "brand look" is great — but that should *never* limit your ability to sell.

If your concern is lots of long, boring paragraphs, communicate that concern to your copywriter. Insist on *engaging, easily scanable copy*. But keep in mind that your various audiences will come to your website and **expect to get the full story.**

With most website Content, it's not a "volumes of Content" problem. More likely, it's:

- *A lack of concise writing* – including **lack of specifics.** You want to focus on your prospects' problems – and how your unique benefits solve them — without useless wording.

- *Poorly organized Content* that isn't scanable. Your copy should be easily scanable and visually "friendly." Subheads should outline your key points.

What could happen without enough copy?

When visitors can't find answers, or they find an incomplete answer, they usually won't contact you to ask about it. **They'll go to another website.**

- Think that won't happen? What do you do when you can't find details of something you want to buy? Don't you just search for another site?

- *If you leave your Personas with unanswered questions,* it's just too easy for them to click to one of your competitors.

Start by creating your complete sales message first, following the Sales Process and addressing the most common objections.

Then map the copy to the available page layout. If you have additional copy, consider adding pages you can link to. Or if ecommerce, you may have tabs you can use for more Content.

Wordsmithing and the "look" of copy

We talked in *Chapter 10* about the need for scanable copy – full of specifics and benefits for each Buyer Persona.

Avoid writing one- or two-word headlines that don't **tell the scanning visitor what's in it for them**, what they're going to learn on the page, and why they should stick around. Your visitors will be gone before they find your fabulous Content and Offers.

Avoid boring, non-involving headlines like this:

(The Name of Our) Software

(Yawn.) What does the software do**? What is the single most important thing you want me to know** about your software? *Why not give me a reason* to read further? How about:

Easily Add Sound to Your Presentations with (The Name of Our) Software

Yes, this particular headline isn't yet a work of art, but it's likely more effective than just "(The Name of Our) Software."

Don't rely on the visitor to figure out what your software does – make it easy for the scanning reader to get your key messages. And give him/her a reason to stay on the page.

Review your headlines and subheads. *Will I learn all the important benefits if that's all I read on your site?*

Here's how to make headlines more effective:

1. Think of what you'd say if you could only use one sentence to get me to read your page.

Don't worry about the number of words at this point, just create one sentence that gives me a very strong reason to read the page.

2. Edit your headline to remove any unnecessary words and make it crystal clear.

Read your headline out loud – is that what you'd say to me face-to-face? Simplify your statement until it reads exactly the way you'd say it.

As you're reviewing your headlines and body copy, look for powerful words — use action verbs whenever possible. Try to avoid useless and general introductory clauses like "As you may know."

Your headline and first sentence should work together, to **deliver the most important thing you could say to a prospect.** A too-generic lead sentence is the most common mistake that many websites make.

7 points to evaluate website messaging

"Stickiness"

When a visitor comes to your Home page (or a Landing Page), does the copy convince the visitor to stay and learn more? Can I see the most unique things about your site – no matter what page I'm on?

Persona-focused

Does your Main Menu and Home Page address key concerns of each Persona – so each knows where to start? Do you have Content for each Persona?

Why should I buy yours?

Is it clear why the visitor should buy from *you*?

223

Too many websites sell the same benefits your competition mentions. What are your unique points of differentiation – and are they clearly defined throughout your entire website? *Can I quickly discover what unique combination of benefits you offer?*

Benefit-laden headlines

Is the Headline on every page the strongest it could be? Does it draw prospects in and convince them to read the rest of the page?

Effective lede (lead)

Is the first sentence on each page the single most important thing you could say to draw visitors into the copy?

Scanable

If I just *scan* headlines, subheads, bullets — can I get the key points of your message on every page?

Friendly look

Does the copy *look* easy to get through? Have you used frequent subheads to break up the copy? Are your paragraphs short?

Where's the Offer

For Lead Generation, is it clear how to take the next step? For sales, do you feature the Offer on every product page?

Is the Offer irresistible?

Have you given me a strong reason to take some action?

Lean but effective

Edit your copy to remove all the junk that doesn't need to be there. If your copy includes a lot of useless "warm-up," is too general, or doesn't tell visitors something they didn't know, visitors will stop reading.

Get to the point with your copy. Be sure every word is there for a reason — and is the strongest it can be.

Your blog Content Strategy

Stock your blog with useful Content focused on your target audiences. You want valuable Content on your blog for five reasons:

- *To help educate* and provide useful information for prospects.

- *To prove your expertise* and help differentiate your offerings.

- To help improve Conversion by:
  - o *Answering objections*
  - o Explaining *features important to a specific industry*
  - o Focusing on the *major hot buttons of a particular Persona*

- *To improve your search engine visibility and drive new traffic.* Each post gives you another page that could appear in search engine results.

- *To attract links to your valuable Content from other websites and blogs.* You want the attention of bloggers, editors/reporters, and other industry influencers.

Create an Editorial Calendar

Your Editorial Calendar is a plan for the topics you'll cover for each of your Personas. You want to address key concerns, objections, and challenges they're facing throughout their Buying Stages.

As you plan future blog posts, consider:

- *Which Persona does the topic address?*
- *Is it unique, valuable Content to drive new links?*
- Which website page or keyword phrases does this topic support? *(See Chapter 14 on SEO)*.

Those companies who blog the most frequently tend to generate the most leads – and the most sales. Try to maintain a regular posting schedule. Each blog post should include:

- A specific, engaging headline
- An involving lead or first sentence
- Something the reader didn't know *(to prove your expertise if selling services, or differentiate your ecommerce offering)*
- Enough "meat" (specifics) to deliver value for the audience's time
- Specific subheads to make the post scanable

Be sure to **add share buttons** to your blog posts to expand their reach.

When you create each post, optimize it with keyword phrases and synonyms in the post URL, headline, subheads, and copy, just as you would with web pages *(see chapter 14 for* SEO).

Assign each post to *only one Category*.

End every blog post with a question that's easy for your audience to answer. Ask if they've experienced a similar problem and how they handled it.

For every blog comment you receive (that isn't spam), reply to that comment. Ask a related question to elicit an additional comment. "Can you tell me more about your …?"

Answer "Why should I buy yours" and follow the Sales Process

To take maximum advantage of every website visitor, every page of your website needs to give visitors a reason to stay and learn more. The answer to *"Why should I buy yours?"* should appear throughout your website.

Your product and service pages are your selling pages. On those pages, follow the Sales Process in copy, just as you would if selling face-to-face or over the phone.

Use blog posts to educate, prove your expertise, improve conversion, drive organic traffic, and attract links. Focus your post topics by Persona.

Results Obsession Skill #3:
Selling with words to develop Content that SELLS

References

Olson, Christi. (2017) *The value of search across the modern consumer decision journey.* Search Engine Land. <https://searchengineland.com/value-search-across-modern-consumer-decision-journey-270021>

Chapter 14

What You Should Know about Search Engine Optimization

Your Search Engine Optimization (SEO) efforts help prospects find you online. Specifically, SEO helps your individual web pages and blog posts appear in search engine listings when people search for certain topics.

For many companies, Organic (search engine) traffic can make up a significant portion of your total traffic. Organic traffic also tends to convert to leads and sales at a high rate. It's qualified traffic, because visitors from search engines are actively searching for what you're selling.

*"Search Engine Optimization
has a high ROI."*

- Search engines **drive 29% to 44% of new ecommerce customers**
- **In 2019, search engines drove from 41% to 64% of all website traffic** (averaging 53% across industries)
- Position in search results can have a significant impact on traffic. The first three or four Organic positions tend to drive the most traffic.

For most companies, Organic traffic is too important to your overall results to ignore SEO.

SEO is a high-ROI marketing investment

You may wonder if SEO is worth the time and money. You can run the numbers to determine just how cost-effective SEO might be for you.

Let's say your total Organic traffic was growing about 5% per year. Then, you spent $3,000 optimizing your site. After Year 1 of your SEO investment, you saw a 15% increase in Organic traffic. Was the additional 10% increase worth the $3,000?

If your yearly traffic is 20,000 visits, a 10% increase would be an additional 2,000 visits. You paid $3,000 which is $1.50 Cost Per Visit.

- You can compare this with your Cost Per Visit – and your Cost Per Lead or Sale -- from pay-per-click (PPC) advertising or other marketing efforts.

- Usually, Organic traffic converts at a higher rate than other marketing efforts, driving its Cost Per Lead or Cost Per Sale down.

Look at leads or sales from Organic traffic for the year prior to your SEO efforts. Compare number of leads and sales generated during Year 1.

Let's say you converted 3% of your additional 2,000 visits for 60 leads or sales. That means you paid $50 per additional Conversion ($3,000 / 60). Is that a reasonable cost, compared to your Profit Per Sale (for a sale), and compared to other marketing activities (for a lead)?

In reality, your SEO efforts should continue to yield increases in Organic traffic far beyond Year 1. And SEO should be an on-going effort.

You may find that your SEO investment is one of the lowest in dollar terms, but the return in Traffic, Leads, and Sales may be one of the highest. For many companies, SEO efforts return an incredibly high ROI.

How do you know your SEO is effective?

Are you sure your SEO is as effective as it could be? It seems few businesses think so. In general, the complaints seem to be:

- *"We're not sure if our SEO is working"*
- *"We're not sure if our SEO was done correctly"*
- *"We're not sure if any SEO has ever been done"*

This chapter will help you answer all three of these questions. The key measures of effectiveness are:

- **Is your Organic TRAFFIC steadily increasing?**
- Is your Conversion to LEADS or SALES from Organic traffic strong? (Is the traffic qualified?)
- Is your website appearing on Google.com (where about 67% of all searches occur) **when prospects search for your most important keywords?** (Are you visible among your competitors?)

If you can't say "yes!" to all of these (or you're not sure), then your SEO may not be as effective as it could be.

If you're thinking about building or redesigning your website, get your SEO resource involved at the beginning of the process. If you hired a company to "do SEO" when you built your website, it's probably time for an SEO review, update, and cleanup.

If you're just getting started, you can set up some of the basics yourself. If you're using an SEO consultant or considering one, you'll learn what to look for to ensure your efforts are as effective as possible.

SEO involves 7 critical steps — none of which are rocket science, all of which are easy to understand, and most of which **should be entirely transparent to you**.

Your SEO should be an on-going effort. It's too important to your results to not review and enhance your efforts regularly by:

- **Building and optimizing quality Content (like blog posts)**
- Linking to appropriate pages on your website
- Promoting Content to generate social shares and in-coming links

There are also technical issues to review periodically.

Diagnosis: Organic Traffic, Leads, Sales

What is your SEO doing for you?

The only reason to undertake SEO in the first place is to drive Organic traffic. Some simple numbers from Google Analytics can help you measure the success of your SEO efforts:

Traffic

Is your Organic traffic growing each month? *You should see a steady increase in Organic traffic*, especially if you're regularly adding new Content through blog posts.

- In Google Analytics, choose "Acquisition," "All Traffic," "Channels" from left menu. Set the date range you wish to review in the upper right corner.

- To see monthly traffic for a timeframe: in the Search box just above the table, search for "Organic" (to isolate just the Organic traffic). Then, choose Secondary Dimension (just above the table) of "Time," then "Month of the Year."

- How does your monthly traffic this year compare to last year? (If your business is seasonal, it may be useful to compare current year to prior year traffic by month.)

Traffic quality

If your Organic traffic is consistently growing, look at **the "quality" of that traffic.**

What is your Bounce Rate? What about **Average Session Duration** or **Pages/Session** trends over the past year?

A high Bounce Rate, and low Average Session Duration or Pages/Session, could indicate:

- A mismatch between what your search listing promised, and what your Content delivered
- If you sell a premium product, it could indicate you're not attracting those willing to pay a premium price

You can address both of those issues by *modifying your Page Titles and Descriptions,* which we'll discuss below.

It could also mean that *blog post visitors aren't looking at many other pages.* Add a Lead Generation (or Sales) Offer or links to your product/service pages on every blog post.

Leads and sales

What's your **Conversion Rate to leads and sales from Organic** traffic?

If you're adding several new blog posts every month, you might find your Organic traffic is growing, but your Conversion Rate is declining. This is another sign that **you need more visible and relevant Offers on blog pages**.

How do you know if your SEO is "correct"?

Unfortunately, there are plenty of websites that have paid for "SEO services" – but the websites haven't actually been optimized for search engines. *A free Google tool – Google Search Console -- will point out SEO elements that need work.*

In Chapter 2, we suggested **connecting your website to Google Search Console.** Go to search.google.com/search-console/welcome and enter your domain name.

- If you can access Google Analytics as an Administrator, you can verify ownership with your Google Analytics account. (Select the "Alternate Methods" tab, click the "Google Analytics" box, then "verify.")

- Otherwise, have your webmaster give you access to Google Search Console. *(Note you'll only have data from the date you connect your website.* Make the connection now so Google Search Console can start to gather data.*)*

Once you have some data, you'll be able to see the effectiveness of your SEO elements. The Overview shows you:

Performance

Click "Open Report" (from the Dashboard) or select Performance from the left menu. Select the date range you wish to review.

Queries — keyword data

Click all four of the options at the top: Total Clicks, Total Impressions, ***Average CTR (click-through), and Average Position.***

Scroll down past the graph. The first option, "Queries," shows you **a portion** of keywords that drove clicks to your site and for which your website appeared in Google search results ("impressions").

- Note those **keywords that don't include your company, brand, or product names**. You want to see the list of these "non-branded" keywords grow over time (and you want to see them attract more clicks.)

- **If you see mostly "branded" keywords,** it's likely your SEO isn't as effective as it could be.

- **Average Position**: Sort by position to see the keywords for which you tend to appear highest. Note those **keywords that appear in positions 1-4.** How many are "non-branded" keywords?

Pages

On the Performance Report, select "Pages" (instead of "Queries") to see your pages appearing in search listings.

Sort by Click-Through (CTR). This indicates the **effectiveness of your "Page Titles" (which become the headlines of your search listings)** and "Meta Descriptions" (which become the descriptions on google.com).

Low CTRs could indicate the Page Titles and descriptions for those pages aren't enough to motivate your visitors to click.

Other helpful charts on the Overview page (or from left column) include:

Coverage

See the number of your valid pages that Google has indexed.

- *If you have a number in the Error box*, scroll down to "Details."

- Under the "status" column, click the error to see the list of affected pages and what the error is. (You can give this list to your webmaster to address.)

Enhancements

Under "Mobile Usability" and "Breadcrumbs," you'll see the number of pages with errors.

- Scroll down to Details to see the type of error. Click on the error in the "status" column to see the affected pages.

Because Google looks at the mobile usability of your website first, it's important to *address errors promptly that Google shows for Mobile Usability.*

- Once your webmaster has addressed any errors, return to Mobile Usability, scroll down to see the errors, click on each error, and then *click "Validate Fix."* Google will then let you know if the problem is fixed.

In the left column menu, you'll also find:

Security and manual actions

See these sections for messages from Google for any penalties or other problems found. If your prior SEO consultant used questionable SEO strategies, Google may now penalize you for them.

Links

Select "Links" from the left menu to see the number of in-coming links to your individual website pages ("External").

Scroll down to see Top Linking Sites to see where your in-coming links are coming from.

Although Google Search Console has its limitations, it does give you a simple (and free) look at some of the keywords driving clicks to your website, your pages appearing in search engine listings, any broken links (more on that below), and specific improvements Google recommends.

Rank

You may also want to do a free trial of a tool to check where specific pages of your website are ranking for specific keyword phrases. One tool that doesn't require a credit card for its 14-day trial is unamo.com.

Keep in mind that Rank is merely a **diagnosis** tool for individual pages. Your actual Organic traffic trends (and Conversion to leads and sales) are the true measures of SEO success.

Key SEO strategy elements

Google uses an algorithm to determine the position of your website's pages in its search results. It typically issues major updates to its algorithm once or twice a year (and is constantly making minor updates).

In 2019, Google rolled out its "mobile first" initiative, meaning **Google focuses on the mobile version of each of your web pages** when applying the algorithm. So, looking good on a mobile phone is critical for SEO.

In general, Google wants to see:

- *Mobile-responsive pages* -- your Content re-positions itself to fit the one-column mobile screen (and I shouldn't have to scroll right to see any element)
- *Pages that load quickly* on mobile devices
- *Content large enough* to be easily read on a mobile screen
- *Buttons and other links with enough white space* around them to be easily clickable on a mobile phone
- *Fresh Content* – new or updated pages or blog posts
- *Unique Content* -- don't use the same Content on more than one page or URL. And don't use Content from any other website (including manufacturer's descriptions)
- *Quality natural (non-paid) in-coming links* – from websites that relate to your area of business

- *Diversity of natural (non-paid) in-coming links* – links that you attract naturally should be from a range of websites, and they should link to a variety of pages on your website

It also appears that social signals — shares and retweets of your social posts — may positively affect your SEO position.

Keyword Research: what your audience searches for

The first step in most SEO projects is Keyword Research. You or your SEO specialist should discover:

1. **Which keyword phrases are driving visitors to your website now?** Your Google Search Console account will get you started.

2. **Which keywords are driving Conversions?** If you're using pay-per-click advertising, you'll have data for PPC.

3. **What are all the potential keyword phrases your audience might use** to search for what you offer? You can identify some potential keyword phrases from your Buyer Persona summaries (review what each Persona is looking for) and from your competitors' websites.

In general, you want to *use keyword phrases with two or three words*. (One-word phrases tend to be too general.)

If you attract clients regionally, add your city or state to the keyword phrase to identify local search volume (e.g., "San Diego Web Consultant").

Google suggestions

As you search for a keyword on google.com, note the suggestions that appear as you type your keyword (which are queries others have searched for).

For each keyword search, scroll to the bottom of google.com to see "searches related to" what you searched for (for more keyword ideas).

Search volume for each keyword

Once you create your draft keyword list, **run the keywords through a keyword tool to identify monthly search volume for each keyword.**

These keyword tools are either free or offer a free trial:

- Searchvolume.io — free tool
- Ubersuggest.io — free for keyword ideas and monthly search volume
- Spyfu — see competitors' keywords
- KeywordSpy — estimates your rank by keyword
- Moz Keyword Explorer — for search estimates by keyword at moz.com/free-seo-tools
- SEMRush — search up to 10 keywords free
- KW Finder

Typically, keywords that are more general have the highest search volume. **But they may not attract qualified traffic** for your products and services – and they tend to **have more competition.**

Keyword phrases your competitors use

Search for each keyword phrase you're considering, to **see the competitive sites that appear and their position.**

Look at the headline of the search listing for each competitor (the "Page Title"), which will usually *include the keyword phrase that individual page is optimized for.*

This can give you some idea of the level of competition for each keyword phrase among those who sell similar products and services. **Are there keywords where few of your competitors appear?**

To help you evaluate competitive opportunities, you can *download a free tool at https://moz.com/products/pro/seo-toolbar.* (This puts "Moz Bar" just below your browser window.) After the download, you'll set up a free account.

At google.com, search for a keyword phrase you're considering. Scroll down to the Organic listings. You'll now see the "Moz Bar" appearing below each listing. The Moz Bar shows:

- "PA": Page Authority. A measurement of a page's ranking potential based on its in-coming links.
- "DA": Domain Authority. A measurement of a website domain's rankng potential compared to all websites in the Moz index.
- Link Analysis: click on this to open a report page. Click on "Ranking Keywords" to **see what keywords the page ranks for**.

A relatively low "PA" and "DA" on a competitor's page mean *a potential SEO opportunity.*

Click on a competitor page within the search results. In the Moz Bar (at the top of your browser), click the far left option ("Page Analysis"). Look for the use of the keyword in URL, Page Title, and "H1" (main) headline. If you don't see the keyword in these locations, *there may be an SEO opportunity (for your optimized page to rank higher).*

Your final "short list" of keywords

Select a "short list" of potential keyword phrases for which you want your pages to be visible on search engines, and where you believe competitive opportunities lie.

You want keyword phrases:

1. *With a reasonable amount of search volume each month.* **It's usually better to rank well for a keyword with lower search volume** than to rank poorly for keywords with more volume.

2. *That aren't being targeted by all of your competitors,* where there appears to be an opportunity for your website to rank well.

3. *That may drive Organic traffic for you now* (or that your Personas are likely to be searching for)

4. *That may drive Conversions in PPC for you now* (or that are most likely to bring **qualified** traffic to your website)

SEO Step 1: Keywords per page and post

The Content on each of your pages typically focuses on one main topic. From your "short list" of keyword phrases, *choose the keyword phrase that best represents the topic of that page.*

You may have heard the phrase "long-tail keyword." These are keywords that may not have a lot of search traffic but are specific to your audience.

- The pages that you reach by clicking on Main Menu topics may cover more general topics, but *sub-pages may reflect long-tail keywords*

- **Long-tail keywords will tend to have the highest Conversion**

- It may be easier to achieve a higher ranking for long-tail keywords (and keywords with a location, such as "San Diego SEO copywriter")

You may have pages that won't be built around a keyword phrase that has significant (or any) keyword volume. But if it needs to be part of your sales story, the page needs to be there.

You may also identify keyword phrases for which you want to be visible on Google.com, and for which you don't currently have Content. These are **Content areas where you'll want to develop additional pages** and/or new blog posts in the future.

Components of SEO

If it's good for website visitors, it tends to be good for SEO

Search engines send out "search bots" (automated software) to "spider" your site (review its Content and links):

- Bots can read text, links, and programming code
- **They can't read images, videos, or Flash**

The process of SEO helps bots get to every page (that you want them to find) and identify the key topics on each page of your site.

Once you choose a keyword phrase for each page, here's how to optimize your site:

SEO Step 2: Keyword-focused page URLs

If you're building a new website, it's critical that **the person handling SEO specifies all of the individual page URLs** to be included in your new or revised website. The list of page URLs is called the "sitemap."

- *Be sure your web designers don't create any pages before* the SEO consultant creates the sitemap.

For each page, you'll create a page URL that incorporates the most important keyword phrase for that page.

- Separate all words in the page URL with *hyphens.*
- Place the most important keyword at the beginning and try to keep the *page URL to 3 to 5 words.*
- Each word you include in your URL shares some of the value of the entire URL. Make every word count, and *don't include small words* like "a," "and," "the," etc.

A Main Menu page: website-development

A sub-page: website-development/ecommerce

A blog post: how-to-SEO-optimize-website

Don't repeat keywords in your URL. It's not necessary to say "website-development/ecommerce-website-development."

Google pays attention to about five words and ignores duplicates.

- *Do you have page URLs that don't use keywords,* like: yoursite.com/products/prod1
- *Or page URLs that use variables* — like yoursite.com/products/?prod1=35

Revise those page URLs to make them friendlier to both your audience and to search bots.

You also want to move to using https rather than http. Google prefers sites that have this extra level of security. You'll install an SSL certificate and migrate all of your page and blog post URLs to https. (You'll need to permanently redirect the existing http pages to https, otherwise Googlebot will see duplicate pages.)

You should **submit your sitemap** (sitemap.xml) to Google through Google Search Console for any new website, or when you're making substantial changes to page URLs and Navigation.

- You should also sign up for Bing Webmaster Tools to submit a sitemap. See bing.com/toolbox/webmaster/

SEO Step 3: Optimize elements for search results

If you're using WordPress, you can load a free SEO plug-in (like Yoast SEO). The plug-in adds a Page Title and Meta Description editing box below the Content on each WordPress page.

Keyword-focused Page Title

Page Title seems to be an important element in SEO.

Your Page Titles become **the headlines** for each of your pages appearing on google.com. So it's important that the SEO resource creating your Page Titles is also a copywriter.

- **Write the Page Title like a headline** – don't make it a list of key-words. It should read like a headline.

- **Put your most important keyword phrase** (the main keyword phrase on the page) **at the beginning** of your Page Title

- Page Titles should include the **specifics** of what's on each page

- Create a **unique** Page Title for each website page and blog post

Technical note: Before you create or redesign your website, tell your web designer you want to specify *Page Title separately from: what you call the page in your Navigation, what the page URL is, and what the main headline is on the page.* **It's important that your web designer knows this upfront.**

- **Don't put the name of your site in Page Title**. Many SEO plug-ins add the site name at the end of the Page Title needlessly. Your URL includes your site name. Including it in Page Title can dilute the value of the other words (and create Page Titles that are too long).

  o **For Yoast SEO for WordPress**: in left menu under SEO, select "Search Appearance." Select "Content Types" from the top tabs.

  o Under "Posts," "SEO Title," remove "site name" and "separator." Scroll down to "Pages," and remove "site name" and "separator" from "SEO Title" box.

Your Page Title should be about 55 characters. Google uses a proportional font, so the number of characters that will be visible on google.com varies.

Page (Meta) Description

You should have a *unique* Description for every page. Write your descriptions to differentiate you and *give searchers a reason to click*. (Assign Meta Description creation to your SEO copywriter.)

Descriptions on Google.com are about 120-150 characters.

SEO Step 4: Optimizing on-page Content

Always write your copy for your target audience first (using the principles we talked about in *Chapter 10*).

If you're not using an SEO consultant that's a copywriter, **be sure the last individual to touch your copy is the copywriter**.

- No amount of Organic traffic driven to your website will generate leads or sales if the copy doesn't sell – or if the keywords have made the copy appear unnatural.

Over-use of the same keyword phrase on a page will not only turn off your audience, but it may cause a penalty from Google.

Headlines and subheads

Incorporate your primary keyword phrase for each page early in the main (H1) headline. Be sure to code your main headline on each page as an "h1" (or "Heading 1" headline in WordPress).

Be sure you code each subhead as a subhead ("h2" or "heading 2" on a WordPress site.).

More **specific** headlines and subheads tend to be more effective at drawing the reader in. They're also more useful for SEO.

- "Specifics" usually mean headlines and subheads beyond a single word or two, and that include a keyword phrase.

Optimizing copy

You'll include your main keyword topic throughout the page, with *variations and synonyms* just as you would naturally when writing copy.

Anchor Text on links

When you create links to *your* pages, **place the link on a keyword phrase** (called "Anchor Text") that relates to the page you're linking to.

Don't miss SEO opportunities by placing text links on "click here" or "see our blog post on this topic."

- For example, "We recently finished a <u>website makeover that incorporates SEO</u> and social media."

- If this was a web page, *the link would be on the actual words underlined above.* (Vary the Anchor Text you use for links to each of your pages, so the links look natural.)

For the links on your website to your social media pages, use text links with your company name: "Response FX® on Twitter," "Response FX® on Facebook," etc.

Look for opportunities on each page to *link to a few of your* related web pages and blog posts.

- Each time you create a blog post, look for opportunities to *create links* within the post *to your appropriate product or services pages.*
- Minimize the number of outbound links to other websites.

Image file names and alternate ("alt") tags

- Your logo file should have your company name in the *file name.*

- Product images should use the product name in the *file name.*

- For other images, save them with file names that include keywords related to what the photo is about.

The more specific your file name, the better. *Use up to five words.*

- Provide your logo file, product images, and all other images to your website developers with **already-optimized file names as above.**

- As you add new images to your website, remember to always *create optimized file names with keywords.*

Once each image is loaded (into WordPress, for example), you can open each media file and **create the alternate or "alt" tag**. Alt text should help to describe the item. It can be helpful for SEO when you incorporate keywords.

- Alt tags are one of the elements of an ADA-compliant website as well, so it's a good idea to include them.

SEO Step 5: Off-page elements

Driving in-coming links with Content

Is your Content worthy of a link from another website or blog? You'll want to create a steady stream of useful or interesting Content, like:

- Calculators, survey results, checklists, cheat sheets, special reports, industry studies, industry lists, top 10 lists, infographics, white papers, or Buyer's Guides.

- An article by Jordan Kasteler on *Search Engine Land* suggests these link-attracting Content ideas: controversial position, timeline or promise for improvement if you follow these steps, the ranked list ("The 50 Greatest . . ."), Directory of the best of something, quiz, and "Complete Guide to".

Once you've created some link-worthy Content, post about it on social media (especially Twitter) to alert bloggers and other websites.

It's true that in-coming links to your website don't all carry the same SEO value. Some links are "no follow" links that tell search bots not to follow the links. Some are "follow" links that have more SEO value.

Also, the "authority" of the website or blog that's linking to you determines the value of that in-coming link to your website.

- Sites that have *been around longer*, include *topics similar to topics on your website*, and contain *lots of quality Content* are more likely to have better Authority.

- *Sites that may be industry associations or publications* will tend to be high authority sites.

- *Links from .gov and .edu websites* may have more value.

Ideally, the page linking to your website will have few outbound links on the page. Avoid having many reciprocal links. Google doesn't like paid text links and may penalize sites that sell them. Your site may also receive a penalty for being part of poor or "spammy" link networks.

To check in-coming links to your competition, see:
moz.com/researchtools/ose/

Incorporate social media "share" buttons

The popularity of your Content may be used as a ranking signal by search engines (especially Bing).

You should use social media SHARE buttons on blog posts and key Content and Offer pages, including "how to" articles or Tools, and pages with interesting Content formats (videos, charts, quizzes, infographics, comics, etc.).

- Addthis.com (Addthis®) and sharethis.com (Sharethis®) offer social sharing plug-ins for WordPress that also track the number of shares.

SEO Step 6: Permanent 301 (URL) redirects

A "301" is an HTML status code that indicates a page has been permanently moved to a new URL.

Using a 301 Redirect on an individual page URL redirects any incoming links to the new page. As long as you redirect each page individually to its corresponding new page (rather than redirecting an entire domain name), you will **preserve the value of any in-coming links to former pages**.

You'll need 301 redirects when:

- You want to "delete" a product, page, post, category page, blog category, or tag. The only way to "delete" a page that's been published is to use a 301 redirect.
- You change the URL for any page or blog post
- You discover broken links to pages that no longer exist
- You discover published page URLs that were never supposed to be public pages

Programmers may use a 302 temporary redirect, but 302s (and 307s) are a problem for SEO. Be sure your programmer *only uses 301 permanent page-by-page redirects* from your prior pages.

SEO Step 7: Technical setup and clean up

Breadcrumbs

Be sure to include breadcrumbs on your website, which can be helpful for SEO. (Your WordPress theme may allow breadcrumbs, or there are plug-ins to add them.)

Duplicate Content

Duplicate Content is a significant issue that you want to avoid. You have duplicate Content if you have:

- Multiple domain names pointing to the same site

- Two different URLs pointing to the same page
- The same Content used on more than one page

Google only wants to index one version of each page of your Content. If you have multiple pages with the same Content, you could have in-coming links to those multiple pages, which diffuses the value of those incoming links.

If you're selling products from a manufacturer, **be sure not to use the same manufacturer-provided descriptions of each product** that appear on many other websites.

If you have pages for multiple locations, be sure not to replicate the same Content. (Just changing the location name on each page does not count as "unique" Content.)

- Ask each location manager to answer some questions and use the answers to develop location-specific Content.

Page load speed

Page load speed on a mobile device affects your rank in Google's search listing results.

To test your mobile site optimization:
thinkwithgoogle.com/feature/testmysite

The tool will give your developers specific ideas for speeding up your site.

SEO Step 8: Local Search

To improve your Local Search visibility, you'll need local Content.

- *Include your city/state in the page URL, Page Title*, Meta Description, H1 main headline, and in the page Content.

You also want to **create or "claim" your listing** in local online directories to create consistent "Citations" (name, address, phone number, hours listings).

Visit each online directory, search for your business, and follow directions to add or "claim" your business listing.

- Always register your company name in exactly the same way: **with exactly the same name, same address, phone number, and hours.**

Company name

If your company name is XYZ Insurance Services, Inc., be sure you list it *exactly* that way in every directory. If you have multiple locations, call each location by a consistent name, like "Response FX® San Diego" and "Response FX® Los Angeles."

Use keywords in your company's name if it doesn't explain what you do. For example, if your company name is "Susie's," make your company name in every directory *"Susie's Flowers."*

Address and phone

If you're on State Street, be sure you list your address in every directory as "State Street" (rather than listing it sometimes as "State St").

If you have an 800 number and a local number, **list the local number** consistently in all directories.

You should also review your company listing in the big national databases for inclusion and consistency. You can get an idea of *how consistently your company appears across the databases* by visiting:

https://moz.com/local/search

You should submit or "claim" your business listing in:

- Yelp®, FourSquare, MerchantCircle.com™, CitySearch® (expressupdate.com/search), yellowpages.com, Facebook®, manta.com, Factual™, Superpages®, Linkedin®, and Youtube® (for starters).

- Most allow you to include a "profile" or "description" that should contain your most important keywords.

Submit your local business to Google at google.com/business and to Bing® at bingplaces.com. Add or edit your business on Google Maps.

SEO Step 9: Optimizing videos

Your videos can be helpful to your SEO efforts when you optimize them:

- Include keywords in your *video filename*
- Include appropriate keyword phrases and your company name in the *title of the video*
- Include an *exact transcript* of the video on the web page on which it appears – to tell search bots what the video page is about. (Search bots can't read videos.)

Sites like Rev.com will transcribe your video for you. (Rev.com is $1.25 per minute with no minimum.)

Additional video optimization for YouTube®

YouTube® is the second largest search engine, so optimizing your videos here can reap benefits.

- Include keyword phrases in the Video Description (and write a substantial Description)
- Include at least 10 "keyword tags" for each video
- Load an exact transcript of each video

Hiring an SEO consultant or specialist

SEO involves both technical (coding) skills as well as copywriting skills. Ideally, SEO would involve a team that brings expertise in both.

But frequently, an SEO consultant brings mostly the *technical knowledge*. In that case, **be sure your SEO Consultant works with your copywriter.**

- All copywriters should understand why SEO Consultants recommend certain things.

- If an SEO Consultant wants certain keywords in a headline, the copywriter should be able to incorporate them.

But keywords on a page don't necessarily add to the sell and help Conversion. That's why *a copywriter must be the final eyes on copy.*

"SEO copywriters" are copywriters who've added SEO to their skill set. Most SEO copywriters know how to conduct an SEO audit, improve Content optimization, identify and address duplicate Content, and create 301 redirects.

An SEO resource should never tell you:

- "We'll buy links for you"
- "We'll automatically link to you from our 27 websites (none of which have anything to do with your product)"
- "We'll create pages just for the search engines"
- "We use writers in (some other country)".

Be sure to **ask where their Content writers are located**. In general, copy that sells effectively in the U.S. should be written by copywriters who are **native English speakers living in the U.S.**

Even writers in the UK don't use exactly the same wording and spelling as U.S. writers.

SEO is too important to not understand

SEO is all about CONTENT -- *regular* development of *original*, high quality Content that others will want to share and link to.

Someone on your Marketing team should understand how to measure – and diagnose -- the results of your SEO effort in Google Analytics and Google Search Console.

If you don't see increases in Organic traffic (the purpose of SEO), your SEO isn't as effective as it could be.

You should never be in the dark as to what SEO work has been done on your website and what still needs to be done.

Ask your SEO consultant to show you exactly what's been done – and what he or she recommends and why. (Most SEO consultants use a spidering tool that can show you all your Page Titles and Descriptions in a spreadsheet.)

SEO is not a "set it and forget it" project. You should strive to add Content (useful to your Personas) regularly to your website. And your SEO consultant should regularly check for broken links, duplicate or missing Page Titles or Descriptions, and other technical issues.

Results Obsession Strategy #1:
Learn how to diagnose your situation step-by-step

References

Sterling, G. (2019) *Organic search responsible for 53% of all site traffic.* Search Engine Land. <https://searchengineland.com/organic-search-responsible-for-53-of-all-site-traffic-paid-15-study-322298>

Kasteler, J. (2011) *21 Types of Social Content to Boost Your SEO.* Search Engine Land. <searchengineland.com/21-types-of-social-content-to-boost-your-seo-103625>

Kasteler, J. (2011) *How to Ensure That Your Content Will Go Viral.* Search Engine Land. <https://searchengineland.com/how-to-ensure-that-your-content-will-go-viral-92473>

Backlinko. <https://backlinko.com/hub/seo/keyword-difficulty>

Chapter 15

Online Pay-Per-Click (PPC) Advertising

Online pay-per-click (PPC) advertising can be highly effective at driving traffic, especially from those who know what they want and are ready to buy.

PPC advertising is a great Testing vehicle. You can test headlines, descriptions, Offers, and Landing Pages. In usually a very short time, you can find the best options to use throughout your marketing. And when you keep testing, you keep learning and continuously improving your results.

"Cost Per Lead or Cost Per Sale are your key measures of PPC success."

255

Google Ads is the largest search engine PPC program. There are other search engine PPC programs, but *you may find that Google Ads delivers the most profitable results.*

Most social media platforms (such as LinkedIn®, Facebook®, and Twitter) also offer ads on a PPC basis. But **these ads don't appear as a result of a search, so they drive less qualified traffic.**

It's also true that PPC advertising is a fast way to spend a lot of marketing budget without much return, unless you really focus your efforts. Here's how to boost your PPC ROI.

Search engine pay-per-click advertising

If your web pages can show up in the "Organic" search engine listings "for free," why would you consider PPC ads (like Google Ads)?

PPC ads increase your visibility. When SEO efforts aren't placing you in a high position on page 1 of Google for certain keywords, PPC can get you there.

- Note that whenever a company says they can GUARANTEE that you'll be on page 1 of Google or in a certain position, there are only two ways to do that: 1) use PPC ads, or 2) do it Organically for key-words that have low or no search volume.

Currently, there are four paid ads above the Organic listings and three ads at the bottom of the page on google.com on a desktop.

- On mobile devices, no Organic listings appear on the screen without scrolling. (And Google is currently testing even more paid ads above Organic listings.) So paid ads have more visibility than Organic list-ings on a mobile phone.

Appearing in the top four paid ads on the first page is critical, and adver-tisers are bidding more to stay in those premium spots.

What are the keys to PPC success?

Whether you manage a PPC program yourself, or hire someone to do it, certain strategies will help you ensure that budget isn't needlessly wasted.

The keys to effectively using PPC are:

- **Correct setup:** Search (or Shopping Campaign for ecommerce).

- **Tight focus** – keywords and ads should deliver qualified traffic looking *only* for what you sell

- **Active management – constant ad testing, reviewing actual keywords searched,** and **tracking of Conversions** with a focus on Cost Per Sale or Cost Per Lead

The setup and management details below are for Google Ads.

Campaign setup: Search only (or Shopping)

Part of your success is in your "Campaign" setup. Each Campaign might focus on a particular product, product category, service, or geographic area.

You can run various types of Campaigns, but the highest ROI will come from a Search-only Campaign.

With a Google Ads Search Campaign, **your text ad appears on google.com when someone searches for a keyword you've bid on**.

For ecommerce, you can also use Google Shopping ads. A Shopping ad includes a product photo, product name, short description, and price of your product that will appear on google.com *as a result of a search.*

There are also "Display" Campaigns, where your ads appear on other companies' websites. Display has lower click-through (and usually lower ROI), because *you're not reaching an audience that's specifically searching for your product or service.*

For each Campaign, **you'll specify geographic areas you wish to target (or any areas you wish to avoid**).

You'll also specify an **average daily budget**. You can allow Google to set your **bids per keyword**, or you can do it manually.

If you're going to actively test and manage your ads, you'll want to be sure ads are rotated evenly. In Campaign Settings (part of setup):

- Click "show more settings." Under "Ad Rotation", choose "Do not optimize" if you (rather than Google) want to decide which test ad is doing better

Keyword setup to attract your audience

Within each Campaign, you'll set up "**Ad Groups**." Each Ad Group will include a small group of related keywords (and one or more ads.)

You'll start with keyword research similar to the process we discussed for SEO. Online tools (*see the list in Chapter 14*) can help you create your keyword list.

Other *online tools will track your competitors' paid keywords (and ads)*. Two competitor research tools that both offer free trials are:

- Spyfu.com
- Ispionage.com

As you gather your keywords, you'll group them into Ad Groups:

- The *keywords in each Ad Group should have a tight focus*, so you can write an ad that relates to all of those keywords.

- Typically, you'll want to *use keyword phrases of two to three words* to get the specificity you need and **not pay for a lot of unqualified clicks.**

258

Targeting point: The common error is **not being specific-enough with your keywords**. The broader your keywords, *the more likely you are to be paying for unqualified traffic.*

If you specialize in a particular industry or type of product/service in your category, you'll want to include that specific industry or type of product in *every* keyword. For example:

- If you sell tennis equipment, the term "tennis" probably needs to be in every keyword – tennis rackets, tennis shoes, tennis clothing, etc. (Otherwise, you'll get lots of clicks from those looking for other types of sports equipment).

- If you only sell auto insurance, don't bid on generic keywords like "insurance" or "insurance quote."

Targeting point: Another common error is with the "match type" you select. *Match type is how you tell Google when the keywords you're bidding on are a match* for what the individual is searching for.

You can set up each keyword as:

- [exact match] — indicated by brackets around the keyword. The search must match this exactly with no additional words.

- "phrase match" — indicated by quotes around the keyword. The search must include this phrase, but words can be added before or after it.

- +modified +broad — the search must include the words with a plus sign directly in front of them. But they can be in any order with any other words included.

- Broad match — search can include something close to these words, in any order, with other words included.

Be sure your PPC specialist understands you need qualified traffic, and will be measuring success on Cost Per Lead or Cost Per Sale.

Set up "negative keywords" to control ad visibility

You'll want to set up "**negative keywords,**" to tell Google for which keywords you *don't* want your ads to appear.

This is a key strategic element for trying to ensure that the clicks you pay for are *only* from those truly interested in what you're selling.

- If you're selling only tennis equipment, negative keywords might be: basketball, baseball, badminton, golf, etc.
  - If someone searches for "basketball shoes" or "badminton racquets," your ad wouldn't appear.

- If you only sell auto insurance, you might set up these negative keywords: homeowners, life, health, medical, etc.

Set up ads and ad Testing

Within each Ad Group, you'll create ads that relate to all of the keywords in the Ad Group. And Google Ads will allow you to **create multiple ads within each Ad Group.**

Those ads will rotate automatically. This allows you to **test different headlines, individual words** within the headlines, **descriptions,** individual words within the descriptions, **Offers,** etc.

- *Create at least two ads for each Ad Group*, so you can test the ads against each other.
- Most Testing has found that *capitalizing every word in your ad headline and description* gets better results.

Be sure PPC resources understand you **expect constant ad Testing** – and **you want to know what they've learned** from the Testing.

You'll want to use the winning words, headlines, descriptions, and Offers from PPC ad Testing across your marketing programs.

See Chapter 18 for more detail on Testing.

Set up Landing Pages

You want to send your PPC traffic directly to the Content referenced in your PPC ad.

If you're pitching a Lead Generation Offer:

- Send visitors to the Offer sign-up page

If you're pitching a direct sale:

- Send visitors to the page where they can buy the specific product

Be sure you don't limit your PPC specialist's effectiveness by not allowing him/her to create or modify Landing Pages. PPC can drive highly-qualified traffic, but it still may not convert – or not convert as effectively as it could – without Landing Page Testing.

- Create separate PPC Landing Pages, not linked through your main Navigation, to allow your PPC specialist to test different copy, Page Layouts, and Offers.

Results tracking

Set up Conversion tracking in Google Ads

Under "Tools & Settings" (in the top menu), "Measurement," select "Conversions" to create code to track your Conversions.

- Click the large blue plus sign + at the top left.
- Select the type of Conversion (website, etc.)
- Then select Purchase, Lead, Sign Up, etc.
- Give your Conversion a name: "15% off Sale."
- Click "Create and Continue."

If someone else makes changes to your code, select "email the tag." Enter that individual's email address.

If you're tracking an ecommerce sale, lead, or sign-up, *select "Page Load" under tracking method.*

- Your web programmer will place the code on the "Thank you" (for purchasing, signing up, requesting the download, etc.) page.
- **Be sure you create a "thank you" page for each type of lead, and a separate one for sales.**
- Click "send and continue."

Once your code is in place and a sale or lead (or other Conversion) occurs, your Reporting in Google Ads will now show Conversions.

Note that Google Ads lumps all Conversions into one column. So if you've set up more than one type of Conversion, you'll need to view results in Google Analytics.

Set up Google Analytics for Google Ads tracking

To connect your Google Ads account to your Google Analytics account, you'll need Admin access to both accounts. You can start from Google Ads or Google Analytics:

- In Google Ads, from the top menu, under "Tools & Settings," "Measurement," choose "Google Analytics."

- *(Now in Google Analytics:)* Choose "Admin" in bottom left column. In middle "Property" column, select "Google Ads Linking."

- Select "New Link Group" and select your Google Ads account from the list.

To track Conversions by individual Conversion Goal, you can set up *Goals* in Google Analytics *(see Chapter 3).*

(If you have an ecommerce website, you can either set up Goals or Ecommerce tracking to allow Google Analytics to track your sales.)

- Google Analytics also tracks results by keyword.

- For individual ad, Google Analytics *only shows results by first line of each ad.*

If you're testing two different ads that both use the same first line, you'll need to *create a UTM tracking URL* to use in each Google ad.

To set that up:

- In Google Analytics "Admin," in the "Property" column, choose "Settings." Under "Advanced Settings," check the box for "*Allow manual tagging (UTM values) to override auto-tagging for Google Ads.*"

UTM codes require Source, Medium, and Campaign. You can add the tracking element of "content" to track a specific ad. For example, the UTM tracking URL below is for:

medium =	cpc	(PPC)
source =	google	(Ads)
campaign =	May 15% off promotion	
content =	superior111	(the name of the ad being tested).

https://www.responsefx.com/?utm_medium=cpc&source=google
&utm_campaign=may15off&utm_content=superior111

For a simple way to create a UTM tracking URL, visit:
https://ga-dev-tools.appspot.com/campaign-url-builder/

Just enter your variables and it creates the tracking code for you.

Management and Results Analysis

Click-Through for ad effectiveness

You should always be testing at least two different ads per Ad Group.

The Click-Through Rate (CTR) for each ad tells you what percentage of viewers who saw your ad clicked. It's a good indicator of the **attractiveness** of your ad copy to your audience.

If an ad is receiving poor Click-Through (0% to 0.4% or so), it's time to start testing another ad or ads.

- Review your test ads at least weekly, to see if one is substantially better than the others.

You may want to Pause the poorer ads, and create additional test ads to see if you can beat the winning ad. But before you do, check each ad's results through leads and sales.

Leads and sales by Campaign and Ad Group

You'll want to compute Cost Per Sale or Cost Per Lead as a benchmark for managing your Ad Groups and Campaigns.

- Cost Per Sale = Ad cost divided by number of sales
- Cost Per Lead = Ad cost divided by number of leads

If you have a single type of Conversion set up in Google Ads, you'll see your leads or sales in Google Ads.

If you have multiple Conversions set up, and you want to see results by type of Conversion, you'll see those results in Google Analytics.

In Google Analytics, select "Acquisition," *"Google Ads,"* "Campaigns." Click any Campaign to see Ad Groups.

- **Compute Cost/Lead (or Cost/Sale) for each Ad Group and for each Campaign**

Above the chart, select "Secondary Dimension," "Advertising," "Ad Content." This shows you results by first line of each ad (if you're not using utm_content tracking).

- **Compute Cost Per Lead or Cost Per Sale by ad**

To see Keywords within an Ad Group: select "Acquisition," "Google Ads," "Campaigns," click on a Campaign to see Ad Groups, and click on an Ad Group for keywords. (At the top right of the Google Analytics screen, you can select "Export" to download the report into Excel.)

- *Compute Cost Per Lead or Cost Per Sale by individual keyword.*

If you're using a UTM tracking URL, you'll see results under "Acquisition," *"Campaigns,"* "All Campaigns."

- Above the chart, choose "Secondary Dimension," "'Advertising," "Ad Content" to see ads by Campaign.

In the top row of any data chart, **use the "Conversions" pull-down** menu to select the Conversion you want to see.

Traffic quality

To see the quality of your visits, look at your *Google Analytics.* See "Acquisition," "Google Ads," "Campaigns."

To see results by Ad Group, click a particular Campaign.

For each Campaign or Ad Group, review **Bounce Rate and Pages/Session.**

Add a Secondary Dimension of "Advertising," "Ad Content" to see results by the first line of each ad.

If you're using utm_content in your URLs, see "Acquisition," *"Campaigns,"* "All Campaigns." Above the chart, select "Secondary Dimension," "Advertising," "Ad Content."

High Bounce Rate and/or low Pages/Session may indicate:

- Your keywords aren't specific enough
- Your ad isn't specific enough

- Visitors aren't finding what they expect on your Landing Page

Reviewing "search terms"

Once your program is running, you'll be able to **review the actual search terms prospects used** that caused your PPC search ad to appear.

- *In Google Ads*, for any Campaign or Ad Group, click the "Keywords" tab in the left menu. Then click "Search Terms."

These actual keywords that prospects searched for can help identify additional keywords you might add.

But more importantly, **you'll discover words for which you don't want your ads to show.** (Add those as "negative keywords.")

- Be sure your PPC resource understands **you expect "Search Terms" to be reviewed regularly**, to add "negative keywords" as needed.

Quality Score

How does Google Ads determine in what order to show ads? Google computes in real time a "Quality Score" of 1 to 10 for each keyword.

Google considers **your bid, expected CTR, how relevant your ad is to the keyword, and the quality of your Landing Page.**

An estimate of this "Ad Rank" is:

Your Maximum Bid per keyword   x   Quality Score

- **Higher Quality Scores (7 or above) can mean a higher position**, giving you more clicks at a lower cost.

- Conversely, poor Quality Scores (2 or 3) may mean your ads will be given a lower position even if your bid is higher than other ads (or your ads may not show at all)

To add a Quality Score column so you can actively manage your keywords: *above a keywords chart,* click "Columns," "Modify Columns," "Quality Score." Check "Quality Score" and click "Apply.")

- Keywords with low CTR may be too generic, or may need a higher bid

- You may need to reorganize your keywords into new more tightly-focused Ad Groups

You may also need to create new Landing Pages. And you want to constantly test ads and Landing Page improvements.

Competitive share

You can get an idea of your "share" of paid search impressions and clicks by adding two additional columns to your reports in Google Ads:

- "Search Impression Share" = the percentage of times your ads appeared for your keywords, compared to competitor ads

- "Click Share" = your share of all clicks from those impressions, compared to the competition

To add them, choose "Columns," "Modify Columns, select them under "Competitive Metrics," and click "Apply."

Note that *Google doesn't consider your negative keywords when deciding all of the potential impressions your keywords could have received.* But it gives you an idea of the Campaigns and Ad Groups where you may have more potential for traffic if you make improvements.

How to identify a smart PPC specialist

To get the most from PPC advertising, you want to **actively manage** your ads and keywords.

Look for specialists who have the Google Ads Certification. They are required to pass a yearly test to maintain that certification.

Before hiring PPC specialists, ask *what they're going to review each week.* At a minimum, you should hear:

- **Cost Per Lead or Cost Per Sale** by Ad Group and Campaign
- **Click-through (CTR) on each test ad**. And when they find a "winner," they should pause lower-performing ads and create new test ads.
- **CTR by Keyword**
- **Search Terms** to identify potential keywords and negative keywords (to add), and see how qualified the searches are
- **Ads that competitors are running,** to identify ways to stand out and differentiate your offering

Once you choose a PPC resource, be sure to give that resource access to your Google Analytics.

Focus on results for cost-effective PPC

We've talked about the key factors that have the most significant effect on PPC results. There are many other elements your PPC specialist may actively review and manage. But if this foundation (of *correct setup, tight focus, and active management*) isn't in place, it will be difficult to generate a positive ROI from your PPC investment.

Don't blindly hand over your PPC budget to someone and hope they'll spend it wisely.

Especially with an outside PPC specialist, he or she isn't likely to understand all the nuances of your business at the outset. Take the time to discuss your specific goals for the program, and determine a plan for regular review of progress.

Be sure everyone involved understands that Cost Per Lead or Cost Per Sale is your key measure of PPC success.

Results Obsession Strategy #6:
Equate your costs to results whenever possible to get to ROI

Chapter 16

High Impact Email Strategies

What's your return on your email efforts?

Marketers consistently say that email is the medium that delivers their highest ROI.

- McKinsey found that *email was 40 times more effective at acquiring new customers than Facebook or Twitter.*
- Campaign Monitor® reported *email returns $44 for every $1 spent.*

When you communicate regularly with customers by email, you can cost-effectively build repeat sales, Lifetime Value, loyalty, and referrals.

"How are you maximizing your Investment in each email address?"

If your website generates leads, an email "nurturing" program is a critical piece of your everyday marketing toolkit.

- Salesforce.com Research found that *the average B2B company spends $150 to acquire an email address.*

- Forrester® Research found *that companies good at lead nurturing generate 50% more sales-ready leads at a 33% lower cost*!

Your Email Conversion Series is where "C" leads are educated to become in-market "B" leads over time, and "B" leads become sales-ready.

In this chapter, you'll focus on a better plan and strategy for your email program to boost your marketing ROI.

4 steps to drive superior email results

How do you get the most from email? Focus on these elements:

1. Segment your email lists to talk relevantly

Use data you have to drive relevant Content and Offers to each Persona. Focus on the highest value customers (and opportunities to create more of them) and send customized messages.

Those who segment their email lists to customize Offers or newsletter Content for each segment get substantially better results (what a surprise). Segmentation can have a dramatic effect on results, even for small emailers.

No matter how small your list, consider segmenting it to make your email Subject Lines, Offers, messages, and newsletters more relevant by segment.

2. Test the most important elements regularly

- Subject Line (which determines whether your email is viewed)
- Offer (the element that drives the click if driving leads or sales)
- Main message
- Length of message
- Message format — "letter" versus "postcard" (with image)

Marketers achieving the highest email response rates tend to do more A/B tests -- especially *Offer tests!* Nationwide, about 77% of marketers report running email tests.

Marketers with the lowest email response rates tend not to test.

- If you're in the "let's just wing it" 23% — or worse, *your agency* never suggests running an email test — you're not maximizing results.

You should be testing your way to email success (by testing one Offer or message against another, for example) to continually search for ways to boost your Conversion Rate. *More on how to test in Chapter 18.*

3. Track Click-Through (CTR) for effectiveness

Click-Through (not Open Rate) is the key indicator of whether your email persuaded your audience to act.

Look at **Unique Clicks / Delivered** for each email. For those emails with lower CTR, it's time to do a rewrite.

4. Focus on Conversion Rate

For emails designed to get a sale or lead, the message should focus on driving the action.

Conversion Tracking helps you identify email messages and Offers that most effectively drive leads and sales. Use **sales/delivered** or **leads/delivered** to see your final response rate.

3 best uses of email

Email is the workhorse of *lead Conversion, maximizing customer Lifetime Value*, and *re-engaging* current and former customers.

Your email program should be cost-effectively driving more sales, improving customer profitability, and shortening your sales cycle.

Some of the most effective (and profitable) email campaigns are "triggered" by a particular event or time period, and use data about the prospect or customer to customize the message.

The first step is creating your contact and message plan.

Triggered emails: by time or event

"Triggered" emails are emails sent out automatically by an email system, either when a prospect or customer takes an action, or when a defined period passes without an action.

After a triggered email, an automated series of emails can continue to mail at defined intervals. (This is a "drip" campaign, because you're sending information periodically.)

You can use drip campaigns to encourage Conversion to a sale *(Lead Conversion Series)*, encourage the next customer order and build Lifetime Value *(Customer Retention Series)*, or try to get former customers back *(Customer Re-engagement Series)*.

Some typical event or time triggers could be:

- *Response to an Offer -- Request Content, Subscribe* (to the enewsletter*), Sign-Up for a Webinar, Download the Demo, Request Quote, etc.* The Response can trigger the start of your **Lead Conversion messages** designed to educate and move the lead to the next step in the Sales Process.

- *Purchase:* The purchase can trigger **Customer Retention messages**, especially to *motivate one-time purchasers to buy again.*

- *Time since last purchase*: Customers that haven't purchased in a time period can receive a series of **Customer Retention or Former Customer Re-engagement emails**.

Segment targeting of a message series

Your segmentation plan doesn't have to be complex. Start with the basics you can easily identify. You'll talk differently to:

Leads

Base your emails on the topic of the Offer that brought in the leads (down-loaded Content, webinar or newsletter sign-up, coupon or discount.)

When you capture information from a lead, you might **request elements that help define each Persona (if your Offer doesn't)**. Then you can also talk differently to each Buyer Persona based on those data elements, like:

- *Different titles or positions* within a company

- *Different geographic areas*, if geography segments your audience

- *Key problem* he/she is trying to solve

- *Key products* he/she wants to learn more about

Customers

You should talk to customers **based on their last (or past) purchase(s).** This is the most basic type of segmentation, yet it can be highly effective. *Are you tailoring your customer messages based on what types of products/services each customer buys?*

You can also use information from your customer database to segment by Buyer Persona, as well as customer profitability measures:

- *Volume buyers and other Best Customers* may be a separate segment in your Customer Retention Series

- *Customers acquired with a discount Offer* may need more aggressive follow-up Offers to buy again

Your copywriter should know exactly how you've segmented your list(s) — and any personalization elements you want to use in the copy.

- You may not need multiple versions by Persona, but you may want to **cover concerns important to each Persona**.

- And depending on the type of customer communication, you may want to *create a separate "Best Customer" version.*

You might start with simple "triggers" that launch a Lead Conversion, Customer Retention, or Customer Re-Engagement Email Series. But as you learn more about each name, you may pull names out of these series to *create new segments that will receive more targeted emails.*

Lead Conversion Series

For both ecommerce and non-ecommerce, an email *Lead Conversion Series* can:

- *Educate* your prospects about the unique **benefits** your product, service, or solution delivers and the problems it solves. In some cases, it may make sense to have each email focus on one specific benefit.

- *For services: prove your expertise* in your solution category. You want to become a trusted advisor or resource.

   o Detail your particular **process** to b*uild trust in your ability to address the prospect's situation or problem.* Walk the prospect through unique elements of your process (that you could parse out in a series of emails.)

- *Prove the value of your solution* by showing how you solved other customers' problems (or **how other customers are using your products**.) You could do a series of case study emails.

- *Differentiate your company* and solution from the competition

- *Move leads through your sales process faster* by:
   o Delivering periodic Offers to motivate the next step
   o Answering key questions and **objections** that may keep leads from taking action

Lead Conversion Series: ecommerce

In your Email Conversion Series for ecommerce, your primary objective is to encourage leads to learn more — and motivate the first purchase.

- *Showcase* your unique products or services, hottest sellers, new offerings, and highest-rated products.

- *Illustrate* the unique benefits and features (of your products or services, or ordering from your company)

- Highlight ways to use your products, or how to maximize the benefit from your products

- *Present Offers to motivate the first sale:* offer a product sample, trial, discount, or product bundle (see Sales Offers in *Chapter 7).*

- *Continue to build* your "brand promise" (the "why should I buy from you?"), so your audience equates your company name with your key points of differentiation.

- If you have a timed trial of your product or service, use email to keep your trial users involved during the trial. Each email might point out one of the benefits or illustrate how to use a particular feature. "Have you tried . . .?"

Lead Conversion message #1

The first email your lead receives from you will likely have the **highest readership**. Make that email count for more than saying, "Thank you, and contact us with questions."

Objective for email #1 (Content or Webinar Offer)

Get leads to read the downloaded document you offered or put the webinar they registered for on their calendar. (If you have an enewsletter sign-up on your website, let visitors download your last issue.)

In your first email, **always include a download link** to the Content marketing Offer or enewsletter the prospects signed up for. Or **remind them of the webinar details**.

1. *Write it as a personal "thank you letter"* from one individual to another. People like to deal with individuals, rather than companies. And it starts a personal relationship with the prospect.

2. *Summarize in bullet points the key things prospects will learn* from your download, webinar, or enewsletter.

3. *Include links to other resources* (blog posts, etc.) on a similar topic. Start to position yourself as an expert resource.

Subsequent emails

Base your series of emails on the topic of each Offer. Revisit your Buyer Persona summaries (from *Chapter 3, 4, and 8)* and consider what key questions each Persona might have. What might be useful?

- Don't assume your leads read the entire document (or watched the entire webinar), understood your key points, or remember what they read or watched.

- Never assume they know *how your product or service works, why certain features are important, or the benefits you deliver.*

- *Don't assume visitors to your website understood the "why should I buy yours" message* (or remember it)

- *Don't assume web visitors are aware of everything you offer.*

Your emails should *tell prospects something they didn't know*. In many cases, you can summarize some of your existing web Content – especially Content targeted to each of your Buyer Personas. (Few, if any, visitors read or remember a lot of information from your website.)

Use a few different **emotional drivers** *(from Chapter 8)* throughout your series, to see if you can find your target's hot button or pain point.

You want to move your prospects to the next step in the Sales Process with a **periodic Offer**. (In *Chapter 4*, we outlined types of Offers for each Persona by Buying Stage. You'll find next-step lead Offer ideas in *Chapter 6* and sales Offers in *Chapter 7*.)

Length of your email Lead Series

When you generate leads, *how long does it take you to convert them?*

The length of your sales cycle is how long you should follow up with leads.

The "3 C's" play a role: How Complex a sale it is, how much you're Changing the customer's current way of doing things, and how Costly your product/service all affect this timeframe.

For longer sales cycles, **many companies (i.e., sales reps) stop following up on leads way too soon**. With an email series, you can continue to follow up, even after your sales reps have stopped.

No matter how long your sales cycle, *a percentage of those who responded to one of your Offers will end up buying from someone*. So it's smart to keep in contact until: you actually get the sale, they tell you they've purchased elsewhere, or you have no response to your last three emails.

For an ecommerce client (where none of the "3 C's" apply), we discovered that virtually no sales were made to prospects 90 days after the date they became a lead.

- We stepped up our efforts to convert prospects to customers in the first 90 days.
- After 90 days, we send "Your last email from XYZ Company," with a link to a simple preferences page. The preferences page allows prospects to opt-in to continue to receive the twice-monthly special promotions by email.
- Otherwise, they're moved to an "inactive" file. We may email them a few times a year when we introduce a new product or have a major sale or special.

It's important to keep track of your own results by "time on file" (in your database or CRM), as every company's results will be different. *(Capture the original date the lead came on your file, and the date of first purchase.)* Keep a running count like this:

Time on file	# of leads	# converted to customers
1-30 days		
31-59 days		
60-89 days		
90-119 days		
120-149 days		

How often should you contact your leads? It's something to test.

- The most critical time is immediately after the individual responds to one of your Offers.

- Once a week may be a reasonable timeframe for contacting the actively-searching potential buyer – but test to find out. (A once-a-month enewsletter is *absolutely not frequent enough*.)

How many emails should be included in your Lead Series? Enough messages to cover the key topics that will *get the prospect to take the next step* in the Sales Process.

It's also true that you want to avoid having your leads unsubscribe. Be sure to *send valuable Content* to educate and help them – so they see the value of remaining on your email list.

Customer Retention Series

An email *Customer Retention Series* can:

- Deliver perks to your Best Customers

- *Ensure customer satisfaction* — by helping customers get maximum value from your product or solution. Educate them about specific features and how to use them

- Show *how others are using* the product or solution, and the great results they're getting. Include case studies of the great results you've achieved for clients (if selling services)

- *Continue to prove your expertise and add value.* Educate about your unique process (if selling services)

- *Remind* customers of your unique benefits to differentiate you, and keep customers buying

- *Identify early problem*s by sending a link to a periodic customer satisfaction survey (with a gift or other bonus for completing it)

- *Expand the relationship* by promoting related products, add-ons, and other services. *Educate* about the benefits of your range of products and services to increase "share of customer"

- *Include periodic Content Offers* to allow them to become leads for additional products/services

- *Stay top-of-mind* if another need comes up

- **Maximize customer Lifetime Value** – (for ecommerce) promote Offers to *upgrade* to more profitable options, *boost average order size,* and boost order frequency *(more on ecommerce below)*

We sent a series of three email messages to C-level customers of a law firm. We asked for their participation in a survey, to find out if the law firm was meeting their expectations. We offered a bottle of wine as a thank you (the law firm had a winery client).

The survey asked about frequency of contact, attention from junior-level versus senior-level staff, etc. These specific questions showed the customer the law firm was really interested in tailoring their service to each customer.

We got 60% of these C-level executives to complete a 6-page survey! (Was it the wine?)

Ecommerce customer messages

For your ecommerce customers, Customer Retention messages will be driven by their purchase or click actions – or lack of actions.

Your email series should keep them buying, and improve customer Lifetime Value.

After the sale

After each purchase or renewal, your "thank you for your purchase" email will get the highest readership, so use this email wisely.

- Outline how to use particular features of the product purchased, include ideas for using the product, link to more details or videos, and remind of the benefits they'll enjoy from your service. *(Or if you have a lot of information, each of these could be a topic in your email series.)*

- *For first-time purchasers:* include an Offer to drive the next sale.

Promote additional sales

Your follow-up emails can include:

- Special Offer for related products —to extend the functionality of or complement the item purchased (consider Amazon's "Customers who bought this also bought this . . ." idea.)

- Special Offer for similar products.

- Auto-ship program. The email asks if customers need to reorder, and if they do, they just click "yes," and the order ships.

- Your newest products and services, best sellers *("This month's Best Sellers")*, and highest-rated products.

Drugstore.com sends an email that includes all the items you recently purchased. Just click to reload any item into the shopping cart – which makes the next purchase fast, easy, and more likely to happen at drug-store.com.

Increase the size or profitability or orders

- **For services**: after a few months of using a service, you might send customers an **upgrade Offer** to try your upgraded service.

The Auto Club of Southern California sends an Offer to try their upgraded service for a few months before your renewal. If you accept the upgrade, they pitch the upgraded service at renewal.

- **For consumable products:** send an Offer for **upgraded or more profitable versions** of products the customer purchased – and point out the specific benefits and value of the upgrade.

- *To increase average order size*: offer special savings (or something free) for orders over **a certain dollar amount (**or a quantity discount). Or offer **a bigger discount the more they spend** (save $5 on a $50 purchase, save $15 on a $100 purchase.)

- Consider a **bundled Offer** (a special on two or more products/services purchased together).

See Chapter 7 for more on sales Offers.

30 days after purchase (or sooner): ask for a review. Ask if they're happy with the purchase. If they click "Yes," send them to a page where they can provide a testimonial or review. If they click "no," send them to your support page, with answers to common questions and your contact information.

After 60 days of no purchase among one-time buyers, consider a separate email series with more aggressive Offers for them. *The faster you can convert a one-time buyer to a two-time buyer, the greater the Lifetime Value.*

Enhance customer loyalty

Your Best Customers may also be buying from competitors. You can use email to help increase your "share of customer" among **heavy users**.

You should reward customers for their business and give them a reason to give you a larger share of their purchases.

Consider **Best Customer perks** — by amount spent within a time period, amount of time as a customer, or a combination of these. *Consider customer-only Offers so they see extra value in continuing to be a customer.*

- Give them special upgrades (upgrade to faster shipping), free services (free shipping), free samples, or other extras.

- Send advance notice of any new products or specials. Nordstrom always gives its customers a few days before a publicly-advertised sale to purchase at sale prices. For good customers, they'll give you an advance showing of new items to be included in the sale before they even hit the selling floor.

Renewals

When you're selling a service that renews, be sure to *communicate with your customers regularly during the service period*.

- Remind them of the unique benefits of your service and working with your company
- Give them ideas for getting the most from your service

Getting your customers to renew early is critical. You essentially want to take them "out of market" for competitive Offers around their renewal date.

- *Consider a special Offer for renewing for a period longer* than their current service. The longer the time between renewals, the less often each customer comes up for renewal.

- *For yearly renewals:* Give more free months the earlier they renew

- Illustrate the *benefits of any new features* in your renewal emails

- After a few renewals, *give your consistently renewing customers a bonus* to thank them and keep them renewing (one free month for every renewal year, etc.).

Customer Re-Engagement Series

For those truly **lapsed customers** (those that cancel a service, don't renew a subscription, or who haven't made a purchase in three months or more), trigger a series of "win back" messages.

Your *Customer Re-engagement Email Series* can:

- *Introduce* the benefits of your newest products, highest-rated products, and hottest sellers ("this month's best sellers")

- *Remind and re-educate* about your unique benefits, or the problems you solve.

- *Present customer success stories* or cases of how others are getting maximum value from your solution

     o *Especially for services:* highlight the great results your company or solution helped a customer achieve

- *Deliver periodic Content Offers* to prove your expertise, and introduce new solutions

- *Deliver a series of special Offers to drive a new ecommerce sale*

○ It tends to be true that those who've only made a purchase when there's a discount may not buy until there's another discount. You might create product/service bundles for this audience, so *they'll still get a discount – but for a higher average purchase.*

Non-triggered emails

Some emails won't be triggered by the action or inaction of a lead or customer. You might plan non-triggered campaigns when you have:

- New products, services, features, benefits, or capabilities.

- Special ecommerce Offers or promotions. A catalog trick is to *email only those who've purchased from you more than once* ("multi-buyers.") Send an email advertising a sale to them first, advising they have a one-week advantage over the public for the sale. (**This reduces out-of-stocks for your good customers.**)

- Products or services that need more visibility

When sales are lagging, you also might create non-triggered emails that target specific types of customers (frequent buyers, etc.)

Enewsletter

Non-triggered shouldn't mean non-targeted. You want your enewsletter to deliver information that's as valuable and relevant to each Buyer Persona as it can be:

- *Segment by product/service usage*: Use information on the products and services your customers are using (or past purchases) to tailor their enewsletter Content.

- *Tracking by recipient:* Track the topics or Offers each customer clicks in your enewsletter, so you can continue to send similar topics to that customer in the future.

Your enewsletter can present a summary of a few blog posts, with a "continue" link to each full blog post on your website. (Or include one full blog post with a related Offer to click.)

- If you use this technique, you'll be able to see which topics are most interesting to your audience, as well as *exactly who clicked on what topic!* Most email systems provide this tracking.

The role of an enewsletter to leads (non-triggered)

If your enewsletter **summarizes and links to your latest blog posts, it can augment** the emails in your Lead Conversion Series.

But your new leads shouldn't *only* receive your monthly enewsletter (especially if you're selling an expensive or complicated solution.)

- Communicating monthly with new leads is probably not frequent enough for effective education.

- To convert your leads (if B2B or where the 3 C's are present), you'll likely **need a "salesperson"** in a series of more frequent emails, each written like a personal email from one individual to another.

Interest in enewsletters can drop off precariously after the first few issues — a sign that your audience isn't finding your emails valuable.

- Most marketers find that *from 25% to 40% of names on your email list don't click* on any of your enewsletter articles.

Work harder to make your enewsletters more targeted by customer Persona, so they're relevant and highly valuable.

Tracking message effectiveness

How effective is your particular email message and Offer at **driving traffic**? Do you know if your audience is reading your enewsletter or other promotional emails?

Tracking setup

For ecommerce: be sure you have Google ecommerce tracking set up to track the number and *amount* of sales.

For Lead Generation: set up a Goal in Google Analytics, so those that complete a form on your website become a **lead** "Conversion" that can be tracked. *(See Chapter 3.)*

You can also use Goals to track *number* of **sales**. (If your website sells a single product or service where every sale is for the same amount, you can assign a Value when you set up the Goal Details.)

To see Conversions to Leads or Sales *from individual emails*, you'll need to use UTM tracking codes.

To add a UTM tracking code to each link in your emails:

To the page URL you wish to link to, you'll indicate:

- *"Medium" (email)* – Google Analytics has a set list of possibilities you can use for Medium.

- *"Source"* – use this field to categorize your email types (newsletter, lead-series, retention-series, promotion)

- *"Campaign"* – use this field to identify the specific email in your series, or a special email topic (8-ways-improve or first-purchase or july-sale)

A tracking URL looks like this:

https://www.responsefx.com/offer-landing-page/?utm_medium=email &utm_source=retention-series&campaign=first-purchase

Visit this link for a fast way to create a tracking URL:

https://ga-dev-tools.appspot.com/campaign-url-builder/

Note: **always use lower case in your tracking URLs** so you'll have consistent tracking. If you start mixing initial caps and lower case, you'll have separate tracking for "Newsletter" and "newsletter."

In Google Analytics, see "Acquisition," "Campaigns," "All Campaigns" to see the Traffic, Leads, and Sales each link drove. (If you've set up multiple Goals, you'll see *a "Conversion" box above the table where you can choose the Goal you want to see.)*

Some emails may get a higher Click-Through percentage but have a lower Conversion Rate to leads or sales.

- That indicates strong interest in the topic.

- *If you're generating leads*, it could also mean the form on your Landing Page is too long — or there's a problem with the copy.

- *If you're driving sales*, it could mean your product copy didn't effectively convince the visitor to take action — or prove the value of the product in relation to its price.

Click-through Rate (CTR)

Look at Unique Clicks (number of individuals who clicked) divided by total **Delivered** (total sent minus undeliverables and bounced names).

> You want to gauge *how effectively your email drove clicks from those that actually had the opportunity to see your email* (total delivered).

What should your Click-Through be? Customer CTR is typically much higher than for leads. But every company's results will be different.

Track CTR by individual email: higher Click-Through indicates more interest in that email.

Email Conversion Rate to leads and sales

How effective is your message and Offer at **driving leads or sales**?

- *Email Conversion Rate*: compare number of sales (or form completions) divided by total emails **delivered**.

Always follow results through to the lead or sale when possible.

As you test emails, you'll also identify winning Subject Lines, emotional drivers, email formats, message length, and images (for the postcard format). *See Chapter 18 on Testing.*

What about "Open Rate"?

"Open Rate" is useful for testing Subject Lines and giving you some indication of the attractiveness of the Subject Line. But Open Rate does *not* mean that recipients clicked on your email to open it or even saw your email.

Open Rate actually means that any images within the email were "opened" (or pulled from the server).

So Open Rate is problematic for gauging email effectiveness:

- Many email programs now have "graphics off" as the default. If the recipient doesn't turn graphics on for your email, NO opens will be counted, no matter how many times the recipient views the email.

- But if the recipient has "graphics on" (in an email program with a "preview pane," where you can see a portion of the email without clicking on it) EVERY email with an image will count as "opened" **whether the recipient ever actually views your email or not.**

- **No mobile views register as "opens"** no matter how many times recipients open your email on a mobile phone.

How can we conclude anything from Open Rate? As we compare Subject Line to Subject Line, we assume that each version went to a similar percentage of "graphics on" and "graphics off" individuals. Any increase in Open Rate for one version may have been due to individuals actually clicking the email with "graphics on." So use Open Rate for comparison only.

Whenever you see "results" or recommendations based on Open Rate, just keep in mind: **Open Rate isn't an indicator of whether the email was effective at generating a click, lead, or sale.**

Tracking by individual recipient

Are you tracking which of your leads or customers are clicking on your email messages?

You want to know *which topics (blog posts, product/service information, or Offers) each recipient has clicked,* to help you tailor future email messages.

If you're using an email service, the service will track the clicks for you by individual recipient. Add to your customer/lead database the **topic each person clicked on and the date**.

Improve response from individual recipients

If your email messages are getting good CTR and good Conversion for new Offers and sales, be sure to look at **results by individual name.**

Those who never click

Identify leads and customers that haven't clicked on your last three emails.

- *For customers:* are you emailing the wrong individual or individuals in the company? (i.e., someone in Purchasing)

  - Is there someone using your system, products, or services who might be more interested in your messages?

  - Is there someone at a higher-level in the company that might be interested in your blog posts and case studies?

To engage more names, it's time to try something different! You might *remove these un-engaged names* from your Lead Conversion, Customer Retention, or Customer Re-engagement Series to try a different type of email to reach and re-engage them.

Start with the Subject Line:

- If your past Subject Lines have been promotional, consider testing more educational ones. If you're been using educational Subject Lines, change the topic or pitch a useful Offer. Consider a fact-based or news-related Subject Line.

- Consider a "Most Read Posts (on Topic)" Subject Line.

- *Ecommerce:* Introduce new products or services, best sellers, highest-rated products or services (if you haven't been doing that)

- *For customers*: Make topics more relevant to the products, services, or systems they use. Give them ideas for using the product or service (and give them a link to more detailed information online, so you can track the clicks)

- *Leads:* Consider sending your latest testimonials from those that have tried a particular product or service ("see what customers say".) And link to a page of testimonials on your website.

- Introduce a case study

- Segment the names and target your Subject Line by Persona

AFTER you've tested new Subject Lines, move on to additional testing of the Offer, message, message format, and message length:

- Test different Offers

- Test different message formats. *If you're sending enewsletters or emails with images, try a more personal message.* If you've tried personal or educational approaches, change up the topic. Or send a more promotional postcard format.

- Test message length: if you've been sending longer emails, try shorter ones with bullet points. If your emails tend to be "short on meat," include more specific details for more value.

- **If your enewsletter includes multiple topics**, consider a simpler one article "tip of the week" or a summary of a single blog post. (Many companies find that interest in articles beyond the first two drops dramatically. **That's a clear sign you're including too many topics in your enewsletter**.)

The point is to change things up in your emails and enewsletters, to find topics your customers (and leads) are interested in.

There are also deliverability reasons that cause no response, especially from certain email systems like Gmail. (*More on deliverability in Chapter 17.*)

Ecommerce leads who clicked but didn't buy

- If your original email didn't include a special Offer, consider sending a follow-up email with an Offer to motivate the sale

Leads who regularly click — but haven't taken the next step

Those names are actively seeking information or a solution. They have the highest probability of making a first purchase.

Have Sales follow up to these regular clickers.

Email qualifies leads and drives sales with segmentation and continuous Testing

Email is highly effective for educating your leads — and improving the profitability and Lifetime Value of your customers.

Segmenting your email lists by Persona and other characteristics will allow you to focus your message and Offers. It's the first key to improved results.

The second key is **constant Testing** in email. It's easy to test, and you can use what you learn to improve your other marketing efforts.

Track Click-Through and Conversion Rate to leads or sales to identify your most effective efforts. And analyze results by individual recipient to identify segments that need attention.

Results Obsession Strategy #3:
Design Systems for Continuous Traffic, Leads, and Sales.

Use email to nurture leads through the Sales Process.

For ecommerce, use email nurturing and customer loyalty messages to create a continuous flow of sales.

References

Aten, J. (2019) Inc. <https://www.inc.com/jason-aten/this-mckinsey-co-study-shows-why-you-should-still-use-email-marketing.html>

Patel, N. *The Top 10 Ways to Engage Dead Email subscribers.* <https://neilpatel.com/blog/re-engage-dead-email-subscribers/>

B2B Personas. Salesforce Research. <https://a.sfdcstatic.com/Content/dam/www/ocms-backup/assets/pdf/datasheets/mc-b2b-personas-targeting-audiences.pdf>

Burdett, D. *Why B2B Lead Nurturing Can Be the Golden Ticket.* Artillery. <https://www.salesartillery.com/blog/bid/141712/Why-B2B-Lead-Nurturing-Can-Be-The-Golden-Ticket-to-Sales-Success>

Chapter 17

Creating Email to Drive Qualified Leads and Sales

W hat are the biggest reasons email messages fail? On the technical side, you may have deliverability issues, especially if you're using a purchased or rented list.

So getting in the "in" box tends to be the first challenge. (We'll cover Deliverability a little later in this chapter.)

The second challenge: getting the email noticed. It's why Subject Line Testing can boost your results significantly.

"Are you writing every email to stand out in the in-box, and motivate the click?"

293

The third challenge: motivating the click. The two most common issues standing in the way: 1) your *Offer doesn't motivate your audience to take action*, or 2) your Content isn't relevant and valuable to your audience.

Now that you have a better plan and strategy for your email program (from *Chapter 16*), let's create more effective emails to drastically improve your email results.

Creating a successful email program

Step 1: Write an engaging Subject Line

Your Subject Line is the most critical headline of your email message. It MUST attract your audience's attention — or you've wasted your efforts.

- *Your Subject Line must convince the recipient that tremendous value lies within your email message.*

Craft your Subject Line to deliver a strong reason to open or read it:

- **Promise a unique benefit** (the *"what's in it for me"*)

- **Promise something useful** — A case study, how another company benefited from the solution, useful tips or "how to" details, or an "Ultimate Guide" deep-dive on a subject

To give your email the best chance of being viewed:

1. Craft a Subject Line that's more FACTUAL, educational, or newsworthy. Or have your Subject Line relate to some breaking news story.

2. Consider a strong recurring Subject Line. WhetstoneGroup calls their weekly enewsletter *"Monday Morning Sales Coach."*

3. Avoid all caps but use Initial Caps to stand out.

4. Include a specific number if possible.

Michael Masterson has suggested using four U's: Urgent, Unique, Useful, and Ultra-Specific.

Write your Subject Line to stand out in the inbox and intrigue your audience enough to get them to start reading.

You should always be testing different Subject Lines

It's amazing how much the change of a single word in the Subject Line can change results.

To test Subject Lines, use "Open Rate" as a (very) rough gauge of which Subject Line is more attractive. *(More details on Testing in Chapter 18.)*

There are also **online tools that will evaluate your Subject Lines** for you. See *influencermarketinghub.com/subject-line-tester/*

Shorter email Subject Lines may work best

Numerous studies of headlines **within** direct mail and print ads have found that longer headlines work better — because they allow you to be more specific about the benefits.

And longer headlines within the email message itself still tend to out-pull shorter headlines.

But there's one area where shorter may be better, and that's the email Subject Line. That's because:

- *Mobile devices usually display only the first 35 characters* of the Subject Line (and about half of all email messages are first reviewed on a mobile device)
- Many email programs truncate the Subject Line
- Some email programs allow the user to reduce the portion of the Subject Line that's viewable (even on a desktop)

When writing your email Subject Line, try to ensure the most critical elements are within the first few words.

∎∎

A young marketing team I've been working with reviewed results of their email campaigns over the past year. (The company uses purchased lists of email addresses from industry associations for Lead Generation.)

The team listed results by Subject Line of each individual email. One had a Subject Line of "Happy Holidays." A nice sentiment – but few (if any) prospects will take the time to open this email. Why send that email at all? It had no message value and could have driven prospects to click the "this is spam" button. Not surprisingly, its Open Rate compared to other emails was poor.

Another email had a Subject Line of "Seminar #4 in our (name) Series." Using the actual topic of the seminar would have been stronger. And the "#4 in a Series" may indicate to some prospects they might not get any value if they didn't attend seminars 1-3.

∎∎

Avoid the ho-hum Subject Line. Work harder to entice me with the copy — make it so irresistible I HAVE to read it. And be as specific as possible.

Step 2: Craft a great Offer

For ecommerce:

- Gift with purchase Offers tend to have the highest average CTR
- Anything new, the "latest", "New arrivals", "latest mark-downs", etc. can generate high interest

For non-ecommerce:

- **Make the entire email about the Offer** that moves your lead along in the Sales Process.
- Include a short introduction, bullet points to "merchandise" benefits of the Offer (or what the lead will learn), and a prominent call to action button or link.

You should always be testing different Offers to see what will appeal to your particular Personas. Competitive comparisons, Buying Guides, or "Ultimate Guide" Offers can be effective.

Step 3: Email Content Strategy to engage

Now that so many emails are read on a mobile device, shorter messages make sense.

You may want to *focus your email on solving a single problem, delivering a single tip, or highlighting a single benefit.* And for Lead Generation, you should always pitch a single Offer in your email.

Deliver maximum value — don't send boring emails

You planned your triggered emails, email series, and non-triggered email campaigns in Chapter 16. As you start to write those emails, consider for each audience:

- What will prospects or customers **learn** from this email – can you *tell them something they don't know?*
- What do they need to know (from your Persona summaries)
- What would help them now or give them an edge – useful tips, steps to improve something
- What would be unique and interesting
- What's NEW that might be of **value** to your audience (new product, promotional Offer, or Lead Generation Offer)
- What new TOOL might be **helpful** to your audience
- Could you link to other materials on your site that your audience might **appreciate?**

Re-think the usefulness of what you're sending out.

- Could you include a link to an easily-printable checklist that summarizes your points?
- Could you send a list of the highest-rated products, "gift ideas under $XX," or a "how to choose" message?
- Do some of your products work together? Tell me how.

Some studies have found that links to videos can receive double or triple the number of clicks as other text links.

Personal message vs "postcard" approach

Your email "format" can be a personal message (with no visual), or it can be more promotional with a visual like a "postcard" (for ecommerce products).

- With a "postcard" approach, you'll have a headline, main visual, and then the main copy.

  - *Consumer emails with images tend to do better* than emails without images. (Although, if you send an all-text email every once in a while to **customers**, you may improve results. Text-heavy enewsletters can do well for consumers.)

- With a personal message approach, you'll write one-on-one to another person with *no image*. Address the reader directly using "you" and "your" as you would in a personal email.

  - *B2B emails without images tend to do better* (and may have an easier time getting through spam filters)

Segments and personalized Content

Before you start writing either type of email, identify any ways the email list has been segmented (or could be segmented), so you know who you're writing to. You want the copy to be as relevant as possible.

Do you need various versions of the email to **address the different segments or Personas?**

Can you use topics the individual clicked on previously, previous purchases, previous Offers responded to, or other information you know about each name to **customize each recipient's email**?

Customizing with "dynamic Content" (specific to each recipient) can boost Click-Through and average order size, create more "best" customers, and even reactivate lapsed customers.

You might talk differently to audiences by:

- Geography
- Title
- Best Customers (vs all customers)
- One-time buyers vs multi-buyers
- Discount buyers vs full-price buyers
- Category or brand of products purchased

We wrote four different versions of our monthly promotion for a golf client, by including a special Offer for the last brand of golf ball the customer had purchased. Our email response skyrocketed by 130%.

- Of course, you don't always want to offer a discount for the product or brand your customer buys. *(Don't "train" your customers to wait for a discount.)* But in this case, we positioned it as a "thank you" to past customers to keep them buying from this company.

What makes great email body copy?

KEY MESSAGE AT THE TOP

Getting the email opened (or scrolled within a "preview pane") is the key hurdle. That means the Content that shows in the preview pane (at the top of your email) is the most important Content in your email.

Be sure you have an engaging headline and/or lead paragraph there.

THE MESSAGE ITSELF

Your "lead" paragraph should remind of some pain and/or promise some pleasure, or intrigue with something the recipient didn't know.

- Ideally, you want your most critical message in the first few lines.
- With a postcard approach, the lead will follow the image.

For a Lead Generation Offer: **use bullet points** to outline the benefits of your Offer.

For an educational email: consider **subheads and bullet points** to make the message easily scanable and **highlight the key points**.

Keep these points in mind as you're writing your copy:

- *Why should I buy yours*: Use copy that clearly proves what your product or service can do *that other offerings can't*

- *What's in it for me:* Make the benefits of your Offer, product, or service clear.

- *Why should I respond now*: give me a strong reason to take the next step or buy now

- *Write copy that's conversational* (because most emails are meant to be part of a conversation). Did yo*u write it the way you'd say it face-to-face?* Be sure to *talk to the reader* using "you" and "your."

- *Use concise, specific writing.* Every word should be there for a reason — and each should be the strongest word you can use.

See Chapter 10 for more copywriting tips.

How long should your email messages be?

If you're pitching a Lead Generation Offer, you might use a short introduction with a pain/pleasure lead, followed by bullet points of what I'll learn by requesting the Offer.

If you're educating your leads, deliver enough "meat" in the email to make it worth their time to read. Be sure you "tell them something they didn't know" to advance their knowledge about your solution area.

- Include a "continue" link to read more, so you'll know what topics appeal to each recipient

If you're pitching a Sales Offer for an ecommerce site, your postcard design will typically include a headline, main visual, and a short message with a link to the Landing Page.

- If your product isn't sold visually (like clothing, furniture, artwork, etc.), you may need more benefit copy.

■■■

We recently reviewed a B2B email effort to prospects. This company sells a *Complex* product at a high perceived *Cost* that *Changes* the way their audience does their job.

Those "3 C's" — Complexity, Cost, and Change — indicate they'll need a high level of education to make the sale.

- But the company's email effort wasn't engaging. It didn't deliver any useful information. No specifics were included to educate the prospects further on this Complex solution.

Worse, the sample email started with "Dear . . ."

- *One surefire way to look like spam is to send out an email that reads, "Dear (name)."*

When was the last time you sent a personal email message that read, "Dear (name)"? Some ISPs actually check emails for things like "Dear" — and then conclude the message is spam because of it.

Write promotional emails in a conversational style, like the individual emails you send. If you'd never say, "Dear Karen," when sending me a personal email, don't say it in a promotional email. It's stiff, formal, and spammy.

The lead sentence in the email message is CRITICAL. If you don't grab your recipients there, it's likely they won't read your email at all.

- The company email we reviewed started out, *"The market is currently . . ."* Let's see — **if we're face-to-face or talking by phone, would your first words be something that impersonal?**

The email did include some bullet points — a very smart way to catch the eye of the scanning reader. But unfortunately, those **bullets were too generic, and didn't deliver enough "meat" to engage** the reader.

After reading the entire email, I still didn't know anything more about the company's solution. And that's a good way to guarantee that prospects won't read the company's future emails either.

- The email concluded with a high commitment Offer to schedule an online demo. (To the prospect, this means "talk to a salesperson.")

It's unlikely that prospects will be ready for this step when they haven't yet been educated on this Complex and Costly solution that Changes the way they do business.

How to turn this email around?

1. **Start the email the way you'd try to engage me on a cold call.** Use the Sales Process, a greed emotional driver, and a hint-of-pleasure (I'm going to reveal a secret) lead-in:

   Hi Karen,

   Two of your competitors just . . . with our solution and I thought you'd want to know how they did it . . .

2. **After you've grabbed me, tell me some useful "meat" to differentiate your solution** and really illustrate the value I could enjoy.

3. **Then get me to take the next intermediate step (Offer)** — download a white paper or podcast to learn more, attend a webinar, or watch a video.

■ ■

What's the key reason most promotional emails aren't read? They don't deliver enough value. Send valuable emails that tell your audience something they didn't know, or something that could benefit them — and watch your Click-Through Rate soar.

Words to avoid in emails

You want every word in your email messages to be as effective as it can possibly be. But with email, there are specific challenges.

ISP (Internet Service Provider) and company spam filters can cause some deliverability problems if you don't watch out for them. ISPs may not deliver your email message if it contains:

- Too many words in all caps
- Too many exclamation points throughout your email, or multiple exclamation points in a row
- Dollar signs in a row

These words and phrases may also signify spam:

Free!	Order Now!
50% Off!	Order today
Save up to	Act Now!
Discount!	Visit our web site
Special Promotion	What are you waiting for
Great offer	Information you requested
Why pay more	Satisfaction Guaranteed
Lowest price	Guarantee, Guaranteed
Click Here	Money-back guarantee
Call now!	100% satisfied
Subscribe	

You can find a list of *924 (!) words to avoid* in this list:

https://damngoodwriters.com/post/spam-trigger-words

So, what's a smart copywriter to do? You find ways to "write around" these promotional words. And try to avoid using multiple spam triggers in a single email message.

But if you've got a great free Offer, don't be afraid to say "free." Spam "trigger terms" are not the deliverability killers they once were. Sender reputation is now more important for deliverability.

Test something in every email campaign

What should you test in terms of copy? These are the first priority items:

- Subject Line

- Offer

- Main Message — *Test different emotional drivers* or highlight different benefits (for a postcard format, test different headlines and images)

- Length of Message — For one client, we found that a short paragraph of maybe two sentences, with an early link, and bulleted benefits of the Offer or product is the winning formula.

- Postcard vs personal message format

See a more detailed discussion of email testing in Chapter 18.

Designing email for better response

The specific design of an email message can affect response positively or negatively. It should always support the look and feel of your brand image. Additional key design issues are:

- Will this email be completely functional and communicate the key message *with "graphics off"* (the default for many email programs)?

- Will this message be easy to click and read on a *mobile device*?

What's really showing in the "preview pane"?

When you write your email message, you may focus on getting the critical words at the top. But what happens once the email is designed?

What's actually in the top 2 to 4 inches of your email message? (That's about all that will show within the "preview pane" of many email programs.)

- If you've got a *masthead, logo, or image* there, your audience may not see anything at all with "graphics off"

- Be sure you *include a benefit-oriented headline* that gives the recipient a reason to read further.

- If you want to use an image at the top, **put your headline above the image instead of within the image.** Use real text HTML for the headline so it will appear with "graphics off."

Early call to action link that's mobile-friendly

Be sure your response link is clearly visible near the top of your email. (And you may want to repeat it at the end of your message.)

- If you use a button, **be sure you also have a text link** so your email is completely functional with "graphics off."

- Be sure your **text links are easily clickable on a mobile device** — include some white space around them.

Easily readable on a mobile phone

Be sure the design makes your Content easy to read on a mobile device (where about 50% of emails are read). **Add space between paragraphs, and use bullets and subheads** to make it look easy to get through.

Test results show:

- B2B emails get higher Click-Through with **text links**.

- Consumer emails get higher Click-Through when using image (button) links or **image with text links**.

Bottom line: *create emails that are completely functional and tell a complete story even if images are blocked*. Test emails with images versus all text to find out which is more effective. And consider switching things up to show your audience something new.

Deliverability

The biggest challenge with email is *getting it delivered to the inbox*. How can you increase your chances of getting in the inbox?

- **Don't include repeated symbols (like !!!), lots of capital letters, etc. in your email Content.**

- Check your sending IP address regularly to be sure you're not on any ISP blacklists for sending spam. One **blacklist checker** is *mxtoolbox.com/blacklists.aspx*

- Email requires very clean code – it's *not* the same as coding a website. As you make changes to your template, the code gets messy and probably needs regular clean up. One free **HTML checker** is *htmlemail-check.com*

- *Try not to send out a volume of email all at once.* Stagger your emails throughout the day (or week), so the receiving ISPs and company email servers don't see a volume of emails all at once from you. *(This is especially important when sending to Gmail addresses.)*

- You also want to avoid periods of *sudden* heavy email volume. When you start a major email campaign, **send small batches of emails to your most engaged names first** — usually customers or leads that have responded in the past. Then slowly ramp up your sending volume to the rest of your list

You can send a test email on *mail-tester.com* to identify potential problems with your email.

"From" field

Your "From" field should include an individual name where possible (especially where the name will be known by the audience), along with your brand name:

"karen marchetti at ResponseFX"<kmarchetti@responsefx.com>

Some spam filters will look for "from" addresses that don't contain an individual name. So using "sales@" or "mail@" can negatively affect delivery.

But be sure to test this. I have a client that gets better results when the email is *not* from an individual name.

Sender Reputation and deliverability

We used to worry only about the lists of email "trigger terms" to avoid being blocked by ISPs. (We once had to promote a *golf ball that had "Long and Soft" as part of its name* . . . we had some challenges with that one.)

Now ISPs analyze the sender IP address and the sender itself. So, it's critical to understand the importance of your "email reputation."

- When you send **email to names that have not opted-in**, those individuals can hit the "spam" button and report your IP address to their ISP. ISPs keep track of spam reports from users, and if you receive too many "this is spam" clicks, ISPs start blocking your messages.

- When you don't remove undeliverable addresses from your lists, or you **send to old lists** (with lots of undeliverables), ISPs may block your messages. Be sure to **remove undeliverable addresses after every email effort.**

- When you send to inactive recipients — those who haven't opened or clicked your past email messages — your messages may be blocked. Keep track of inactive recipients and **remove those who haven't opened or clicked in 6 months.**

ISPs may use the **SPF (Sender Policy Framework)** authentication as a Content filter. SPF compares your return path domain (e.g., www.responsefx.com) and your IP address to the list of approved IPs you include in your DNS record (something you maintain with the service that registers your domain name).

- If you're going to use an email service provider (ESP), you should update your SPF record to include the ESP's own IPs that will be sending out your email.

Note that if you "rent" a list of email addresses, the list provider will send out the email for you. In this case, it may be a one-time rental, so you may not think to **update your SPF record for that email effort** (but you should). Not having the sender's IP in your SPF record is another reason why rented email lists typically get poor results.

Check your sender reputation with ReturnPath's Sender Score at *https://www.senderscore.org/*.

Are you writing every email to stand out in the in-box and motivate the click?

Your Subject Line determines whether recipients will read your email or not. Be sure you're constantly testing new ways to get your emails read.

Include an Offer in your emails to drive action. Always include a link (which could be to more Content) so you know how many actually "read" your email – and thought it was interesting enough to want to learn more.

Craft a smart Content Strategy to tell each Persona something he/she didn't know. Be sure every email is as relevant as it can be.

Use the Sender Policy Framework and adopt other deliverability best practices to help more of your emails get in the inbox.

Each of your Personas receives too much email. Work harder to stand out in their inbox.

Results Obsession Skill #3:
Be sure your emails sell effectively with words

References

Walker, C. *4 U's of Web Copywriting*. Yahoo! <https://smallbusiness.yahoo.com/advisor/4-u-copywriting-tips-writing-great-headlines-copy-220008437.html>

Rubin, K. (2012) *The Ultimate List of Email SPAM Trigger Words*. Hubspot®. <https://blog.hubspot.com/blog/tabid/6307/bid/30684/The-Ultimate-List-of-Email-SPAM-Trigger-Words.aspx>

Moorehead, L. (2019) *Images vs. No Images in Email Marketing Newsletters*. IMPACT. <https://www.impactbnd.com/blog/images-vs.-no-images-in-marketing-emails-newsletters>

Patel, N. *12 Ways to Improve Email Deliverability*. Neil Patel <https://neilpatel.com/blog/improve-email-deliverability/>

Kalossakas, O. *Deliverability Basics*. Litmus <https://litmus.com/community/learning/19-deliverability-basics>

Chapter 18

Testing Your Way to Marketing Success

Testing is the secret to continuously improving marketing results.

What do we mean by "Testing"? You **compare two or more versions of something at the same time**, to learn which version is best.

What we DON'T mean by Testing:

- *"We tried that Offer and it didn't work"*
- *"We tried that copy and it didn't work"*
- *"We tried email or pay-per-click and it didn't work"*
- *"We tried that Mailing List and it didn't work"*

*"When you continually test, you will
test your way to success."*

If you just try something once, there are too many variables affecting results to know whether the Offer, copy, or the media channel "did or didn't work." You need to compare your results to something.

You want to be able to say *"We tested 2 versions, and this one did (or didn't) do better than the other one."*

You can test your web pages, Landing Pages, pay-per-click ads, and email messages. *Why guess* which headline, Offer, key benefit, emotional driver, Mailing List, or exact words you should use? **Why not actually find out what works best?**

When you continually test, you "test your way to success." Each test can help you identify new ways to boost response. And *small increases in response, when taken together, can have a huge impact on ROI.*

That's why we test!

At a major marketing conference, the keynote luncheon speaker was Emily Soell (pronounced "sell" – perfect name for a copywriter.) Emily wrote some of the most profitable sales-driving copy in history, including the copy that launched Conde Naste *Traveler* magazine.

Emily told the audience she was going to show a number of tests her agency had done. And she invited us to vote for the winner in each test.

As she went through the tests, she told us which version *she* thought would win in each case. Surprise:

> *Even the expert Creative Director – Emily Soell – wasn't always correct in picking the winner before the test!*

At the luncheon, I sat next to Bill Brown, who was then Creative Director for a major West Coast agency. He was also the recipient of multiple Direct Marketing Association ECHO Awards *(awards based on results)*.

Before Emily began, Bill said to me, *"Let's see if we can pick the winner in each test, and see how we do."*

Of course, I didn't always choose the winning package. *But neither did Bill*! As the consummate Creative pro, he turned to me afterwards and said:

THAT'S WHY WE TEST!!!

If even the pros who regularly drive millions of dollars in sales have to test to find the best option, **we should all be testing.**

What will you learn?

Testing can make a tremendous difference in your profitability! It allows you to identify big winners, as well as incremental changes, that will improve your results. You can identify:

1. **Better Offers**: *If you want a significant change in response, test Offers.* If you aren't testing Offers, your sales or lead-driving efforts aren't as cost-effective as they could be.

2. **The Most Effective Copy**: Have you identified the best *headline, main message, emotional drivers, and key benefits* that really sell?

    - For Qualcomm®, we tested two different emotional drivers and **found the emotion that tripled results!**

    - In pay-per-click ad tests, we've learned exactly what wording to use for a client's audiences -- and which benefits drive sales. Once we *applied what we learned to the client's website and email messages*, we saw results climb everywhere.

3. **The Amount of Copy**: Are you still arguing over whether you need "all that copy"? Or maybe you ask your copywriters to "write leaner"? But you're not sure which is more effective. Why not test two different messages (one shorter, one longer) and find out which works better?

4. **Design**: Do you know which Page Layout is most effective? Have you tested the color and wording on your response button? Especially with Landing Pages, small changes can have a huge impact on results.

5. **Format:** In email, should you use a highly promotional look with images? Or would a personal "letter" Format be more effective? Why not test and find out?

6. **Audience:** When you select names for email, have you tested different segments of your customers and prospects? You'll waste even the greatest copy and Offer on Mailing Lists that aren't as targeted as they could be.

These are key elements that can have the biggest impact on response — and where you'll get the most value from your Testing.

Testing truths (or why we keep testing):

- *What works today may not always work.*
- *What works for a particular market or product may not work for every market or product.*
- *Things that used to work may wear out.*

That's why you should always be testing.

Single variable (A/B) tests vs multivariate

The easiest types of tests to start with are **single variable tests (or "A/B tests").** You create more than one version of your *web page, PPC ad, or email* message — *where you change only one element between the versions.* Any difference in response between your versions will be due to the single element you changed.

If you have at least 100,000 unique web visitors per month, or your visitor Conversion Rate is 10% or more, you can consider **"multivariate Testing"** on web pages. Multivariate Testing uses software to help you test multiple variables at the same time. You specify which elements you want to test and create different versions of each element. The software then creates the combinations and tests them for you.

The more elements you wish to test, the more potential combinations there are – which require larger test quantities.

Components of effective tests

You want to create tests that compare options — to help you identify which option works better. To do that, you'll *create two or more versions* of your marketing effort, *assign a separate tracking code* to each one, and execute the versions *at the same time*.

Test one "element" at a time

When you create your versions, you want to modify one element at a time. **Everything else (as much as possible) should be the same** between versions. This helps ensure that any difference in results will be due to the single item you changed.

Testing two or more versions of your headline, lead paragraph, or emotional driver

Use the same Design, Format or Page Layout, List, Offer, and the rest of the copy in each version. Any difference in response will be due to the individual Creative element you're testing (headline, lead, or emotion).

Testing two or more versions of product copy as a whole

Use the same Design, Format or Page Layout, List, and Offer in each version. Any difference in response will be due to the copy as a whole.

In this case, **the single "element" you're testing is the copy as a whole**. You won't know whether one headline did better than another, you'll just know that *one version of the entire copy did better than the other* version.

Testing two or more Lead Generation Offers

All of the copy is going to change with the Offer. The Design, Format or Page Layout, and List should remain the same between the test versions.

Test two or more versions at the same time

When you change one thing at a time, you'll know what made the difference in results.

But if you do one version now and another version later, you introduce the variable of time. When you review results, you won't know if a difference is due to the different version – or the different timeframe, because:

- Your competitors may have launched a promotion or reduced their pricing between your tests.
- Maybe the economic climate has changed.
- Any seasonality in your industry could affect results.

So always run your test versions at the same time.

What should you test first?

Test your biggest questions

Which elements are you most unsure about?

Are you having disagreements about which Offer to use, or you can't decide which headline is better? Test to find out.

Test the big things

For each media channel, certain elements have the most impact on response. These are where you should focus your Testing. (We'll go through these elements by media channel below.)

Test significant differences

For the biggest change in results, test completely different layouts, or Creative approaches. Or test single elements like completely different Offers.

How to track results from test versions

Tests of media that drive traffic to your website

For pay-per-click advertising and email tests, use UTM tracking in your link to the Landing Page. With a UTM tracking link, you specify:

Source = whatever you want to name your particular test
Medium = email (or cpc)
Campaign = the name of the version

For a test of list segments using *email*, your tracking link for your one-time buyer segment will look like this:

https://www.responsefx.com/?utm_source=segments050120&
utm_medium=email&utm_campaign=onetimebuyer

For a test of headlines using PPC, your tracking link for your "superior coverage" headline would look like this:

https://www.responsefx.com/?utm_source=headlines060120&
utm_medium=cpc&utm_campaign=superiorcoverage

You'll also need to **set up Goals in Google Analytics** so you can track Conversions. *(See Chapter 3 to set up Goals.)*

- In Google Analytics, under "Acquisition," "Campaigns," "All Campaigns," you'll then see the results of your test by Campaign version.

Tests of pages or elements on your website

There are software services that allow you to do single-variable testing within your website. (If you're using WordPress, Nelio (neliosoftware.com) is an easy testing plug-in to use.)

These services will allow you to *select one of your web pages, create a variation of that page, and start a test of the two different page versions*. The service will randomly funnel traffic to the test page for you.

How many for a valid test?

You want **enough responses per version** to be confident that your results weren't an accident. What's "enough responses"? Typically:

- 50 responses per version – for an 85% degree of confidence that the results are repeatable.

- 100 responses per version will give you 90% confidence.

Pay-per-click ad Testing

One of the easiest vehicles for Testing is pay-per-click (PPC) advertising through Google Ads.

You create a headline and a short description for each ad. Create multiple versions of the ad, and Google Ads will rotate your ads for you.

You can test different headlines – or test changing a word in the headline. Test different Offers, different benefits, or the wording you use to talk about the benefits.

To track results (through leads and sales) of different ads that may use the same first line, create a UTM tracking URL to use in each Google Ad. *See Chapter 15 for information on tracking PPC elements.*

To see which ad version works better, review Click-Through, Cost/Sale or Cost/Lead.

With PPC, you can easily learn exactly which Offers, messaging, and benefits attract your audiences.

Email Testing

Email Testing is also one of the easier Testing options – and it can be the most cost-effective. You want to test the elements that have the biggest impact on email response. That includes:

- How the names were selected
- Subject Line (which determines whether your email is viewed)
- Offer
- Overall copy with your key benefits
- Length of message
- Format of the email – personal email vs a promotional approach with an image.

You want to **test big differences** in each of these elements to find a significantly better version.

You'll create a unique UTM tracking code for each version, and email the two versions at the same time (as much as possible).

You'll review Unique Clicks/Delivered, Leads/Delivered, or Sales/Delivered for each Campaign version to pick the winner. In Google Analytics, see "Acquisition," "Campaigns," "All Campaigns."

To test list segment vs list segment in email

Create one list with your segmentation criteria, and create a second list with different criteria (or choose names with no particular criteria but from the same general population, like "customers.")

- Keep everything else the same between the Lists: use the same email Subject Line, Offer, email message (copy, message length, Format), and Landing Page

To test Subject Lines

- Keep everything else the same between versions (same List, Offer, copy, message length, Format, Landing Page).

- Split the email list into as many groups as you have Subject Lines to test. (You want to **create random groups** as much as possible.)

Compare Open Rate, Unique Clicks/Delivered, and either Leads/Delivered or Sales/Delivered to see which Subject Line was best.

It's common to find a Subject Line with a better "Open Rate" but a poorer Conversion to leads or sales. Be sure to *follow your results through to leads or sales* when possible.

To test Lead Generation Offers

Everything about your email should focus on the Offer. The steps below assume you want to promote each Offer in Subject Line and in your body copy.

- Create a different Subject Line and email copy for each Offer. **Each email version will contain a link (with UTM tracking code) to a different Landing Page (one per Offer).**

- List, message length, and Format of the message should remain the same between versions.

- Create as many random email groups as you have Offers to test.

Compare Unique Clicks/Delivered and Leads/Delivered. You'll conclude that one Offer, its Subject Line, copy, and Landing Page generated a higher percentage of leads than the other one.

Because the Offer, Subject Line, and copy all change between the email versions, *you can't conclude any difference in response was due to any of those elements separately.*

To test sales Offers

- Create a different Subject Line that promotes each Offer and modify a portion of the copy that pitches the Offer. (You'll likely need to include a particular "bonus code" in each email.)

- Use the same Mailing List, general message copy, message length, Format, and Landing Page.

- Split your Mailing List randomly into as many groups as you have Sales Offers to test.

To test overall message

- Use the same list, Offer, Format, and Landing Page.

- You'll have two different messages, and you may want two different Subject Lines.

- Create list groups for as many message versions as you have to test.

To test length of message

- Create a long version of your message, and a summary version of the same message – using the same headline, lead sentence, emotional driver, and key benefits. (One will go into more detail, one will be more of a summary.)

- Use the same list, Subject Line, Offer, Format, and Landing Page.

- Split your list randomly into two (or more) groups.

To test message Format

- Create a personal message approach and a more promotional approach of the same message. (Or you could test two different layouts or designs.) In this case, your headline, lead sentence, and the way you write your copy may all be different between the versions, but you should have the same benefits in the same order in each version.

- Use the same Mailing List, Subject Line, Offer, and Landing Page.

- Split your Mailing List into two (or more) random groups.

To test different images in a postcard format

- Use the same list, Subject Line, Offer, message copy, message length, and Landing Page. Split your list into two or more random groups.

- If you want to test two completely different products, use the same list, Offer, and message length. In this case, you'll conclude one email did better or worse than the other.

Website Testing

Which pages should you test? Focus on your Lead Generation Offer pages, other Landing Pages, key product or service pages, and pages with a high Bounce Rate.

What should you test? For Lead Generation:

- Length of your response form – number of questions, and required versus non-required fields
- Copy on your Lead Generation page that accompanies the response form – amount, bullets versus no bullets, headline, specific wording
- Layout of the page
- Action button – wording, color

For ecommerce:

- Copy: product page headline, product description, length of product copy, order of benefits, paragraphs versus bullet points
- Visuals: images, charts or other graphics
- Layout: what elements are included on the page, order of elements, placement of elements

You'll want 50 to 100 Conversions per version, and at least 10 Conversions per day per version. You'll want to *test for at least a week* to get day of week and time of day variations in response.

Web page Testing software

Google Optimize and other Testing software (like Nelio for WordPress) will allow you to:

- Run A/B tests where you change one element on a page, and then test the revised page against the original version.

- Test two completely different pages against each other.

- Conduct multivariate tests, where you can test two or more elements at the same time. You can identify the best combination of elements, as well as the most effective version of each element. (You'll need to have at least 100,000 unique visitors per month to use multivariate testing, or a Conversion Rate of 10% or more.)

Analyzing results

What if the purchase amount varies?

If you're selling more than one product via ecommerce, you'll want to compare total sales amounts between the versions you're testing.

With email to your in-house lists, you'll look at total Sales **Revenue divided by number of emails delivered** (for each version) to pick the winner.

- To do that, *you'll need ecommerce tracking set up in your Google Analytics*. Talk to your webmaster.

If you're testing a rented or purchased email list: subtract the cost of the list rental from your Sales Revenue for that version. Then divide the remaining revenue by number of emails delivered for that version.

Test of statistical significance

How do you know if your test results are statistically significant? (And why should you care?)

When you complete a test, you want to be sure that you can count on your conclusion. You want to know that the winning List or Offer or Creative is really the better-performing option.

Let's say your email test of two versions got these results:

Version A: 0.53% response

Version B: 0.65% response

Was the difference between Version A and Version B a statistically significant difference? Can we rely on these results and conclude that Version B is really the better-performing Version?

To determine if we have a statistically significant difference, we need to compute what the **actual range of Response Rates would be** if we replicated the test repeatedly (because we won't always get exactly the same Response Rate.)

To compute the range of Response Rates for Version A (assuming 9813 emails delivered):

Part 1: $\dfrac{(100 - 0.53\% \text{ Response Rate}) \text{ x } (0.53\% \text{ Response Rate})}{9813 \text{ Delivered}}$ = c

Example: $(100 - 0.53)$ x $0.53 = 52.72 / 9813 = .0054$ = c

Part 2:   (Square root of c) =
            Standard Deviation x 1.96 for 95% Confidence Level = e

Example: $(.0735)$ x $1.96 = .1440 =$ e

The 95% confidence level means that we want the range of responses that will result from our tests 95% of the time.

We'll *compute the low end of our response range*, by subtracting .1440 from the Response Rate.

We'll *compute the high end of the range* by adding .1440 to the Response Rate. For Version A:

Low end $0.53 - .1440 = 0.39\%$

High end $0.53 + .1440 = 0.67\%$

This means that 95% of the time, our Response Rate from Version A would range from 0.39% to 0.67% (if we repeated the test).

Note with PPC tests, you'll use "impressions" for a test version, rather than "delivered" as the denominator in the equation above.

Are differences statistically significant?

When we run the same numbers for Version B, let's say its response would range from 0.49% to 0.81%. So, to compare versions:

Version A: 0.53% response = range of 0.39% to 0.67%

Version B: 0.65% response = range of 0.49% to 0.81%

In this test, the response ranges overlap. *If there is overlap: you do not have a statistically significant difference between versions.* That means that we can't conclude that Version B will consistently generate better response than Version A.

If there is no overlap between response ranges: you can be confident that one of your versions will do better than the other version 95% of the time.

This points out the critical importance of running the test of statistical significance. Version B had a better Response Rate from this one test. But now we know we can't rely on this result and should probably continue Testing.

There are free tools that will simplify this calculation. This one seems the easiest and most helpful to use:

https://neilpatel.com/ab-testing-calculator/

On-going learning

If you can test cost-effectively using email or PPC, I'd do as much Testing as you can in those media – and then apply what you learn to *other media.*

You can also learn from the tests of others. *Marketingexperiments.com and marketingsherpa.com* have extensive archives of case studies with test results.

Testing drives consistently better results and higher marketing ROI

Testing is the key to steady improvement, and it's the most cost-effective way to boost marketing results.

When you test, you don't guess what you should do next – your Testing tells you what worked and what didn't.

Even small incremental changes can have a significant impact on results.

Testing helps you focus future efforts on the most effective list segments, headlines, Offers, messages, and more.

You don't need a large budget to test. You can run cost-effective tests using PPC, email, or website Testing software. The key is to run two or more versions of something at the same time, compare results – and always be testing.

Results Obsession Strategy #4:
Continuously learn and improve through Testing.

Chapter 19

The Numbers

You want to know the cost-effectiveness of your marketing programs. Simple marketing formulas can be very useful in:

1. **Planning** your programs, to ensure what you've proposed has a reasonable chance of hitting your goals

2. **Analyzing your results**, to discover the cost-effectiveness of different media channels or promotions

3. **Setting benchmarks** for how much it costs you to bring in each new customer or sale

4. **Analyzing profitability** of your customer segments

5. **Creating a marketing Budget** based on what your marketing campaigns have actually accomplished.

*"Analyzing results makes the difference between
just spending money –
versus achieving company objectives cost-effectively."*

In this chapter, we'll try to simplify all of the key marketing formulas that tend to be most helpful.

Planning your programs

Incremental Breakeven Analysis (pre-program)

Before you *spend a dime* on a marketing program, you should run a Breakeven Analysis. (We introduced *Breakeven for Lead Generation in Chapter 5 and for Sales Offers in Chapter 7*.) You want to know if the program you've planned has a realistic chance of breaking even.

The first Breakeven Analysis we'll look at is "incremental." It addresses only the costs of selling and delivering one more order. (It doesn't include any contribution for overhead costs.)

- Incremental Breakeven assumes you have other active marketing programs, and you want to evaluate something new.

First, you want to *know how much profit you make on just one more sale, called Gross Profit Per Sale*. Take your sales price and subtract all the direct costs of delivering just one more sale (cost of raw materials, packaging costs, cost of processing the credit card sale, etc.).

- **Gross Profit Per Sale** = Purchase Price minus direct product costs per order

- If your Purchase Price = $79 minus $29 direct product costs   =
  $50 Gross Profit Per Sale

If your average sale includes multiple products, compute the Gross Profit Per Sale for your average order size.

Second, plan your marketing effort, so you can get cost estimates. Take the Total Cost of the campaign divided by your Gross Profit Per Sale. This tells you *the number of orders you'll need to cover the costs of the campaign.* That's your breakeven quantity:

- **Breakeven quantity** =
  Total Marketing Cost   /   Gross Profit Per Sale

- If you're reaching an audience of 65,000 for $50,000,
  Breakeven Quantity = $50,000 / $50 = 1,000

We need to sell 1,000 units to recover marketing costs and just breakeven.

Breakeven Response Rate

Is it reasonable to expect to sell 1000? Take the Breakeven Quantity divided by the number of names you plan to reach with your campaign.

That's your Breakeven Response Rate. This tells you what SALES response rate you'll need just to breakeven.

- **Breakeven Response Rate** =
  Breakeven Quantity   /   quantity reached

- 1000 orders   /   65,000 reached = 1.54%

Is it reasonable to expect a sales response of 1.54%? If you've never gotten a response rate (in terms of orders) near this number, the answer is probably no. In that case, you may want to re-think the cost of your marketing program.

If you're marketing to customers, you might expect a higher response rate than from prospects. This is especially true if you've kept in close contact with your customers since their last purchase.

If you're planning a new marketing effort to prospects, and you don't have any past results to rely on, you might assume 0.5% sales response as a ballpark.

What if it looks like you won't breakeven with the campaign you've proposed? There are three elements you can modify:

- Increase the **sales price**
- Reduce the **costs of delivering the product** or service
- Reduce the **cost of your marketing** campaign

Note this is just BREAKEVEN. If you need to make a profit on the first sale, you'll need to factor that into your calculations (which we'll do below).

Can we afford to . . . ?

How can you determine if you can afford to try something new? A Breakeven Analysis can help you figure it out.

Maybe you'd like to hire a professional copywriter. Or you'd like to try a free gift with purchase. How can you decide if you should proceed?

First, figure out how much your experiment is going to cost. Maybe a copywriter has proposed new copy for $2,000.

Divide that cost by your Gross Profit Per Sale. That tells you how many more sales you'll need to cover the cost of what you want to try.

In this example, $2000 copywriting cost divided by the $50 Gross Profit Per Sale we computed earlier = 40 **more** sales to cover the cost.

Divide the number of additional sales by the number you're targeting. That tells you how much your response rate would need to increase:

- 40 sales divided by 65,000 = 0.06%.

- Is it likely a professional copywriter (*who knows how to sell*) can get you 0.06% more in sales response?

- Highly likely, but it's also dependent on your total Breakeven Quantity. Now, your program needs to generate 1.6% total response (1.54% Breakeven Response Rate + 0.06% more) to break even. If you've never come close to 1.6%, you may need to rethink your program.)

Full Breakeven Analysis

You can also look at a more complete Breakeven Analysis that adds a contribution for overhead and profit margin:

STEP ONE: Compute **Gross Revenue Per Sale** =
Average Sales Price + shipping (total dollar sales)

STEP TWO: Compute **Gross Profit Per Sale** =
Gross Revenue Per Sale minus
- Returns and bad debt (usually a percentage of sales)
- Cost of Goods Sold
- Credit Card Processing Fees
- Actual packing and shipping costs

STEP THREE:
Compute **Breakeven Allowable Cost per Sale** =
Gross Profit Per Sale minus
- Contribution for overhead
(typically a percentage of sales)

STEP FOUR:
If you have a profit margin your company wants to maintain, you can subtract that profit margin (typically a percentage of Cost of Goods Sold).

Marketing Allowable Cost Per Sale =
Breakeven Allowable Cost Per Sale minus Profit Margin

STEP FIVE: **Breakeven Quantity** =
Proposed Marketing Cost / Marketing Allowable Cost Per Sale

STEP SIX: **Breakeven Response Rate** =
Breakeven Quantity / Quantity Reached

Analyzing program results

One of the most useful equations is Cost Per Order (or CPO), also called Cost Per Sale. (If you're prospecting, it can be Cost Per Acquisition or CPA.) Cost Per Order tells you how much you spent to bring in each order.

Cost Per Order =
Total Cost of your marketing effort /
# of sales (or orders) that resulted from the effort

If a $12,000 marketing campaign resulted in 60 orders,
$12,000 / 60 = $200 Cost Per Sale

If you spent $200 to bring in each order, and your Gross Profit Per Sale is $100, that may or may not be a good thing.

You lost $100 on every order you brought in.

But what if you know that on average, each customer orders about 3 times per year from you:

$100 Gross Profit Per Order @ 3 orders per year =
$300 gross profit/year/customer

Perhaps your average customer continues to order from you for 2 years. Now you have $300 gross profit/customer @ 2 years = $600 gross profit/customer (or $600 Lifetime Value).

You'll need to factor in the cost of getting those additional orders over the 2-year period, as well as your desired profit (and overhead), to determine if spending $200 to get each initial order was a good deal.

If $200 was unacceptable, you can:

- Try a different marketing channel
- Reduce the cost of your marketing effort.

To improve Gross Profit Per Order, you could:

- Raise your sales price
- Reduce the cost of producing your product
- Test a more aggressive Offer to try and drive a higher response.

Cost Per Sale can be useful for comparing the cost-effectiveness of different list segments, audiences, Offers, media channels, and campaigns.

Analyzing effectiveness

It may also be useful to look at how much you spent to bring in each dollar of revenue, especially *if the size of each sale varies.*

Expense to Revenue Ratio =
Marketing Costs / Dollar Revenue

If marketing campaign costs were $5,000, and the campaign generated $27,500 in revenue, $5,000/$27,500 = 0.18 (or 18%)

Marketing expenses were 18% of the revenue generated (or *it cost us $0.18 to bring in every dollar of revenue).*

We can also reverse the equation, and look at Revenue divided by Marketing Costs:

Revenue to Expense Return = Revenue / Marketing Costs

This tells you how much **revenue you generated for every $1 of marketing expense.**

In this example, for every $1 spent on marketing, we generated $5.50 ($27,500 / $5000) in revenue.

- You should *run Revenue to Expense by Channel* so you can compare each channel's effectiveness.

Lead analysis by source

It's extremely valuable to know the **Dollar Value of each Response**.

If you're generating leads, you can compare the Dollar Value of each Response to your Cost Per Lead (how much it costs you to generate each Lead). That will help you evaluate the cost-effectiveness of each Lead Generation channel.

Cost Per Lead =
Total Cost of Marketing Effort / number of Leads Generated

What's the dollar value of each lead?

If your average sale is $500:

- If 2% of leads convert to sales, then *each lead is "worth" at least $10.*
  - $500 x .02 Conversion = $10

- If 3% of those who download a white paper convert to a sale, *each white paper download is "worth" at least $15*
  - $500 x 0.03 = $15

- If 10% of those who request a product sample end up purchasing, then *each sample request is "worth" at least $50*
  - $500 x 0.10 = $50

By knowing the value of every response, you will cost-effectively allocate your marketing dollars – and prove your logic to your boss.

In the example above, *a white paper download is worth at least $15.*

- If you spent $1,000 on an advertising test on a particular website, and generated 20 white paper downloads, you got *white paper downloads at $50 Cost Per Lead* ($1000 / 20).

- In this case, that's probably not a cost-effective marketing option for you.

If 20% of those who attended webinars consistently converted to customers, then each webinar attendee is worth $100:

- $500 x 0.20 = $100

If you tested a promotion to CTOs to pitch a webinar for a total cost of $2,000 and got 50 attendees, *it cost you $40 per webinar attendee.* You should **expand your webinar efforts to this audience, because each webinar attendee is worth $100** to you.

When your average purchase is higher, then additional options become profitable. What if your average sale is $5,000?

- If 90% of the prospects who visit your plant to check out your equipment buy, then *each plant visit is worth $4500* ($5000 x 0.90).

If you offer to pay travel expenses to bring prospects to your plant, it's highly likely that expense would be a cost-effective way to spend your marketing dollars.

ROI and Marketing Contribution

There seems to be a lot of confusion around computing the Return on Investment (ROI) of Marketing programs. It's important to remember that all formulas are tools (there is no "marketing formulas police") – so use the ones that help you make better decisions.

Here's how to compute a number of metrics on the way to Marketing Contribution and ROI:

1. Dollar Sales + Shipping and Handling Fees =
   Gross Revenue

2. Gross Revenue MINUS Returns and Bad Debt =
   Net Revenue

3. Net Revenue MINUS Cost of Goods Sold (COGS), shipping costs, 800 number costs, credit card costs =
   Gross Profit

4. Gross Profit MINUS Marketing Costs =
   Marketing Contribution (to profit and overhead)

5. Marketing Contribution MINUS Overhead Contribution (typically a % of sales) = **Net Profit**

6. **ROI** =
   Net Profit (income) / $ Marketing Cost (marketing investment)

For example, $10,000 Net Profit divided by $50,000 Marketing Cost equals 20% ROI.

This is the **Return on Investment before interest and taxes**. That means we took $50,000 of the company's money and invested it in a marketing program. That program returned the money along with a 20% return.

Marketers frequently use Gross Profit divided by Marketing Costs as "**Marketing ROI**." In this case, we're looking at how much of our marketing investment was returned in the form of Gross Profit (from the effort).

If we calculate "Marketing ROI" as Gross Profit divided by Marketing Costs, and Gross Profit is $70,000 and Marketing Costs are $50,000, then $70,000/$50,000 = 140% return.

That means our marketing costs were "returned" 1.4 times.

Looking at **Marketing Contribution** can also be helpful. If your marketing effort generated $70,000 in gross profit, and you spent $50,000 on the effort, *Marketing Contribution is $20,000.*

Is that good? It depends on your company's particular situation. If you have revenue coming in from other efforts, you might use the $20,000 Marketing Contribution to fund further marketing efforts.

Consider also **Lifetime Value** (LTV) of customers you bring in from your marketing program. Is it likely they will generate repeat orders? Can you expect a significant portion to continue ordering from you for several years?

- If these customers have a significant LTV, you may be happy to bring them in with a $20,000 Marketing Contribution.

Returning at least 100% of your marketing investment is always promising, but not always required for a successful program. *Many times, it makes economic sense to bring in customers at an initial loss, if you know they have a significant LTV.*

Customer database metrics

Repurchase rate

When you receive the first order from an individual or company, they're a "first-time customer." But they may have just been "trying you out," or the individual may have been purchasing a gift for someone.

The critical order is the second order:

Repurchase Rate =
number of second-time customers /number of single-order customers

You might also look at your percentage of one-time buyers:

Percentage of One-Time Buyers =
Number of single-order customers / number of total customers

You should track the percentage of single-order-only customers, to see if your marketing efforts to generate the second order are working.

Lifetime Value

Your database should track:

- All dollar sales made by each customer

- Date of first sale
- Date of each subsequent sale

This allows you to determine *average dollar sales per customer per year*, and *how many years the average customer continues to purchase* from you.

With those numbers, you can compute Lifetime Value per individual customer to *identify your most profitable customers.*

Overall **Lifetime Value** (LTV) for your customer base is:

Average Dollar Sales Per Customer Per Year   x
Average Number of Years as Customer

The first step is identifying the number of years for which you have sales data on each customer and former customer.

Part 1: Average Sales Per Customer Per Year

- Add the total sales for all customers = Total Sales (for a period)
- Divide Total Sales by Number of Customers = Average Sales per Customer for the period
- Divide Average Sales per Customer by number of years you reviewed = Average Sales Per Customer Per Year

Part 2: Average Number of Years as a Customer

- For each customer, compute number of months from first *sale during the period* to last sale.

    o Last Sale = May 2020 (202005) and First Sale = February 2019 (201902)
    o Subtract Last from First = 0103 = 15 months
    o Divide months by 12 to convert to years = 1.25

- Add all of the years as customer = Total Years for All Customers

- Divide Total Years for All Customers by Number of Customers = Average Number of Years as Customer

Part 3: Compute LTV

- Multiply Average Sales/Customer/Year by Average Number of Years as Customer = Lifetime Value

LTV Database Snapshot

Obviously, there are limitations with the Lifetime Value calculation above:

- The average time as customer *may be understated* for those who were customers before the timeframe you specified.

- Time as customer and revenue per customer may be *understated for those current customers* who may continue to buy from you.

- The revenue per customer may also be *understated for customers who stopped purchasing* from you during the period (but may have actively purchased from you in prior periods)

- It ignores data from customers who did not make a purchase during the timeframe (who were not active customers)

So it is a "Database Snapshot." It looks at your Active Customer database as a whole for a particular period.

LTV Historical Approach

Because of the limitations of the Database Snapshot approach, you may also want to consider the "Historical Approach" to compute Lifetime Value.

The Historical Approach looks at each inactive customer's actual completed "lifetime" with your company.

For former customers, you know exactly how much they spent with you and how long they continued to buy from you. (This assumes you have the data available.)

To use the Historical Approach:

1. Decide how to define "inactive" or former customers (for example, customers with no order within the last X months).

2. The number of **customers you identify as inactive = A**.

3. For each inactive customer, compute total dollar sales over their lifetime. Add all of these **"total dollar sales over lifetime" for your inactive customers = B**

4. B / A is **Average Dollar Sales Per Customer over their lifetime with you** = Lifetime Value

If you have the data available, it's also useful to:

5. Compute "total months as customer." For each customer, calculate the number of months between the first order and last order. Divide by 12 for total years as customer.

6. **Add all the "total years as customer" for inactive customers, and Divide by A = Average Years as Customer.**

It's useful to have both the Historical and the Database Snapshot LTV for a more complete picture of Lifetime Value. The two measurements also show you how Lifetime Value may change for your customer base over time.

Based on customer LTV, you may be willing to spend more on marketing to bring in new customers (even at a loss), because of the revenue they'll bring in over their lifetime.

If you're bringing in customers at breakeven or a loss, this analysis will reveal how long it takes a new customer to become profitable.

Establishing your marketing budget

Why not dazzle your boss with a measurable marketing plan? What's a measurable plan? One that includes *quantifiable objectives* and a *budget to reach those objectives based on past results.*

When management gives you the company's sales objectives, be sure you're ready with a grounded-in-fact budget proposal to achieve them.

Where the budget begins

Let's say your company's goal is to generate $1,000,000 in sales and your presumed **average sale** is $500.

- You may need 2000 sales ($1,000,000 divided by $500) to achieve your goal.

But you really want to be sure about that "presumed average sale," especially if you sell multiple products or services (or your sales force has the flexibility to offer discounts).

- Determine Total Revenue for last year and divide by Number of Orders or Sales to find out for sure. *If you want management to believe your numbers, base them on reality.*

- Total Revenue / Number of Sales =
  Average Dollars Per Sale

What was your total marketing budget last year? How many orders or sales did the company have?

- **Total marketing budget / number of sales last year =
  Cost Per Order (CPO)**

Multiply your Cost Per Order by the number of sales you'll need to achieve the company's goal.

- Let's say your CPO was $80 @ 2000 sales = Marketing Budget of $160,000.

This is the type of analysis that illustrates you're basing your budget on reality. CFOs will especially appreciate this detail. If you want to preserve your marketing budget, this is how to show your boss and CFO that you're investing your budget wisely.

When you can bring CPO to the table, you can base your budget negotiations on actual results, rather than guesswork or dreams.

New customer goal

Here's another example, based on an objective of bringing in a specific number of new customers, as well as having an overall dollar sales objective (which we'll address below).

Objective = 10,000 new customers. Past Cost Per Sale was $10.

10,000 new customers @ $10 Cost Per Sale =
$100,000 prospecting budget

Dollar sales goals

You can also estimate your dollar sales, using your **new** customer objective and your average dollar sale from **new** customers. (We're using $100 average first sale.)

10,000 new customers (goal)   x $100 average sale = $1,000,000 sales

If you have a $3 million overall sales objective, that means $2,000,000 in sales needs to come from *existing* customers.

If your average sale from existing customers is $150, you need 13,334 orders to hit $2 million in sales:

- $2,000,000   / $150 = 13,334

How much does it cost you to drive sales from existing customers? Let's say it's $10 per sale.

13,334 orders @ $10 per sale = $133,340 budget

Add your $100,000 prospecting budget and your $133,340 customer marketing budget to establish your total marketing budget: $233,340

Budget negotiation

What if your boss or CFO says that budget isn't acceptable?

- You could create new Offers designed to **generate higher average orders** (for new customers and/or existing customers)

- If you've been tracking your Cost Per Order by media channel, you may have identified some **channels that bring in orders at a lower cost**. You could use only those channels, assuming they can generate enough sales to hit the company's objectives.

But realistically, you may need to revise your objectives. This is the time to have a fact-based discussion about objectives and the marketing budget, to ensure that everyone has realistic expectations about what you can accomplish.

How much to spend to bring in a customer? Cost Per Acquisition and Lifetime Value

You can also look at proposed marketing programs by your past Cost Per Acquisition.

If you're like most marketers, you might struggle with the question, "How much can we spend to bring in a new customer?" The answer depends on your company's particular business model.

Are you willing to just breakeven on each new customer (or even bring in customers at a loss)? In that case, you'll rely on customers making future purchases and becoming profitable over time. If you're willing to just breakeven:

Cost Per Acquisition (CPA) = your Gross Profit Per Sale

If you're willing to spend up to your Gross Profit Per Sale to bring in each new customer, then your marketing budget is:

Gross Profit Per Sale   x   desired number of new customers

If you're willing to bring in customers at a loss, you may be willing to spend more.

What if you need to make a profit on the first sale? Then you can't spend your entire Gross Profit Per Sale.

Or maybe each new sale must contribute to overhead and profit immediately. In this case, the amount you can spend to acquire a customer will be the **Marketing Allowable Cost Per Sale**:

Marketing Allowable Cost Per Sale =
   Gross Profit Per Sale   minus
   Overhead and Profit (typically a % of COGS)

You should also run a Breakeven Analysis (along with this type of "how much can I spend" analysis), to be sure your marketing programs have a reasonable chance of achieving your objectives.

What to track regularly

Your key metrics start with Traffic, Leads, and Sales. You'll also want to track results of your on-going marketing programs.

1. Traffic: number of unique visitors to the website

You want to see the number of Users to your website steadily increase. (In Google Analytics, see "Audience," "Overview.")

2. Traffic quality: Bounce Rate, Pages/Session, Session Duration

What are the trends in Bounce Rate, Average Pages/Session, and Average Session Duration? Ideally, you want to see Bounce Rate decline while Average Pages/Session and Average Session Duration increase.

3. Organic traffic

You should see a steady growth in Organic traffic, especially if you're adding new blog posts (or other pages) regularly.

In Google Analytics, see "Acquisition," "All Traffic," "Channels." Compare the number of Users per month to leads or sales from Organic per month, to see trends in your Conversion Rate.

4. Growth in non-branded keywords

You want to see more traffic driven by non-branded keywords – those that don't include your company or product names. (See *how to do this with Google Search Console in Chapter 14*.) That's one sign your SEO efforts are effective.

5. Traffic trends in other media channels

Monitor traffic trends in email, paid search, social media, and paid social. Look at Bounce Rate, Pages/Session, and Average Session Duration. Compare the number of Users to leads or sales by channel to see trends in your Conversion Rate by channel.

6. Leads: growth in your prospect database

Is your prospect database growing? Are you getting new enewsletter subscribers? How about responders to your other Lead Generation Offers (white papers, other Content Offers, webinars, etc.)?

What percentage of your website Users are converting to leads?

7. Conversion of leads (to take next step and to sales)

Keep track of Conversion from your email nurturing efforts. Are you "testing your way to success" by finding ways to improve that Conversion?

8. Sales: number of sales, dollar sales, Sales Conversion

Look at overall sales, and then sales by channel to see where improvements and declines have occurred.

What percentage of Users are converting to sales (if ecommerce)?

Review Sales by Product if you're selling multiple products by ecommerce. (In Google Analytics, see "Conversions," "Ecommerce," "Product Performance." Set up Ecommerce Tracking if needed.)

You can also add a Secondary Dimension of Source/Medium to see which channel is driving sales of each product.

9. Cost Per Order

How much did you spend in marketing during the period? How many orders did you bring in? *Marketing cost divided by orders = Cost Per Order.* What is Cost Per Order overall, and by channel?

10. Engagement

In your enewsletter: compare *number of Unique Clicks to Number Delivered to compute Click-Through* by individual article. This will help you identify the topics your audience is most interested in reading about.

When you track which articles in your enewsletter are clicked by each individual name, you can then determine: which names have been "engaged" with you over the last 90 days, and which names haven't been "engaged" with you (over the last 3 months, 6 months, 12 months, or never).

In your blog: how many new comments did you receive? What percentage of blog posts have received comments? What's the average number of comments per post?

Which topics received comments, and which received the most comments? Which topics haven't received any comments?

On each of your social media pages: how many comments, likes, retweets, and shares did you receive? Which topics got the most engagement?

- On your Facebook page, see "Insights."
- On your Twitter home page, see "More," "Analytics." See "Notifications" in the left menu to see actual retweets and mentions.
- On your LinkedIn page, see "Analytics," "Updates."

(See Chapter 3 for more on social media analytics.) Social media engagement helps expose your posts to new prospects — and helps keep your posts visible to your page followers on Facebook.

You can add all comments, likes, shares/retweets, and clicks per social media site. Divide that total by your number of followers or page likes to compute the percentage of followers engaged.

11. Other Metrics Specific to Your Business

If you sell memberships, subscriptions, or other products or services that renew, keep track of the number up for renewal, the number renewed, and the number not yet renewed.

12. Page Visits

Are you getting more visits to your key selling pages? What's the Bounce Rate? What's the Average Time on Page? (In Google Analytics, see "Behavior," "Site Content," "All Pages.")

For the new pages and blog posts promoted during the month, how many Unique Pageviews did each receive?

Each month, you want to look at metrics that directly address how well you're achieving your particular objectives.

Become obsessed with the numbers, and laser-focused on results

Gathering the marketing numbers and learning a few calculations will make you a better marketer. It will make the difference between marketing programs that just spend money – and *marketing that achieves the company's objectives cost-effectively.*

It will elevate Marketing to a more strategic role when you can advise management *how much it costs to attract a new customer* – and *how much your customers are worth over their lifetime.*

This is the way to prove the value of marketing and your own value to your company. When you can show *how cost-effectively your marketing is growing the customer base and building sales*, you should be able to justify higher marketing budgets.

Results Obsession Strategy #5:
Measure every step you can measure

Results Obsession Strategy #6:
Equate your costs to results to compute ROI

Chapter 20

The New Marketing Leader

The new marketing leader (called the Chief Marketing Officer or CMO here) is **performance driven** – focused on measurable results to drive a positive marketing ROI.

The new CMO **understands the buyer journey** through building Buyer Personas, Offers, and Content by Buying Stage.

This new-age marketer should be the Voice of the Customer and drive Lifetime Value. Bruce Rogers from Forbes sees the CMO's role as *"leveraging, protecting, and expanding the value"* of customer relationships.

"The most important skills for a great marketer today lie in Digital and Data."

The new CMO effectively **manages the Customer Experience** – which is primarily digital through the website, email, and social media.

This new marketing leader develops a more powerful brand through proven messaging and emotional drivers. Bob Van Rossum says the CMO needs to **drive an emotional connection to the brand**. The Forbes Accountability Report says marketing contributes to enterprise value by **building Brand Value and Customer Equity.**

The new CMO tests continuously and converts analytics into action. You need a *"data-driven mindset"* (according to Deloitte). The most important skills for a great marketer today lie in *"Digital and Data."*

There is no longer the "Demand Generation versus Brand Message" question. The new CMO creates the Brand Message that drives sales.

Demand Generation (driving traffic, and generating and nurturing leads) can't be done without developing an effective Brand Messaging Strategy. Marketing must do both. Jenifer Kern says CMOs need to build *"scalable . . . demand gen engines"* and hire *"data-driven demand gen experts."*

Is this your marketing focus?

Today's leading marketers need a combination of strategy, Demand Generation, and marketing communications skills. This book has helped you develop and enhance each of these as Results Obsession Strategies and Skills.

Marketing's strategic role in your company

As the marketing leader, it's critical for you and your CEO to get on the same page.

Sadly, *56% of marketing executives say their C-level Executives don't understand Digital Marketing*. As a result, their company isn't setting effective strategies. Well, whose problem is that? **That's a Marketing problem**.

It's up to you (the marketer) to prove the value and effectiveness of Digital Marketing. That's how to get your recommendations funded.

Among CMOs, 74% say their job doesn't allow them to have maximum impact on the company. That's also **a problem marketers can solve.**

You need to prove your strategic value by:

- Knowing more about your customer Personas than anyone else in the company. *That is your critical role!*

- Knowing what your competition is doing in terms of *messaging, Offers, and new product or service introductions*

- Understanding *how much it costs to bring in a new customer*

- Knowing *how much revenue you bring in per marketing dollar*

- Understanding the *Lifetime Value* of your customer

This is your strategic marketing base. You need these elements to craft the marketing strategies that will achieve your company's goals.

When you can show how your marketing programs add to your company's bottom line, it will help to:

- Elevate Marketing from a cost center to a *profit center*
- Give Marketing a *more strategic function*
- Elevate the Marketing leader to a *strategic role* in the company

But you have **to prove the value you can bring to the table first**.

Managing activities vs. leading the strategy

Thomas Barta ("The 12 Powers of a Marketing Leader") asks, *"Do you 'do marketing'* – or do you **lead marketing?"**

In other words, do you **create the strategy** for your brand(s) and Buyer Personas? Or *do you just manage marketing activities* (like outside resources and inside team members)?

Are you focusing on Testing, so you can learn what works? *Or are you just getting marketing projects done?*

Are you more concerned about getting something done on time and on budget – than getting it done as *effectively* as possible?

Market leaders are farther along in *creating a culture of Testing and learning,* and 77% have *specifics on how success is measured.*

Do you?

A study by the CMO Council and Deloitte found that smart CMOs have **elevated their activities from just managing the marketing plan to being a revenue-driver.**

When Marketing doesn't have a strategic role

What if Marketing doesn't have a strategic role in your company?

Your senior managers may have never worked in a company where Marketing — and a senior-level marketer — had a strategic role. So they may not understand what Marketing can bring to the table.

If your company views marketing as "advertising" or "an expense," your marketing budget is likely to be one of the first things cut when the economy takes a downturn.

Ideally, Marketing should be in senior-level meetings about company direction, product development roadmaps, expansion into new markets, and other strategic initiatives.

So how do you get there? To prove your strategic value, start by preparing some strategic discussions for your boss:

- If you know your company is considering new product or service areas, **give your boss the "Voice of the Customer"** to help guide product or service development.

- Prepare *monthly marketing progress reports* that calculate the **Cost Per Acquisition, Cost Per Sale** for existing customers, and **Revenue per Marketing Dollar** Spent.

You want to **prove how effectively** you and your team are bringing in new customers, maximizing the value of existing customers, and driving revenue!

What if you were hired for a more strategic role, but your day-to-day work turned out to be something else?

Open the lines of communication with your boss. If you were hired to accomplish certain goals that you're not actually working on, it's likely your boss isn't happy with the situation either.

If you're too overwhelmed with managing marketing projects, that's a priorities issue. **Take the first step**:

- Make a list of the projects you're involved in and **establish priorities with your boss.**

- Suggest some options for getting projects done to free up your time, so you can focus on the reason you were hired. (Consider interns, freelancers, an agency, a consultant, etc.)

Can any smart manager run Marketing?

When I worked in a large financial services company, a common practice was to rotate the senior-level managers through various departments. Marketing was always on that rotation; not surprisingly, Accounting, Finance, and Legal were not. Is that because to run those departments, you needed specific skills — but "anyone can run Marketing?"

It seems that many companies don't know what well-run marketing looks like — and that it takes specific marketing skills.

A smart marketer's main job is to create the strategic marketing plan for the company and for each brand — and manage that plan:

- The marketer should bring in-depth knowledge of each of your Buyer Personas to the task.

- The marketer will craft the **strategy for competing** – the *"why should I buy yours"* unique messaging strategy designed to appeal to your specific Buyer Personas. Once developed, this brand message **needs to be enhanced and constantly proven to your prospects**.

- The marketer builds continuous Lead Generation and sales systems, and continually tests to make them more effective over time.

- The marketer crafts specific strategies to maximize the value of every website visitor and lead, and build customer Lifetime Value.

Marketing today requires much more than agency coordination if you plan to maximize your marketing budget.

- If the manager doesn't **understand how to build strategies** to accomplish the company's sales (and other) goals, the marketing effort will be ineffective before it ever begins.

- If the manager doesn't know how to **build budgets based on Cost Per Order**, Marketing will be seen as an expense – and less likely to have a strategic seat at the senior-level table.

Can you use agencies or consultants to bring these skills to the table? Absolutely. But the strategic role of Marketing in a company is usually much more effective when the person driving the strategy:

- *Works regularly with the CEO* and other C-level executives to offer strategic Voice of the Customer input
- Has the opportunity to *continually build knowledge of your specific customer Personas*

It's also true that anyone can *learn* marketing – especially when you have a smart, more experienced marketer to teach you.

What if you don't have that person to learn from?

- B*ring in a consultant* to educate your marketing team

- *Encourage team members to add to their marketing knowledge* by taking classes or attending seminars/webinars (which should happen on an on-going basis).

Use your new Results Obsession skills

If you, the marketer, **know more about your customers than anyone else in the company** (including why each Persona buys), you bring the "Voice of the Customer" and prove your strategic value.

If you **understand the competition better than anyone else** – including their brand positioning, product and service benefits, and latest messaging and Offers – you prove your strategic value.

If you know the cost of generating a new customer, how much revenue you create per marketing dollar, and each customer's Lifetime Value, you can talk strategically about budgets and sales targets.

Armed with customer knowledge, competitor knowledge, and key financial results metrics, you're well-equipped to deliver value to your company in strategic discussions.

Overall, **80% of CEOs are unimpressed with their CMO**. So:

- Take regular steps to prove you understand your customers.

- Send your boss regular reports showing *how effective your messaging strategy has become through Testing*.

- Prove how your *marketing programs* continue to become *more cost-effective*.

- Prove these things regularly.

Why some marketing departments are so much more successful than others

The most successful Marketing departments get the most from every marketing dollar. Here are the key components of their marketing plans . . .

1. Unique brand messaging drives sales

The answer to **"Why Should I Buy From YOU"** is your brand positioning. The most successful Marketing departments have the answer to this question posted on their wall so everyone knows it.

The key is to **PROVE why you're different** from the competition. Your brand positioning shouldn't just be a tag line of empty words.

The test of every web page, every email, and every other communication generated by Marketing is this:

- If it's *clear why someone should do business with your company — rather than your competitors* — the communication is doing its job.

2. Fanatical about knowing your customer(s)

Having a deep understanding of your Buyer Personas is one of the most valuable skills a Marketing team can build (and a key to being invited to the senior management table.)

Is Marketing a clear "Voice of the Customer" in your company?

In meetings about new product/service introductions, is it Marketing that can say, *"Because our customers value ..., we should consider..."*

All marketing starts with the customer. Understanding your customer(s) is perhaps the greatest skill to guide copy strategy, SEO strategy, PPC strategy, website design strategy, email strategy, etc. — in other words, I couldn't function without it.

3. Use data by Persona to craft relevant messages

The smartest thing you can do is send *relevant* communications to your Buyer Personas.

Use your data to *customize your communications* based on what you know about your customers and prospects.

The results include*:* better return on marketing investment, better readership of each communication, stronger customer loyalty, fewer unsubscribes, and better prospect Conversion.

4. Continually educate your audiences

Don't send emails that waste your Personas' time. Communicate by sending **valuable** information — *tell them something they didn't know.*

Most customers have no idea of all the products you offer, or all the benefits of the products they've already purchased. Few, if any, customers have read every page on your website.

Make it your goal to **turn every customer into a fan** that wants to do more business with you!

Nurture every prospect over time by educating them about your solution. Effective nurturing should generate a steady stream of sales-ready leads or direct sales.

5. Track everything: Be Results Obsessed!

This is the only way to spend your marketing dollars most effectively. The smartest Marketing departments *dazzle the CFO with their knowledge of Cost Per Order by channel* – and use it to justify the marketing budget to meet the company's sales goals.

6. Test everything to test your way to success

Testing your way to success is the key to doubling and tripling your response. For each media channel, there are certain elements that have the biggest impact on results (which we've talked about in this book). Focus your Testing there.

This is the **secret for getting far greater return** from your marketing efforts — without increasing your budget.

7. Build Lifetime Value of every customer

Maximize the value of your customers by meeting more of their needs. You want to *secure a bigger piece of each customer's business* — and make your company more indispensable to every customer.

Communicate with your customers regularly. Be sure they're the first to know about any new product, service, benefit, special Offer, award, or positive press you've received.

8. Run the numbers before you spend

Know what your *breakeven* is before you ever spend a dime, so you can modify your program if needed. You should never be surprised when a program is unprofitable.

Plan programs to be successful before they ever begin.

"The Secret of Marketing": everything from your customer's point of view

It's critical for every marketer to learn to see everything from your particular customers' points of view.

You should never assume: your customers are like you, perceive things the same way, react the same, or take the same actions that you do.

"You are not your target audience."

It's what business schools try to teach marketing majors: *"Learn how to think like a marketer."*

When you think like a marketer, you always start with the customer. You build Buyer Personas to understand their needs, concerns and why they buy. It's the foundation for creating relevant communications.

Hiring the right marketing team

What if you're hiring someone for a position where you don't really know what skills you need (in that position) to be successful?

If *your website has the primary purpose of ecommerce*, then you need to build a Marketing team that knows:

- How to drive qualified Traffic (through various media channels) cost-effectively

- How to effectively position individual products against the competition to appeal to your Buyer Personas

- How to craft or recognize effective Sales Copy to sell online

- How to test and analyze results

- How to segment communications to effectively sell through email, and maximize each customer's Lifetime Value

If *your website is primarily for Lead Generation*, then you need a Marketing team that knows:

- How to drive qualified Traffic (through various media channels) cost-effectively

- How to craft effective Offers by Buying Stage by Buyer Persona

- How to choose the level of commitment to drive A, B, C leads

- How to craft or recognize effective Content for each Buying Stage for each Persona

- How to educate and nurture Leads to make them sales-ready

- How to test and analyze results

You may be dazzled by a marketer with experience working for a big-name company. But a larger company tends to have an in-house specialist in every area, as well as outside agencies to bring expertise.

Each marketer is **much less likely to have been hands-on** with more tactical areas – especially with specific skills like Lead Generation, website Testing, or results analysis. So be sure to ask what the individual's specific involvement was (beyond coordinating resources).

Younger marketers for digital marketing?

When social media began, many companies turned to younger marketers who understood the tactical side.

But as companies began to scream "Where's the ROI?" it became clear that **social media — like all marketing channels — needs a well thought-out strategy** to be effective.

The fact that younger marketers may use social media (or any digital media channel) more doesn't mean they **understand how to use it most effectively for marketing.**

Some of the best social media campaigns marry innovative hands-on ideas of younger marketers — with well thought-out plans and strategies of more senior marketers that will actually achieve the company's goals.

Become an educated marketing buyer

Your marketing efforts likely revolve around **the most important sales and Lead Generation vehicle we have – a website**.

If the key objective of your website is Lead Generation, you want a website team that focuses on Lead Generation.

Lead Generation is a marketing specialty. Your website team may need to craft unique Offers by Persona by Buying Stage, prominently place Offers throughout the website, and create Conversion paths.

- Doesn't every digital agency know how to generate leads effectively (and cost-effectively)?

- Doesn't every digital agency know *how to sell* — and *maximize Customer Lifetime Value?*

Challenges with outside resources

Sadly, there are agencies, consultants, and freelancers who just 'get the project done" or "keep the program going." They **aren't involved in Testing, may not be tracking results,** and **aren't focused on continually improving your results** to maximize your budget.

Never blindly assume vendors of a particular service are actually experts in that particular service. Ask them for the **strategies they'll use to complete your project**. Unfortunately, there are plenty of marketing vendors and freelancers selling particular marketing services without actually knowing how to get great results from those services.

Beware of vendors who rely on big-name past clients or statements like *"we've done hundreds of (insert tactic here)."*

Doing a lot of something is very different from being an expert in doing it effectively (when you continually *test to discover what actually works*.)

You always want to see the results they've achieved.

Evaluating proposals

Too many marketers seem to have a blind belief in marketing companies. Hiring marketing resources has become similar to hiring an auto mechanic or plumber – it's **"buyer beware."** You want to believe (or you assume) that the vendor knows what they're talking about. You believe the vendor has the right solution and can deliver it effectively.

In this book, you've learned the **key success factors in each digital media channel that have the most impact on results**. You should see a focus on those success factors in the proposals you review. So now, you're ready to find better resources.

How? Always request a proposal from at least two potential agencies, free-lancers, consultants, etc., so you can **compare their strategies to achieve your particular goal**.

Do they ask what you've done before, what you've tested, and the results you've achieved? *If they don't, it's not likely to be their focus.*

- Can they talk about the **Testing** they've done? How have they **improved results** for other clients?

- Can they discuss how they **craft Lead Generation Offers**? How do they manage the Lead Quality/Lead Quantity tradeoff? Do they ask about your need for generating A, B, and C leads?

- Can they discuss how they've **tested ecommerce Landing Pages** to improve results?

- Do they ask **how much you can spend to create a customer** or what is the value of each customer? Can they talk about how they've reduced CPO (Cost Per Order) for other campaigns they've created?

These points illustrate how a traffic-driving or Lead Generation agency should be investing your money.

How to get the most from outside resources

You want to hire resources that bring potential solutions to the challenges you've correctly diagnosed (*from Chapter 2*). And those resources should **plan to be actively Testing.**

- They should also provide regular reporting to show progress and **prove the effectiveness** (and cost-effectiveness) of their solutions

If efforts aren't hitting your objectives, your resources should know how to revise and re-think the program and move in another Testing direction to improve results.

If you're not seeing a high quality of work, it could be:

1) You (or they) may not have correctly diagnosed your problem. So you may have selected a resource that isn't solving the real problem

2) They don't have the skills needed to solve your problem

3) You haven't provided your resource with the Buyer Persona knowledge they need to do their job effectively

Many times, an agency takes a job and doesn't really understand the problem. That's why a very specific proposal is so important.

The ideal client-agency partnership involves each party bringing very specific knowledge to the table:

- **The agency's job** is to be an expert in solving your problem — and having the particular deep expertise you need.

- **As the client**, *it's your job to be an expert in your Buyer Personas.* No matter how long I work with you, I'm not going to have as much contact with your customers as you – so the client ALWAYS needs to be the expert on the customer.

If you don't bring that Persona knowledge to the table (even after reading *Chapter 3*), be sure to build your Buyer Personas before agency work begins.

Direct marketing success applied to digital media

Many of the activities of "Demand Generation" used to be referred to as "Direct Marketing."

Direct Marketers were the ones usually responsible for (and experienced in) generating measurable Traffic, Leads, and Sales. It was typically a Direct Marketer who handled education of prospects through lead nurturing.

Great Direct Marketers effectively **managed customer profitability.** They analyzed the customer file and worked to create more Best Customers and increase Lifetime Value.

- A Direct Marketer usually created the cross-sell, up-sell, loyalty, and reactivation Offers.

- And they have been the ones focused on *making each sale more profitable*, by boosting average order size

I gained incredible Direct Marketing wisdom from visionaries like Jim Kobs, who produced the list of 99 Offers that I used in my Direct Marketing classes for many years. And the incredible Herschell Gordon Lewis, from whom I learned the "wordsmithing" tips in this book.

The media channels have changed, but these direct marketing success factors run through everything in this book. Direct marketing was the first "Results Obsession" for marketers.

Results Obsession Strategies and Skills are keys to consistently stronger results

This book has taken you through six Results Obsession Strategies and three skills to continuously improve results across media channels. Now you're ready to put them into practice:

Results Obsession Strategy #1: Always start with a step-by-step analysis of your marketing, to diagnose exactly where you could improve. It will help you pursue solutions tailor-made to drive the improvements you need.

Results Obsession Strategy #2: Learn why your customers buy from you, so you focus your marketing story on exactly what your Buyer Personas want to hear.

Results Obsession Strategy #3: Create a system of continuous Traffic, Leads, and Sales, to prove how essential and valuable your marketing plan is for your company.

Results Obsession Strategy #4: Focus on testing your way to success, so you learn what works and don't waste your efforts.

Results Obsession Strategy #5: Measure everything — to identify the best performers. *("If you can't measure it, don't do it.")*

Results Obsession Strategy #6: Equate costs to results, to focus on the most cost-effective options.

You've developed an understanding of Google Analytics and the key metrics to review. And you've learned the key elements of *Lead Generation, Offer construction, and Selling with words.*

With your new knowledge of how to manage Lead Quality versus Lead Quantity, how to craft dozens of unique Offers for your Personas' Buying Stages, and how to use the Sales Process to really sell, **you now possess the three Results Obsession skills that perhaps 90% of marketers are missing**.

Incorporate these ROI-related strategies and tactical skills into your everyday marketing life.

*Your newfound Results Obsession is what every marketer needs
to succeed — and transform your marketing efforts.*

References

Top Characteristics of Transformational CMOs of Tomorrow. Nvision®. <https://nvision.na.com/blog/top-characteristics-of-transformational-cmos-of-tomorrow>

Marketing Accountability. (2017) Forbes. <https://www.forbes.com/cmo-practice/wp-content/uploads/2017/08/Forbes-Marketing-Accountability-Executive-Summary-10.2.17.pdf>

The key to delivering analytics advantage. (2017) Deloitte®. <https://www2.deloitte.com/content/dam/Deloitte/ca/Documents/deloitte-analytics/ca-EN-Building-Analytics-Capabilities-AODA.pdf>

Kern, J. (2017) *The CMO Mess & How We Can Clean it Up.* Linkedin®. <https://www.linkedin.com/pulse/cmo-mess-how-we-can-clean-up-jenifer-kern/>

Barta, T., & Barwise, P. (2016) *The 12 Powers of a Marketing Leader.* McGraw-Hill

Murphy, T., O'Brien, D., & Veenstra, J. (2018) *Redefining the CMO.* Deloitte®. <https://www2.deloitte.com/us/en/insights/deloitte-review/issue-22/redefining-the-role-of-the-cmo-chief-marketing-officer.html>

Kobs, J. (1991). *Profitable Direct Marketing, second edition.* McGraw-Hill

Lewis, H.G. (1989). *On the Art of Writing Copy, second edition.* Prentice Hall.

About the Author

Karen J. Marchetti, SVP Client Services for Response FX®, brings 30+ years of Internet marketing and direct marketing planning, testing, and creative expertise for leaders worldwide including:

- Qualcomm, Union Bank of California, Bank of America, Lifeline Cell Technology, RIMES Technologies, CRES Insurance Services, Brilliance Financial Technology, and American Nurses Association.

Her strategies have: **doubled client sales**, *boosted online leads by 67%, driven 60% response to a survey by C-level executives, increased email click-through by 200%, and generated a 22% opt-in rate!*

She has taught Internet Marketing and Direct Marketing at San Diego State University, University of San Diego, UC San Diego, CSU Long Beach, and the University of San Francisco.

Marchetti is a Google Ads Qualified Search Consultant and a Google Analytics Certified Consultant.

Among her accolades are: **"Woman Who Means Business" in Marketing** by the *San Diego Business Journal;* **"Direct Marketer of the Year"** by the San Diego Direct Marketing Association; and Judge of the Direct Marketing Association's International ECHO Awards

She has served on the Board of Directors for the San Diego Software Industry Council, San Diego Direct Marketing Association, and the San Diego American Marketing Association.

Index

Made in the USA
Coppell, TX
26 November 2020